Contents

Foreword 1
Introduction 2
Acknowledgements 4
Map of Northwest Indiana 6
 1. Croatians 7
 2. Serbs 11
 3. Macedonians 16
 4. Ukrainians 22
 5. Slovaks 26
 6. Romanians 29
 7. Italians 34
 8. Lithuanians 40
 9. Greeks 45
10. Polish 50
11. Filipinos 56
12. Assyrians 61
13. Vietnamese 65
14. Hungarians 69
15. Saxons 72
16. Jewish 76
17. Slovenes 81
18. Norwegians 86
19. Mexicans 90
20. Spaniards 95
21. Chinese 99
22. Pakistanis 104
23. Germans 107
24. French 111
25. East Indians 116
26. Czechs 121
27. Russians 124
28. American Indians 128
29. Afro Americans 132
30. Puerto Ricans 137
31. Japanese 141
32. Koreans 145
33. Swedish 149
34. Irish 153
35. Scots 157
36. Lebanese 161
37. Dutch 165
38. English 169

Post-Tribune

serving Northwest Indiana daily

...ooms offered as school-prayer com...

Students not wishing to join in prayer would be given a separate area.

Ernie Hernandez (signature)

...me to Indiana almost empty-hande...

Northwest Indiana Midwest melting pot

This — the 33rd in the Post-Tribune series on the Northwest Indiana Melting Pot by Ernie Hernandez — is on the Swedes, who were among the first settlers of the area.

Ethnics
in Northwest Indiana
By Ernie Hernandez

*Book design by Maryann Bartman of The Post-Tribune.
Administrative coordination by Mary Ellen McGrain of
The Post-Tribune.*

© *1984, The Post-Tribune of Gary, Indiana.
A Knight-Ridder Newspaper. All rights reserved.
Printed in the United States of America.*

*This publication may not be reproduced,
stored in a retrieval system,
or transmitted in whole or in part,
in any form or by any means, electronic,
mechanical, photocopying, recording or otherwise,
without the prior written permission of
The Post-Tribune, 1065 Broadway, Gary, Ind. 46402.*

Library of Congress catalog number 84-60536

ISBN 0 917495 00 4

Foreword

This book presents the people and flavor of a region unmatched for its ethnic diversity: Northwest Indiana. The Region, defined in large part by the circulation of its major newspaper, The Post-Tribune, stretches eastward from the Illinois line through Lake and Porter counties of Indiana. It also includes parts of Jasper, Newton and LaPorte counties, and its northern border is marked by the graceful, dune-filled shoreline of Lake Michigan.

Three-quarters of a million people live in this fascinating, complex region. They represent dozens of nationalities or ethnic groups. Here, among the dunes and the steel mills, Macedonians meet Vietnamese, Serbs meet Greeks, black Americans meet white Americans, French meet Germans. They melt and yet they don't; they become part of the larger America, yet many retain their own clubs, churches and other organizations.

Ernie Hernandez of The Post-Tribune staff wrote a series of 38 articles exploring the past and present of the ethnic groups of Northwest Indiana. When the articles were published in the newspaper, readers suggested the stories be gathered into a book. This is the result of that suggestion.

The book is meant for the general reader as well as the member of a specific ethnic group. It's meant for libraries and schools as well as the coffee table. It's meant for relatives who live elsewhere as well as residents of this region.

Enjoy it, please, and keep it around. It's meant to last.

James G. Driscoll
Editor, The Post-Tribune
Gary, Indiana
March, 1984

Introduction

In September 1982, after a casual conversation with Marcella Otasevich, who was executive director of Gary's International Institute from 1966 to 1978, I passed a note to David C. Allen, then Metropolitan Editor of The Post-Tribune, suggesting a short series on Northwest Indiana's foreign-born, since many of them were getting old, retired or retiring, had left the area or had died. Mrs. Otasevich, who had worked for the Institute assisting the foreign-born since 1947, said we shouldn't let such valuable resources slip by.

The series would cover who the foreign-born are, where they came from, what holds them and their descendants together, their communities' impact and history in Indiana, their leaders, customs, foods, etc...

Being of foreign descent, I felt a certain affinity with the various nationalities, as we all posed as proud Americans while maintaining our ethnic identities. In 1979, I had reported on a speech by Professor N. Lance Trusty of Purdue University's Calumet Campus in Hammond, and I was deeply impressed by his description of the area we lived in, known as Calumet Region, as "a microcosm of the history of the United States," with people of over 75 diverse nationalities living and working together.

As a member of International Institute's Board of Directors for seven years, I had come to know many representatives of those nationalities, learned something about their varied cultures. I felt fortunate.

When I got the go-ahead from Allen, Editor James G. Driscoll and Managing Editor Terence O'Rourke, I started compiling lists from notes I had written to myself through the years. I formulated a letter, to be sent to each of the ethnic groups I could locate, expressing the plan to find out all I could about them, and seeking their assistance.

My plan was to send the letter, ask each group to give it some thought, then schedule interviews with the leaders and spokesmen.

The first in the series appeared on May 8, 1983, after a meeting with Wally Bahun of the Croatians at Wicker Park in Highland. He led me to the "pioneers" among the Croats, who told me of life in the old country, the trip to America, and settlement in Indiana. I was on my way on a voyage through time and around the world.

Little did I know, as I "leaped" from one nationality to another — to Serbs, Macedonians, Ukrainians, Slovenes, Romanians — how anxious they were to tell their stories, their histories, their strengths and weaknesses, their pains and pleasures, their foods and games, their holidays — even their ancient enmities which were being dissipated by time.

And I found these New Americans had such profound experiences. They were witnesses to historical events. Marty Shahbaz' uncle, Ben S. Benjamin, saw the Turks massacre of Assyrians in 1917. Birute Vilutis watched Soviet tanks invade Lithuania in 1941. Reidun Paulsen stared at German stormtroopers in Norway in 1940. M. Akbar Ali was in the great cross-migration of India and Pakistan in 1947. Tivarda Horsza and Bela Janko shared a cell in a Soviet slave coal mine in 1948. Catherine Yamamoto was interned in California in 1942 and Takamitsu Nakamura was fleeing from the atomic bomb in Hiroshima in 1945. Ernie Gabriel was in the Bataan Death March of 1942. Sol Rosner survived Auschwitz in 1945. From each nationality group was a poignant tale, a statement of patriotism, a revelation of an untold or little-known historical fact, a proclamation of ethnic preference, or an acceptance that a group is disappearing because of intermarriage. A refugee left her baby in Poland. The Romanians love the U.S. Flag. Samagitians of Lithuania repelled Genghis Khan. Dutch marry Dutch. Slovenes and Saxons are losing identity.

Luck helped too in preparing the series. Dimitar Basevski, Macedonian journalist, arrived in Gary while I was interviewing Macedonians. Virgil Candea, professor and author from Bucharest, was visiting in Merrillville when I was researching Romanians.

And a good appetite. "You'll gain weight tasting the ethnic foods," said Mary Leuca, who served Romanian *mamaliga,* Thuy Thi Vu Rosenfelt offered Vietnamese *nhoc mam,* Josephine Fox baked Indian fry bread, Mrs. Akbar Ali cooked Pakistani *polawa.* Mrs. Leuca was right, 20 pounds.

When the series started, we didn't have a specific goal. There are 102 ethnic groups identified by Harvard Encyclopedia of American Ethnic Groups, and the U.S. 1980 Census enumerated 127. "I'll keep on until you tell me to stop," I told my editors.

We stopped with the English at No. 38 on Jan. 22, 1984. By then, we had covered every major group in America except Portuguese, Swiss, Austrian, Finn and Belgian, which have few representatives in the area. It was a fitting end, since the English provided the foundation for the melting pot, and one of the descendants I found had the longest, identified, genealogical line — Mrs. Olive Hartsough is descended from Elder William Brewster who led the Puritans from England to Holland, back to England, and to the New World aboard the Mayflower.

— *Ernie Hernandez*

Acknowledgements

The Post-Tribune series on Northwest Indiana's Melting Pot, which began on Page 1 on Sunday, May 8, 1983, and continued for 38 consecutive Sundays until Jan. 22, 1984, couldn't have happened without the advice, assistance and acceptance of the newspaper's editors, particularly Editor James G. Driscoll, Managing Editor Terence O'Rourke and Metropolitan Editors David C. Allen and Paula Ellis. To them, I'm grateful for the support and encouragement.

I also owe debts of gratitude to the people who edited the copy, including O'Rourke, Dave Hawk, John Adkins and others, and to Graphics Editor Larry Bretts for painstakingly providing the maps.

Many others helped in so many ways toward a project they considered "our own." It's not possible to name them all; each story involved interviews with at least 20 people (and each one had a tale to tell, if only we had more space).

Most significant, however, were:

Marcella Otasevich, retired executive director of International Institute and a bottomless well of ethnic information, who directed me to people in virtually each of the nationality groups.

Mary Leuca, principal at Black Oak School, and her husband, Walter, who told me not only all about Romanians, "an island of Latins in a sea of Slavs," plied me with Romanian morsels and all sorts of ethnic informational tidbits, but also maintained a steady flow of encouragement. Then, she gave me her most valuable reference book, Harvard Encyclopedia of American Ethnic Groups.

Larry Sharp, present director of International Institute, who led me to groups I couldn't find.

Wally Bahun, leader of the Croatians, who got me started in the right direction. The first story set the pattern for the rest.

Thuy Thi Vu Rosenfelt, beautiful "mama san" of the Vietnamese, and Refugee Assistance director of Gary Catholic Charities, who helped me communicate with the boat people. She even cooked meals.

Barnett Labowitz, director of the Northwest Indiana Jewish Foundation, who taught me the meaning of Tzadakah and convinced Sol Risner, who will never forget Auschwitz, to talk freely with me, despite the pain.

Father Evagoras Constantinides, parish priest of Saints Constantine and Helen Greek Orthodox Church, for setting me straight about the Greeks and the Middle East whenever I seemed to stray.

Jackie Flotow and Josephine Fox, for gathering Indians to powwow with me, and Frank Roman, for opening his personal archives. From him came 57 books and booklets, all about the Polish in Indiana.

Kathryn Lorraine Duncan Washington, the first black baby born in Gary in 1909, for helping me find the other oldtimers.

Julie Sawaya, born and raised near Beirut, my landlady in Michigan City in 1957, who taught me all about the Lebanese and led me to other Arab Americans.

Malcolm Karam, former International Institute president, who took my mind to ancient Assyria and traced those proud, persistent people's exodus.

Pearl Baboo, descendant of first Americans pre-1650, who led me to the Mayflower progeny among us.

And of course, my wife, Darla Peterson Hernandez, a Swedish American, who didn't teach me a thing about the Swedes, but pointed me to Slovak, Chinese, Indian, Thai, South African, Appalachian and Greek people at Portage Fegely School where she teaches, and kept our son, 5-year-old Peter, company while I did research. "One hundred?" she said when the series started. "Does that mean we won't see you for two whole years?"

— *Ernie Hernandez*

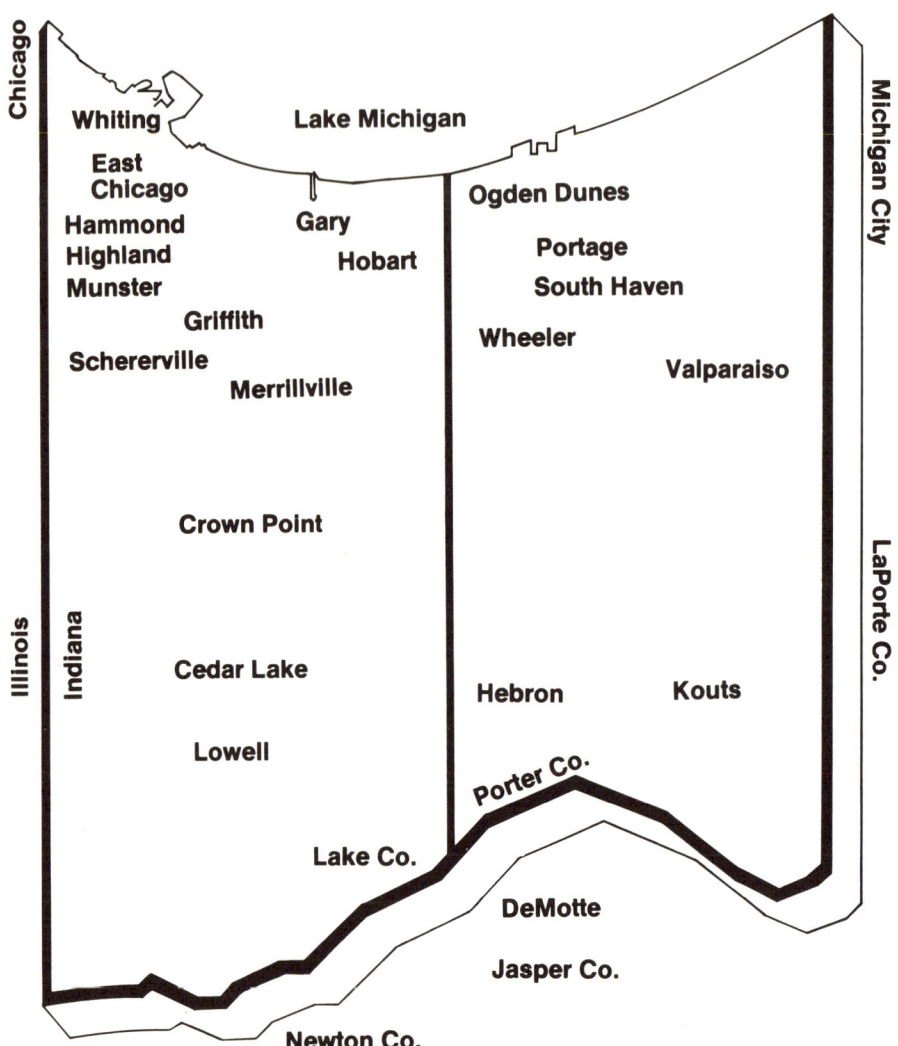

1.
Croatians

"What do I do now?" he repeated. "I make sure that they stay Croatian."

Nicholas J. Erbesti is 94 and alert, the elder statesman — some call him the patriarch — of the 6,000 Croatians in Northwest Indiana, a Gary pioneer, who at the age of 17 left his native city of Kostajnica, in Croatia, to avoid the three-year mandatory army service required by the Austria-Hungary government and joined friends in Pittsburgh.

He was pointing to Elizabeth Moragavan, president of the 1,300-member Lodge 170 of the Croatian Fraternal Union, the largest unit of the organization with 110,000 members in the United States and Canada.

The fraternal union, along with its affiliate Preradovic singing societies and Tamburitzan junior folk musicians, has been at the task of preserving Croatian culture in America since it was founded in Allegheny, Pa., in 1894.

It's an endeavor that's growing difficult, as ethnic groups scatter and marry other people and forget the language, said Mrs. Morgavan, herself American-born, the daughter of George Chelich, who came to Gary to work in the mills in 1909.

But Betty Morgavan and others like Wally Bahun, 68, and Sylvia Pokopac Niksic, who also are U.S.-born to Croatian immigrant parents, have kept the faith, so to speak. They learned Croatian at home and in church, and speak it "almost like natives."

It's a different story with the next generation, those in their 20s and 30s. They were in Erbesti's mind when he admonished Mrs. Morgavan and others to redouble their efforts.

Croatia, dating back to the 9th Century under King Zvonimir whose people were converted to the Roman faith, exists as a people rather than as a nation. It is one of the six states of Yugoslavia, along with Slovenia, Serbia and Macedonia.

The other states, Bosnia and Herzegovina, are also considered Croatian.

It was part of the Austria-Hungary empire until after World War I, when it joined the Kingdom of Serbs, Croats and Slovenes, later identified as Serbia, then named Yugoslavia in 1929.

Madeconians, Serbians and Slovenes migrated to the United States in large numbers also, around 1900. They met in the tents and tarpaper shacks and mills of Gary, speaking essentially the same language.

The Croatians of Northwest Indiana came from communities such as Zagreb, Karlova, Dalmatia and Lika. Today, their descendants still visit those cities in Yugoslavia to fortify their cultural knowledge.

Erbesti, unusual in that he didn't work in the U.S. Steel mills, came as a young businessman. He liked to sell, and eventually owned a restaurant, a small hotel, a grocery store, four pawn shops and a cleaning establishment.

"During the 1930s depression, I lost them all except the cleaners," he said. "My wife cried, and I told her we started with nothing and we had nothing. So what's new?"

His wife, whom he married in 1913, died in 1967. They had three children, Alvin, Valerie Blaney and Minnie Stevens.

When Erbesti arrived in Gary, "there was nothing here, just dunes and swamps," he said. In his first year, he lived in a tent along the Grand Calumet River. Mrs. Niksic recalled that her mother's first home was a cold and leaky tarpaper shack.

As Gary grew — rapidly — so did the Croatian community, with leaders like Frank Riblan, a real estate man; Frank Keleminic, a tailor; Petar Stritof, a saloon keeper; Steve Sarko, a millworker; Janko Badovinac, Paval Lokar, Andrew Sladic, Janko and Helen Keseric, John Benic, Nikola and Marta Brncic, Roko Povrzenvic and Zlatko I. Kerhin, who founded the Croatian Glee Club, Preradovic, in 1914, with 60 members.

It's the oldest singing society in the area, and Erbesti was president for five years in the 1940s. Mrs. Niksic, who has been Croatian Lodge secretary for 34 years, is in her 14th year as president of Preradovic.

Her family was among the first to settle in Glen Park, at 34th and Massachusetts, in 1913, but Gary's Croatian community was centered at 22nd and Adams during those days.

Bahun recalls the 1920s, when the first Croatian hall, built by Riblan — who was called a Croatian Frank Lloyd Wright — at 23rd and Washington, was the place to be in, for stage plays, Tamburitzans, folk dances.

The local Croatians then would be seen at Matt Oreskovich's Packing House, or Gracin's grocery store, or Liberman's Drug Store, and at the Holy Trinity Church, now called St. Monica, at 22nd and Adams.

Today's Croatian Church is St. Joseph the Worker, at 45th and Delaware, with the Rev. Benedict Benakovich as pastor, and the Croatian Center is at 3673 Broadway.

Tamburitza is the name for a series of a dozen string instruments, ranging in size from a ukelele to a bass fiddle.

It's one way to attract the young, American-born Croatians, fascinated by its versatile melody. There are today 42 Junior Tamburitzan groups for Croatian children 7 to 18, across the country. The Gary unit, with Myra Juras as president, is one of the best, and Mrs. Morgavan, who teaches Tamburitza, said local members aspire for four-year scholarships provided to 40 Tamburitza-playing students each year by Duquesne University, Pittsburgh.

Another way to keep the home ties together is the Preradovic, the adult singing group, with about 30 active members, renderian Croatian tunes such as "Lijepa Nasa Domovina," the national hymn, and folk songs like "Moje Selo" and "Da Mi Je Znati."

Then there are Croatian Fraternal Union's youth groups called "Nests," which are encouraged by low-premium ($6 a year) life insurance to attract the youths, up to 18. Nest No. 10 is the Gary group, and it has its own activities.

Musical, hardworking and social people, the Croatians enjoy their cultural get-togethers. On the 1983 agenda were:

— The annual concert of Preradovic on Oct. 16, this being the 69th anniversary.

— CFU Lodge 170's 75th anniversary banquet, also on Oct. 16, when lodges throughout the nation were represented.

— The annual Croatian picnic on July 3 at the Izaak Walton grounds at 57th and Mississippi, sponsored by Lodge 170, Croatian American Democratic Club, Preradovic, Retired Croatians Club, where prase (roast suckling pig) and janjetlina (roast lamb) and assorted strudels were served and a soccer tournament held.

— CFU's national convention in St. Paul, Minn., and the national Tamburitzan festival in Cleveland, both in September.

Bahun, president of the Democratic Club, and Erbesti point out that Croatians have made a name for themselves in the community.

Among them have been Peter Mandich, former Gary mayor; Robert Lucas, a lawyer whose father, Blaz, was a pioneer; Dr. Jobert J. Milos, physician; Dr. Danial M. Bade, dentist; Dr. Fedor I. Cicak, IUN professor; Charlie Vlasic, former Lake County treasurer; state Rep. Peter Katic, Hammond city judge, whose mother is Croatian; and Peter Visclosky, vandidate for 1st District U.S. Representative, whose mother is Croatian.

Erbesti said that even though Croatia doesn't exist today as a nation, "there will always be a Croatia" — in America, where cultural identity blends with national patriotism.

"We have a place here," he said, lecturing young Croats that

10 / Croatians

they should learn their "kako vi and kako ti."

the two phrases for "hello" mean the same, but one is reserved for the elders, with respect, and the other is for the younger people.

* * * * * * * * *

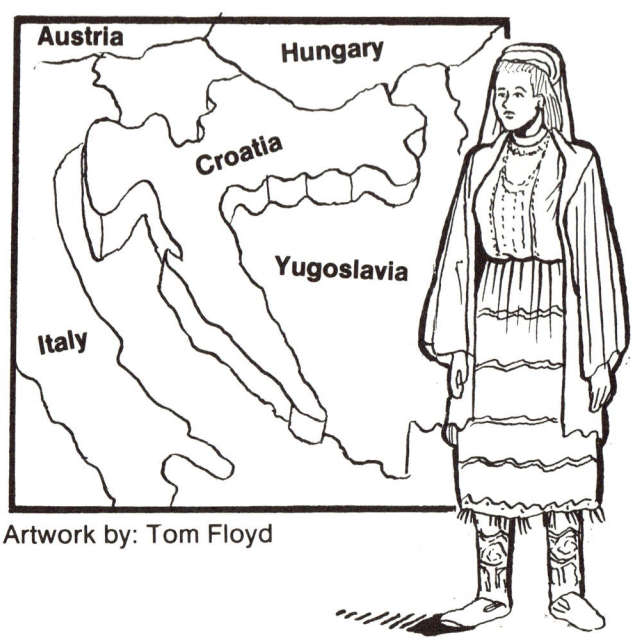

Artwork by: Tom Floyd

Mr. Dobciajaich called the following day to reassure that Bosnia and Herzegovinia in Yugoslavia aren't considered Croatian. Ned Marich did too, and stressed why it's a touchy subject. The Serbians claim Bosnia and Herzegovinia are peopled by Serbs, who recall that in 1912 Croats fought for Austria-Hungary against the Serbs.

Tom Sanders of Gary called to say his family, which Anglicized its name, is Croatian. His father, Steve, arrived in 1914, and founded Sanders Ready-Mix in 1922.

Paula Vuich of the Post-Tribune's credit union called proudly to express her interest in the series. She's of Croatian and Serbian descent.

2. Serbs

"You are a good American because you are primarily a good Serb."

George Rapaich, who was 96 in 1983, 15 when the Karageorge Serbian Singing Society observed its 70th anniversary, likes to use the quote, which he heard himself.

President Woodrow Wilson told it to his friend, Professor Michael Pupin (1858-1935), who in 1916 was president of the Serbian Unity Federation. Rapaich was an executive board member at that time.

"It describes what we are," said Rapaich as he reminisced at the Senior Citizens Home at 3280 Pierce St., Gary.

Alert, articulate and still tireless — he swims and jogs in Miller in the summer, sings bass every Wednesday with the choral group and assists at Sunday services — he talked about his favorite subject: Serbians.

There are more than a million of them in the United States, including about 7,000 in Northwest Indiana. About 500 families are affiliated with St. Sava Serbian Orthodox Church in Hobart, another 300 with St. Elijah Serbian Orthodox Church in Merrillville and others with St. George Serbian Orthodox churches in Schererville and East Chicago.

There weren't as many Serbs in the United States during the pre-World War I days when Woodrow Wilson spoke, but the president was impressed by their abiding patriotism.

Hundreds of Serbian immigrant workers left Gary to go back to the Balkans in 1912 to help fight and defeat the Turks, an ancient enemy. And in 1917, the small Serbian community in the town was again depleted when 450 men, including Risto Vajagich and his eight brothers, volunteered to fight for America in World War I.

"They're fiercely independent," said Marcella Lawler Otasevich, who should know. She was a clerk with the International Institute after World War II when she met and married a Yugoslav patriot, Krisman Otasevich, who in 1939 won that nation's highest award for valor, the Order of the White Eagle, for repelling a battalion of Italian invaders.

While an intense love of freedom and expression described these Slavic people, who have a history dating back to 15 B.C., the Rev. John Todorovich, who has been parish priest at St.

Sava Church for 13 years, says it is more than that.

It's Svetosavlje, or loosely translated, "Orthodox Christianity, Serbian style."

Through St. Sava — Ratsko Nemanjic, 1169-1237, who established the Serbian church within the Orthodoxy — a combination of religion and nationality was formed, he said.

Orthodox Serbians are unique in observing Krsna Slava — each one's Patron Saint Day, or spiritual birthday — as more important than just a personal birthday.

"No one has what the Serbs have," Todorovich said, quoting from a bumper sticker promoted by the Serbs.

From the time Rapaich and John T. Marich, Mitchell Duchich, Steve Orlich, Bozo Trbovich, Louis Christopher and other Gary pioneers met in 1914 to organize St. Sava Church, Svetosavlje has been the dominating goal.

The Serbians are proud of their history.

Serbians in the Roman province of Moesia around the year 637 settled in the northwest corner of the Balkan peninsula. Under Stephan Nemanya, the first Serbian kingdom was established in 1168. A Serbian empire under Tsar Stephan Dushan in the 1300s established one of the world's first civil-rights codes, banning slavery, allowing serfs to take legal action against leaders and forbidding official misconduct.

But Dushan's empire was destroyed in 1389 by invading Ottoman Turks, who ruled for 488 years, until the Russo-Turkish War of 1877. "It's characteristic of the people to remember that date (June 28, the major battle with the Turks), Kossovo and a battle cry, 'For the Holy Cross and Golden Freedom,' "said Otasevich. "June 28 is a national day of mourning, Vidov Dan."

In 1908, the Austria-Hungary empire, which had occupied neighboring Croatia, expanded to Serbian-speaking Bosnia and Herzegovina.

In June, 1914, "the spark that set off World War I" — the assassination of Austrian Archduke Francis Ferdinand — led to war and Austrian occupation of Serbia until 1918. In that year the war ended and the Kingdom of Serbs, Croats and Slovenes, under Alexander I, was formed. It was renamed Yugoslavia in 1929.

President Franklin Delano Roosevelt called March 27, 1941, "the turning point in Hitler's fate" when the Yugoslav army overthrew the country's pro-Hitler government and enthroned Peter II as king. Germany invaded Yugoslavia a week later, but in doing so, its march to Russia was delayed and snow and cold weather halted Hitler's armies in the suburbs of Moscow.

The wars played a part in bringing Serbians to Northwest

Indiana. Rapaich, whose father died when he was an infant, migrated to America in 1907, joining two brothers who worked in the iron shops in Chicago. He worked briefly at the mills, then moved to Gary in 1910.

He was one of Gary's first tavernkeepers, with an establishment at 4th and Broadway. He later operated Broadway Hotel at that site. In 1912, he and two others opened Turner Hall, the largest arena at that time, where they promoted boxing, wrestling and plays.

It was at Turner Hall that he started Karageorge, the area's first ethnic choral group, in 1913.

Rapaich later owned a clothing store, a tavern called "Little Hawaii" and a real-estate and insurance agency at 848 Broadway.

He promoted ethnic and historic plays at Turner Hall and established a theater group that traveled to Milwaukee, Chicago, Detroit and other cities. One of his stars in the production of "Sudjaje" (Fate) was young Mladen Sekulovich, who became known as a movie actor under the name Karl Malden. Malden's mother, Minnie Sekulovich, in her 90s, still lives in Miller.

Malden is among many successful Serbians. Others include Peter Mandich, a former Gary mayor; Mitchell Duchich, who owned Cloverleaf Dairy; Gary-born Bisho Varnava, who later died in a Yugoslavian monastery; Dr. Sloboan M. Draskovich, of the University of Belgrade; Milan Opacich, a violin maker; Zarko Zekerez, a lawyer; Milan Dakich, a professor and politician; Roy Dakich, a lawyer; Nick Stepanovich, a lawyer; Dan Dakich, an Indiana University basketball player; Danilo Orescanin, Indiana University Northwest chancellor; Ray Komenich, an assistant superintendent for personnel in the Gary public schools; former Pittsburgh Pirates baseball player Jumbo Strincevich; retired teacher Ned Marich, a graduate of the University of Belgrade; East Chicagoan Nick Stepanovich, a retired U.S. Army colonel who headed counterintelligence in the Mediterranean in World War II; film writer ("Breaking Away") Steve Tesich; and opera star Diane Chirich.

Nationally, Serbians point to Michael Pupin (1858-1935), the inventor of copper coil wires that made long-distance calls possible; Nikola Tesla (1856-1943), who developed alternating-current motors in harnessing Niagara Falls; pro basketball star Pete Maravich; and the late Bill Vukovich, a two-time Indianapolis 500 winner.

The Serbian community came in waves. The first came before World War I, with Rapaich, John T. Marich, Luka

Grkovich and Stevan Orescanin among the leaders.

A second wave came after World War II, when a million refugees fled the war's destruction in Europe. Half of them came to the United States through the Displaced Persons Act.

Mrs. Otasevich recalls her husband was among the 350 personally sponsored by David Bundalo, who was St. Sava Church's president from 1943 to 1955.

Another post-World War II entry was Mike Popovich, who owns a service station in Gary and is president of the congregation of St. Elijah Serbian American Church, which was formed at 41st and Adams after a split in 1962.

The split on religious-political grounds was, according to partisans from both sides, "painful and soul-searching," but both groups now appear to be thriving.

There were two Serbian churches — St. Sava and Resurrection of Christ — earlier in Gary history. St. Sava started its first building at 20th and Connecticut in 1915.

The two were merged in 1936 when efforts were devoted to a new church on U.S. Steel Corp.-donated land at 13th and Connecticut. That structure, described as "the foremost Serbian church on this continent" by Father Todorovich, was completed Sept. 23, 1938, at a cost of $53,000, and dedicated on Nov. 24.

It was to be the Serbians' religious home until it burned to the ground, mysteriously, on Feb. 16, 1978, forcing St. Sava parishioners to relocate at the 42-acre picnic grounds in Hobart. That site was purchased in 1956 during the presidency of Rudy Tuttle, the first U.S.-born president of the church.

In 1983, Todorovich, church President Nick Sever and the congregation at St. Sava held the June 5 ground breaking of a new church building on land at 9100 Mississippi St., Merrillville.

Meanwhile, St. Sava Church and its co-affiliates with the Free Serbian Orthodox Diocese for the USA and Canada are building a new monastery and diocesan seat at Third Lake, near Libertyville, Ill.

The previous monastery in Libertyville was turned over through litigation to the Serbian diocese that heads the St. Elijah church.

There are two other Serbian churches in the area, St. George in East Chicago and St. George in Schererville.

At St. Elijah, church President Mike Popovich said a church, schoolhouse and picnic complex in Merrillville, costing $6 million, is almost complete. The church, designed in 7th century Byzantine style, is "the most beautiful in the Midwest," he said.

Serbian activities focus on church and family, and thus both St. Sava and St. Elijah units have full calendars.

St. Sava's Service List:

The church presidents and parish priests who served St. Sava Serbian Orthodox Church since its inception in 1914 are named here in sequence.

Presidents — Bozo Trbovich, Steve Orlich, Petar Prica, John T. Marich, Luka R. Grkovich, Marko Lukach, Stevan Orescanin, Marko Lukach, George Miljanovich, Krsto Bratich, Mitchell Duchick, M.B. Mihailovich, R. T. Martin, Jefto Vuletich, George Miljanovich, David Bundalo, Rudy Tuttle, Nick Cabraja, Joe Sever, Sivojin Cokic, Nick Sever.

Priests — Dushan Bogich, Paul Veljkov, Milan Jugovich, Philip Sredanovich, Paul Veljkov, Peter Stijachick, Bogolub Gakovich, Paul Markovich, Dushan Shoukletovich, Vladimir Mrvichin, Nikola Sekulich, Svetozar Radovanovich, Dushan Shoukltovich, Velimir Petrkovich, Peter Bankerovich, John Todorovich.

Artwork by: Chuck Lazar

3. Macedonians

Macedonia.

The name is steeped in history. It is antiquity, Alexander the Great, the gladiators of ancient Rome, a land populated for at least 4,000 years.

It's Cyril and Methodius, founders of the Slavic alphabet. And it's a people now divided among three nations — Greece, Bulgaria and, mostly, Yugoslavia.

For some 800 families in Northwest Indiana, and 400,000 people in the United States, it's the motherland that they look back to with mixed feelings of anguish and anticipation.

"We know how to appreciate freedom. Our people had been enslaved for 500 years (1389-1912) by the Turks," said Loretta Popyc of Lakes of the Four Seasons.

As a 4-year-old in 1937, Mrs. Popyc — known by her maiden name, Rutka Gulaboff — was brought to America by her parents, Mr. and Mrs. George Gulaboff.

She learned Macedonian — the language, customs, devotion to hard work and family, thrift, humility, hospitality and discipline — in Gary. Today she's principal of the Sunday School, president of the ladies' auxiliary and council treasurer at S.S. Peter and Paul Macedonian Orthodox Chuerch, 51st and Virginia in Gary.

It is through the church, with the Rev. Boris Popovski as parish priest, Gary policeman Boris Velovski as president, that the younger American-born Macedonians are learning their Slavic language, their glorious history, and the songs, strudels and soccer so popular in motherland cities like Skopje, Ohrid and Bitola.

"We're Orthodox Christians, Americans and Macedonians — in that order," said Mrs. Popyc, who learned about Alexander the Great and St. Clement of Ohrid from her father, now 90, who in the 1940s ran Famous Grill at 5th and Washington and was the first cafeteria operator at The Post-Tribune building in the 1950s.

Macedonians, like their Balkan neighbors the Croats and Serbs, were among Gary pioneers, with the first wave arriving from 1908 through 1912 to work in the new U.S. Steel mills.

Indiana University Northwest professor James B. Lane, in his 1978 book, "City of the Century," records the story of Duko Costo, who emigrated from Macedonia at age 20 in 1912 to avoid being drafted into the Turkish army.

His was a frugal life. He stayed in a boarding house with other mill workers and slept on a bed when it wasn't used by others. Eventually, he married a Polish woman and they saved money for a bungalow in Glen Park. He died, at age 50, in 1942.

Costo's story parallels that of many of Indiana's first Macedonians, who settled in Tolleston, near the Balkan Bakery at 1337 Adams St., which was unofficially known as "the Macedonian post office."

Since the 1940s, the Macedonians have moved on. Today, they're scattered, living in Crown Point, Merrrillville, Munster, Lowell, Kokomo and Valparaiso, notes Steve Stephan, who retired to Valparaiso in 1979 after 45 years running the Downtown Tap in Gary.

Popovski, who was his schoolmate near Skopje, said the first major migration to America took place about 1865 when Macedonian serfs, overburdened and overtaxed under the Turkish government, fled. Today, there are large Macedonian communities in St. Louis; Buffalo, N.Y.; Akron, Canton and Cleveland, Ohio; Trenton, N.J.; and Detroit.

His father, who died in Pittsburgh, crossed the Atlantic three times — to Canada, to Cuba, and finally to Boston, where he worked building sewers. He moved on to railroad jobs in Detroit, Chicago and Lorain, Ohio.

Another wave of Macedonian immigrants came after World War II and more arrived in the 1950s, like Velovski, who was 16 when he joined his grandfather.

He matured in Gary, served with the U.S. Army in Korea, and became a policeman in 1968. In 1973, he accompanied Gary Mayor Richard G. Hatcher on Hatcher's visit to Macedonia.

Active in the church, Velovski is on his fifth term as president, having served in 1972, 1973, 1975 and 1982.

The church is new, the first of 16 congregations of the Macedonian Orthodox Church that gained independent status in 1958 with Skopje, Yugoslavia, as its holy center. S.S. Peter and Paul opened in 1963.

Before 1963, local Macedonians went to Orthodox churches of other nationalities — Greek, Russian, Serbian — and maintained their cultural ties through the Alexander the Great Macedonian Benefit Organization, the Macedonian Political Organization and the Elinden Club.

When SS Peter and Paul was built, for a congregation of 450 families, it was "a dream come true," Popovski said.

Content as they are to have a church of their own, and to freely go to Yugoslavia, the federated nation in which Macedonia is one of six states, Macedonians have another dream — the unification of their people, here and in Eastern Europe.

"We hope to God that we can be united as a nation with our brothers and sisters," said Velovski.

Since the Balkan Wars of 1912-13, the Macedonian population has been divided into three parts — 2 million in Yugoslavia, with Skopje as capital; 250,000 in Greece, with Salonika as capital; and 100,000 in Bulgaria, with a capital at Blogoevgrad. Many of the Macedonians in Greece and Bulgaria have been absorbed in those nations.

Most of the Greek Macedonians in this area go to Greek Orthodox churches, and the few Bulgarian Macedonians have a church of their own in Indianapolis.

"All Macedonians — from Yugoslavia, Greece and Bulgaria — are welcome here," said Popovski.

There also are about 30 families who followed the Rev. Spiro Tanaskovski, the first priest of SS. Peter and Paul, when he moved on to the St. Clement of Ohridski American Macedonian Orthodox Church in Merrillville.

Macedonians have a strong "survivor" instinct, says Hristo Mangovski of Merrillville, who was a history teacher in Skopje and now is a representative of the Stopanski Bank of Macedonia.

"Hundreds of years of domination will not destroy Macedonians," he said. "Our own history tells us that."

It is with pride that Macedonians speak of their heritage, their language, which is similar to Croatian-Serbian, and the Slav alphabet, which was developed by SS. Cyril and Methodius in 855 A.D.

The first occupants of Macedonia were the Thracians in 2000 B.C., who later were absorbed by tribes from the northwest. After 1100 B.C., the Macedonians came under the influence of the Greeks from the south. The first Macedonian state (707-645 B.C.) was under King Perdiccas, of Slav ancestry. King Philip II extended the Macedonian rule in 338 B.C., and his son, Alexander the Great, destroyed the ancient cities of Tyre, Gaza and Babylon and founded the vast empire that reached east to India, known then as "the end of the world."

Alexander died in 323 at the age of 33. His empire was divided by his generals and Macedonia began to decline. It became a Roman province in 148 B.C., and in Caesar's era of gladiators, 30,000 of them were Macedonians.

The pre-Slavic Macedonians were among the first Christians, said to have been converted by St. Paul in the first century. Christianity never left the land.

Macedonia was made part of the Byzantine Empire in A.D. 395, including the first Bulgarian empire in the 800s and being on the via Ignatia, the ancient road to Asia Minor, it was invaded by the Normans in 1072, and by the Crusaders in the 11th and 13th Century. It became part of Dushan's Serbian empire in 1346, and was conquered by the Turks in 1352. The area remained under Turkish domination until 1912 when it was split into the three present regions.

For the SS. Peter and Paul parishioners, 1983 was a special year. The 20th anniversary of the church was celebrated July 16 and 17 with Macedonian Bishop Metropolitan Kiril, head of the American-Canadian Dioceses, officiating. The SS. Peter and Paul patron saint day is July 12.

Local Macedonians traveled to Toronto, Canada, for the annual diocesan picnic July 31, and to Chicago's Hilton Hotel Sept. 3 and 4 for the national Macedonian convocation.

For the 80 youngsters of the two soccer teams, Warder and Macedonia, every Sunday is special. That's when they have their games. EDITOR'S NOTE: A foreign dignitary from Macedonia visited Gary while reporter Ernie Hernandez was preparing the article on Macedonians for The Post-Tribune series on ethnic groups. His story: A traveling journalist from Macedonia, a guest of the U.S. State Department, finally found the Gary he had long wanted to see.

His curiosity satisfied about the land where his father once lived, before he was born, Dimitar Basevski said he was determined to continue commuications between Gary and Skopje, capital of Macedonia.

Basevski, 40, editor-in-chief of "Macedonia," a monthly magazine published in the Socialist Republic of Macedonia, one of the six states of federated Yugoslavia, found old friends at the St. Peter and Paul Macedonian Orthodox Church at 51st and Virginia.

The former newspaperman learned that the president of the church council, Boris Velovski, a Gary policeman, is his third cousin, and they're from the same city of Bitola.

Velovski left his native Macedonia 25 years ago, and he accompanied Mayor Richard G. Hatcher there in 1973.

Basevski was on a month-long trip to key United States cities under the spnsorship of the State Department.

He specifically asked his hosts for a chance to see Gary because of its special significance to Macedonians, he said.

His father had lived in the Gary area for about four years before 1927, long before he was born, he noted.

Basevski visited The Post-Tribune offices and printing presses and met editor James G. Driscoll.

Basevski and his wife left their two children, 11 and 7, with relatives while on their U.S. trip.

Addressing members of the St. Peter and Paul congregation, he told them that the government in Macedonia is keenly interested in the Macedonian Americans in the Gary area.

"We should get together and communicate our needs and wishes," he said in Macedonian while Velovski interpreted.

"We are interested in your progress, in your education and your business," he said. "I would like to report about you for the rest of the Macedonian world."

Basevski said he was "overwhelmingly happy" to meet local Macedonians who have relatives in his own home city or Bitola, and to learn that young people are learning the language and customs of their parents.

And he congratulates the community for being loyal American citizens while being united as Macedonians.

"Don't let anyone separate you, Be loyal citizens and show your love for your new country," he said. Then he offered a toast "to the success and prosperity of the Macedonian people in this community."

* * * * * * * * * *

The Macedonian Information Bureau, Willowdale, Ontario, Canada, sent a large package to "clarify" that Macedonians of Gary's Saints Peter and Paul Church are only a fraction of the many other Macedonians in the United States in Canada. The vast majority, arriving around 1909, are nationalistic and anti-communist, and are affiliated with Macedonian Patriotic Organization of USA and Canada, founded in 1921, said W.B. Stevens, director.

While the writer was still researching with Gary Macedonians, he was given an invitation to visit Macedonia by visiting journalist, Dimitar Basevski.

The Rev. Boris Popovski tells the story of meeting a dark man while he was in Lahore, Pakistan, who claimed to be Macedonian, a descendant of the the troops of Alexander the Great who reached India in 300 B.C.

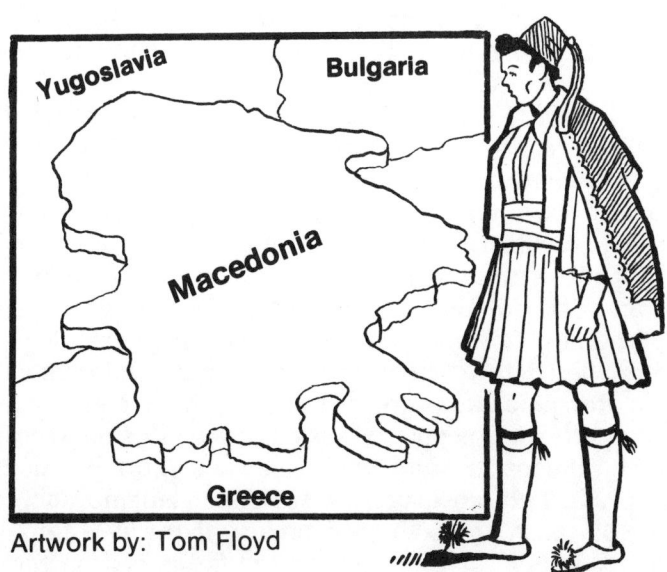

Artwork by: Tom Floyd

4. Ukrainians

> "The Soviets are strong today. So was Rome. England was strong ... It is very hard to destroy a people." — **An American Ukrainian**

Never mind who said it, not so long ago. It is the essence of the Ukraine — ever since the Cossacks, especially since Taras Shevchenko.

"What we're not is, we're not Russian. Ukraine is a nation, with its own language, its own tradition," said the Rev. John Scharba, pastor of St. Michael Ukrainian Orthodox Church in Hammond and a fourth-generation Ukrainian.

Worldwide, there are almost 50 million Ukrainians, with 6 million outside the Soviet Union. About 300 families live in Northwest Indiana, with 150 families at St. Michael's, and another 150 at St. Josaphat Ukrainian Catholic Church in Munster.,

It is a small group when compared to Chicago, Philadelphia and New York, where the population of Ukrainian communities reaches 100,000.

The Rev. Walter Wozniak, parish priest of St. Josaphat, built in 1958, said there also are communities of Ukrainians in Alberta, Saskatchewan, and Manitoba provinces in Canada. The world's largest Ukrainian Easter Egg is the dome of a church in Vegreville, just east of Edmonton, Alberta.

While Ukrainians around the world are known for their elaborate and colorful Easter eggs, intricately designed with pictures of horses, flowers, crosses and village inscriptions, the people from the southwest corner of the Soviet Union, next to Poland and Romania, take greater pride in their endurance.

"We are a suffering people, a serious people," said Wozniak.

In 1983, Ukrainians in Munster, Mishawaka, Fort Wayne and elsewhere prayerfully observed Holod, their remembrance of their own Holocaust, the 50th anniversary of the 1933 famine, which killed 7 million of their people and is blamed on the Soviet Bolshevik government.

Mass death is part of Ukrainian history. In World War II, 2.5 million Ukrainians were killed, while 1.5 million more were reported missing and 3 million were taken as slave labor to Nazi Germany and never returned.

Today, the area famed for its black soil and known during the centuries of the czars as "Europe's granary," producer of half of the USSR's wheat, two-thirds of its iron and coal, and one-third of its rolled steel, remains, in the minds of some Ukrainians, a captured nation.

Father Wozniak, who came from Lvov near the Polish border, said there is ever-present repression and fear in the Ukraine. Unlike in some other Slavic socialist nations, such as Yugoslavia, there is no free access in the Russian state, he said.

"In Ukraine, you can visit your relatives, but you cannot go to their village. You can go to the city, and they'll have to visit you there," he said.

More and more Ukrainian-Americans — descendants of those who left Galicia and Bukovina, Kiev and Lvov from 1880 to 1914 because of economic hardships — are making trips to the motherland.

George Liber, a Ph.D. candidate in history at Harvard, a graduate of Andrean High School and a "full-blooded"Ukrainian, is one of them.

He's one of two sons of Miroslaw and Mary Liber, considered "newcomers" in the Ukrainian community. They didn't arrive in Gary until 1958, coming from Perth, Australia, where George and his brother, Peter, were born.

Their father, who teaches chemistry at Indiana University Northwest, recently retired as chief chemist at Inland Steel. Mrs. Liber, a microbiologist, works at St. Anthony Medical Center in Crown Point. They were married in Germany after World War II.

Peter, a fourth-year medical student at Indiana University, Indianapolis, provided his parents with a special joy in 1983 when he was married in what many consider America's most beautiful Ukrainian church — St. Nicholas Catholic Cathedral, built at Rice and Oakley in Chicago in 1913.

The bride, Adriana, was a Ukrainian from Naperville, Ill.

"It makes life a little easier," was the wry comment of the smiling mother of the groom.

Mrs Liber served torte, a fruit-filled layered cake, while talking about the life and times of local Ukrainians, who are also described as Ruthenian, Rusyn, Russniak, Carpatho-Russians or Little Russians.

Ukrainians — independent-minded, hardworking, physicially strong, artistic, family-oriented, serious — enjoy the quiet pleasures of life, she said.

They like to do intricate work and colorful embroidery, and to sing and dance to the music of the stringed bandura.

Their national hero is Taras Shevchenko (1814-1861), a slave who became renowned as a painter and lyric poet, who described Ukrainians' passion for freedom. March 9 and 10 are annually celebrated as his days.

Other festivities in 1983 were St. Josaphat Church's Silver Jubilee on Nov. 27, the annual Father's Day lunch June 19, the parish picnic Aug. 21, and the Jan. 22 Ukrainian Independence Day, celebrated together by the Catholic and Orthodox congregations.

They are events for serving syrnyk cheese cake, babka bread, nachynka cornmeal casserole, among others.

St. Josaphat Church, with Masses in Ukrainian, is of the Eastern rite, loyal to the pope in Rome while under a patriarch, Cardinal Joseph Slipjyj. Wozniak draws on the Holy Name Society, with Michael Bilik as president, and the Women's Altar Rosary Society, with Myroslava Iwachiw as president, for church-related assistance.

Secular activities are through the Ukrainian National Association with Svoboda as its newspaper, Ukrainian Fraternal Association, Ukrainian National Aid Association and Congress of Free Ukrainians in the United States and Canada. President of the Hammond-Munster chapter is Oris Szewciw, a lawyer.

The Ukrainians are derived from the Rus, a Slavic civilization that developed at Kiev and along the river Dnepr in A.D. 800. Kiev became the first of the independent Russian city-states.

During the 1200s, the Tartars from Asia conquered the area, but were defeated in the 1300s by the Polish and Lithuanians from the west. In the 1400s, discontented peasants joined free soldiers known as Cossacks in the territory between the Poles and the Tartars, and their region became known as Ukraine meaning "borderland."

Russian czars gained control of the area in the mid-1700s and ruled it until the Bolshevik Revolution in 1917. The czars began the practice of exiling Ukrainians and the Soviets continued it. Under the Communist government, millions of Ukrainians were sent to Siberia. Wozniak noted there are still Ukrainian communities there. One is called Zelenyj Klyn, the "green wedge" near the Siberia-Japan border.

Ukrainians had periods of freedom, briefly in 1917 and again in 1942-43 when an insurgent army warred against Hitler's occupation forces and controlled East Ukraine until the Russians returned.

* * * * * * * * * *

Ukrainians / 25

Myron and Maria Liber, talking about their former homeland, noted that when their son visited Moscow as an American exchange student, he asked to see old relatives near Lvov. He spent a weekend with his aunt, but wasn't allowed to go to the countryside to visit his grandmother's grave. He was diverted back to his hotel in Moscow.

Artwork by: Tom Floyd

5.
Slovaks

"If you go to Ely, Minn., or to Cleveland, you'll find the Slovenes," said Louise Keleminic. "Here, we're slowly disappearing." Mrs. Keleminic, of Portage, left her village near Novo Mesto in Slovenia at the age of 17 in 1927. She is one of the few remaining "full-blooded" Slovenes in Northwest Indiana.

Another is Otto Skarja, 78, of Gary, who grew up near Ljubjana, Slovenia's capital. At age 15, he migrated to America in 1922 to work at the hardware store of his uncle, Louis Schmidt.

They are among the 100 Slovenes in the area. The number is diminishing, although Mrs. Keleminic insists that "our tradition remains alive."

She married a Croatian, Frank Keleminic, and their children — Frank and Gloria — were raised in the Slavic culture. Gloria, now living in Seattle, still sings Slovenian folk songs.

Skarja, who worked 40 years at U.S. Steel in Gary, married a Polish woman, and their children were raised American, he said. Otto "Skeets" Skarja Jr., who owns the Silver Dollar Saloon in Lake Station, doesn't speak Slovenian or Polish.

"I'm proud of being both," he said. "I'm a Slovene-Polish American."

The heaviest influx of Slovenes to America occurred between 1880 and 1914, when Austria-Hungary controlled the land. Young men fled from army service and sought their fortunes in America and Canada.

The Harvard Encyclopedia of American Ethnic Groups says 550,000 Slovenes emigrated to the United States by 1945 — 314,000 of them before 1914.

The first major concentrations, in the 1890s, were in northern Michigan and the Minnesota iron-range towns of Ely, Hibbing and Virginia. Slovenes also settled in Cleveland and the Chicago-Joliet area.

Mrs. Keleminic, active with Slovene National Benefit Society Lodge 271, with Frank Skala as president, said the society consists of about 400,000 Slovenes in North America.

That includes immigrant Slovenes and their descendants. The U.S. Census Bureau in 1980 reported that 126,463 Americans claim Slovene ancestry.

Distinct from the Croations, Serbians and Macedonians in what is now Yugoslavia, Slovenes are a Slavic people who speak Slovenian, which is closer to Ukrainian.

Like the Croatians, they're Roman Catholic. Like the Polish, they love the polka. Their favorite foods also are similiar to those of the Poles, with slight variations. The Slovenes serve dishes like potica nut roll, sarkel fancy bread, palenta corn meal with beef stew, and strukla, a kind of strudel.

The Slovenes came to Northwest Indiana before World War I. They settled in Gary's Tolleston neighborhood, an area bounded by 9th and 15th avenues and by Grant and Taft streets.

There, the Slovene Button Box, a type of accordion, was familiar to Serbians, Croatians and Greeks nearby, says Mrs. Keleminic.

Kathy Vatusic, who is Croatian but as secretary of SNPJ Lodge 271 is considered an "adopted" Slovene, said many of the local Slovenes have died or retired to Florida, but their children remain in the area.

Thus names such as Malensek, Pishkur, Jarc, Batzer, Furkul, Unetich, Luzar, Musek, Gazvoda and Kaps still appear in directories and school rosters.

Among the early Slovene businessmen was Ignatz Prosinak, Gary's first harness maker, who had a shop at 9th and Madison.

Starja and Mrs. Klemenic have never met. She's been active in the local lodge, while he maintained his ethnic ties by joining the lodge in Joliet.

"My heart is still in Joliet," he said. He never had a desire to return to Slovenia, not even for a visit, he added.

"America is my country, my children's country," he said.

But to Louise Keleminic — whose father, Joseph Ahcin, had been in America three times before he transferred his family — her two visits to the country where she was born were memorable. After 25 years in Gary, she toured Slovenia for the first time in 1952.

Her early days in Indiana weren't so thrilling.

"Life was hard in Slovenia," she said. "But it was harder in Gary. I begged my father to send me back."

He didn't. And she learned to accept America by becoming active in the Croatian glee club Preradovic. A soprano soloist, she sang for schools and churches and on special programs.

She was even offered a music scholarship in Chicago. But by then, she was the mother of two children and decided her place was at home, she said.

When she visited Yugoslavia in 1952, she said, she was pleasantly surprised. The war had long been over, there were new buildings in Ljubljana and people were going to school.

She said that during her last trip, in 1971, "everything was in better shape, and every house has a car."

"My sisters there now wouldn't think of sending their kids to America," she said.

The Slovenes today have a country of their own, as one of the six republics in the Federal Republic of Yugoslavia.

The Slovenes settled in what is now Slovenia in 500 A.D., but were conquered by German invaders in the 800s. About 400 years later, Austria conquered the region.

Slovenia remained under Austrian rule until 1918, except for a period of French occupation from 1809 to 1815. After World War I, Slovenia became part of the Kingdom of Croats, Serbs and Slovenes, later named Yugoslavia.

In 1941, Italy and Germany conquered Slovenia and divided it between them. When the war ended in 1945, the area was freed again, and then became part of Yugoslavia.

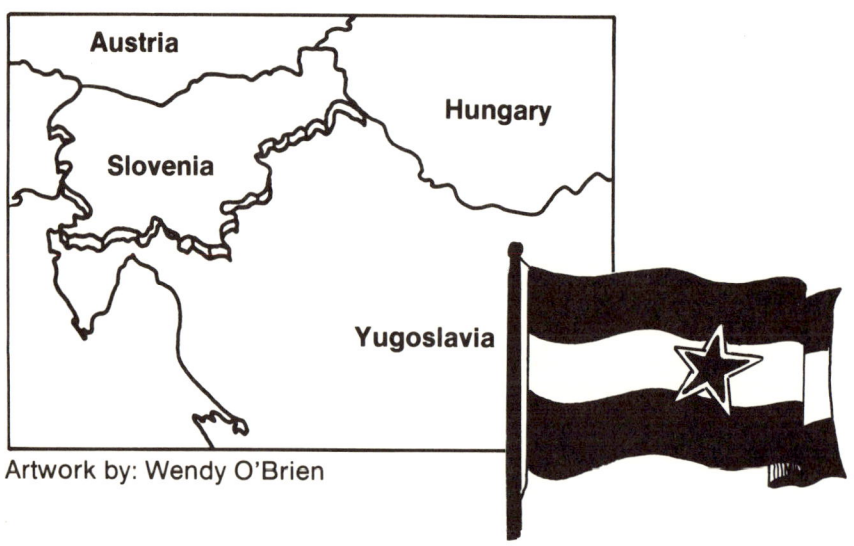

Artwork by: Wendy O'Brien

6. Romanians

U.S. Flag Day on June 14, has special meaning to Romanian Americans and their cousins in the old homeland.

So dedicated to the Stars and Stripes were the early Romanians of Northwest Indiana that no photograph was complete without the honored banner. For group pictures, there were dozens of flags.

"How devoted they were," said Mary Leuca of Crown Point, based on her own personal experience and extensive studies.

There are about 700 Romanian families in the area, belonging to four churhes that date back to 1906. The 1980 U.S. Census reported that 315,258 Americans claim Romanian ancestry.

Ambitious, hospitable, gregarious and proud of their heritage, Romanians consider themselves different from their neighbors in East Europe.

Descendants of Roman legions who absorbed the ancient Dacian people in the 1st Century, Romanians are "an island of Latins in a sea of Slavs," said the Rev. George C. Muresan, pastor of St. Nicholas Romanian Catholic Church in East Chicago, a native of the parish whose grandfather immigrated from Transylvania before 1900.

Present-day Romania is bounded by the Soviet Union, Hungary, Yugoslavia, Bulgaria and the Black Sea. The nation of 21 million, nourished by 900 miles of the Danube River, was occupied by the Dacians beginning around 300 B.C.

They were conquered by the Romans, whose power in the area declined in 273 A.D. Their descendants are the Romanians, who didn't form a state until 1859. Transylvania, where most of Northwest Indiana's Romanians come from, was under the Austro-Hungarian Empire until 1918.

The first immigrants were from that area, where their flag was banned. In America, they found the opportunity to show the colors — their own red, gold and blue and the U.S. Stars and Stripes — said Mrs. Lueca's husband, Walter, a Gary patent attorney and second-generation Romanian.

"They were unable to display the flag until they came to America," he said.

Today, it is a practice of the Romanian fraternal organizations — Transilvaneana, Nicolae Iorga, TriColor, Unirea, Romanian Lodge 148 — to do the sfintieria drapelelor, blessing the flags for special places and occasions.

It is an honor to sponsor the flags. In 1913, East Chicago patrons bid as high as $200 for that privilege.

Mrs. Leuca, principal at Black Oak Elementary School, is the daughter of one of the early Romanians, Danila Stanciu, who migrated from Transylvania to Hannibal, Mo., in the early 1900s to work at the cement plants along the Mississippi River.

He later returned to Romania and got married. A year after Mary Stanciu was born, the family moved to Indiana Harbor and operated the Block Avenue Hotel at 3212 Block Ave.

She grew up in the Harbor, learning the Romanian language and culture through after-school classes. She married Leuca whose Romanian father had migrated to Buffalo, N.Y., settled in Gary and became an educator-researcher.

For her Ph.D. at Purdue University in 1979, Mrs. Leuca wrote her thesis on curriculum study of Romanian Americans. Encouraged by her professor, Peter John Georgeoff, and a $32,000 federal grant, in 1977, she developed "Romanian Americans in Lake County, Indiana: An Ethnic Heritage Curriculum Project."

With 130 oral interviews, and photographs, filmstrips, cassettes, recordings, videotapes and recipes, the work has become a basic university reference on ethnic studies. Harvard calls it the best study of a selected Romanian American community.

Although more than half of the pioneer Romanians interviewed by Mrs. Leuca, Pearl Mailath and Mary Bogolia have died, their stories remain on record.

They were shepherds and peasants, young men who left Transylvania from 1895 to 1910 for a better worklife at 15 cents an hour, away from the clutches of the Austria-Hungary empire.

Romanians describe those years as mia si drumul — "a thousand dollars and home again."

"All they wanted to do, at first, was make enough to buy land in Romania," said Ms. Leuca, pointing out that many did return.

"Because of that intent, they started the supplementary schools for their children," said Mrs. Leuca, who was taught by Letitia Cucui in the 1930s. Earlier, Nicolae Benchea established the first of those culture schools Scoala Regele Ferdinand I.

But intent is often altered by circumstance, and many others, like the Stanciu and Leuca families, stayed in America, and focused their energies on the education of their children.

Among those who stayed are the families of Nick Angel, former Lake County treasurer and commissioner; the late

Walter Jeorse, former East Chicago mayor; Dan Simon, former East Chicago school superintendent; Helen Doria, retired elementary supervisor; Ray Sufana, former county prosecutor; Sufana's brother George, a musician; Eli Popa and Nicolae Novac, writers; Marianne Collier (Mary Ann Chulay) and Claire Malis, actresses; and George Stroia, educational supervisor.

The early Romanians settled around Block and Pennsylvania in Indiana Harbor, and 13th and Jefferson in Gary. Mrs. Leuca reported in her resource guide that in 1905, when there were 4,000 Poles in Indiana Harbor, there also were 1,000 Romanians. While there were 7,000 Croatians in Gary, there also were 3,000 Romanians. In East Chicago, there were 4,600 Poles and 400 Romanians.

In 1901, John Covach and Pete Cionta were in the first 40 men to arrive by train from Midland Iron & Steel in Muncie to Inland Steel.

They lived first in boxcars, tents or tarpaper shacks, later moving to $6-a-month boarding houses such as Casa Romana, where the bortarita — wife of the owner — would serve tocana de pui chicken stew and the staple mamaliga cornmeal mush at breakfast, lunch and dinner, and an occasional ciorba sour soup, scover doughnuts or sarmale stuffed cabbage; and perhaps a little tuica plum brandy.

Almost as soon as they arrived, the early Romanians built their churches — St. George Orthodox at Beech Street (later named Pulaski in East Chicago) founded March 11, 1906, under the leadership of the Rev. Moise Balea, was the first Romanian Orthodox Church built in America. It was damaged and relocated in 1914. In 1976, the New St. George Romanian Orthodox Church moved to Lansing, Ill., with the Rev. John Ionita as pastor.

From 1908 to his death in 1963, the Rev. Simon Mihaltian was pastor.

"He had a profound effect on virtually every Romanian in his community," wrote Mrs. Leuca. By Mihaltian's 50th anniversary as pastor in 1958, he had married 462 couples, baptized 1,531 children and officiated at 1,332 funerals. He also did his own housekeeping, mowed the lawn and played the violin, she recalled.

Meanwhile, in Gary, the Descent of the Holy Ghost Romanian Orthodox Church was founded Oct. 11, 1908, through efforts of Iacob Popa, Ioan Stebla, Nichita Stoica, Ilie Adlea, Ioan Ganea, Mihalca Mafteiu, Peter Ilcau and Nicolae Radovan.

The first service was at 1517 Washington St. on Dec. 25. The first building, costing $1,800 and located at 19th and Hayes, was consecrated June 10, 1910. But as more Romanians settled near

Broadway between 10th and 15th, the church was carried 20 blocks to 12th and Madison in 1915, with a band playing.

Renovated by parishioners Nick Chirila, George Draghiciu and Ilie Grusia in the 1930s, the church was consecrated Sept. 22, 1935, by the first Romanian Orthodox Bishop of America, Bishop Policarp.

The church was sold and torn down in 1969, and Descent of the Holy Ghost Parish relocated at 61st and Harrison, in Merrillville. The current pastor is the Rev. George Gage.

Two other Romanian churches in East Chicago are St. Nicholas Romanian Rite Catholic Church at 4311 Olcott, founded in 1913, which Rev. Muresan serves, and St. Demetrius Romanian Rite Catholic Church, 13th and Butternut, founded in 1914. The Rev. John Popa serves there.

Another Romanian church is the Romanian Baptist Church, started in Gary in 1919. Its first building, at 14th and Delaware, was dedicated Dec. 4, 1921. It was sold in 1964, and members dispersed to other churches.

While churches kept the faithful together, Mrs. Leuca said, the fraternal societies kept traditions alive. First to be formed, in 1905, was the Societatea Transilvaneana with 22 members, followed by the 105-member Societatea Treicolorul Roman in 1908 with Bucur Manta as president. Through it, the Descent of the Holy Ghost Parish was founded.

Romanians, known for their Fourth of July festivals marked by singing and folk dancing, celebrate the anniversaries of the consecretion of their churches. They like large picnic gatherings, usually at harvest time and late in the spring.

For 28 years, the Midwest Romanian Radio Hour, based in Gary, has been working to keep the language alive. Initiated by Eli Grusia, it is carried on by Nicolae Novak at 8 a.m. Sundays on WLTH.

But most third- and fourth-generation Romanians speak only English. That bothers their American-born grandparents, whose love for their Latin-like language is intense.

Yet, there's hope that all the young will start yearning for their roots. There's a new spirit of ethnicity in the land evidenced by clubs like the Justinian Society formed by young English-speaking Italian American lawyers.

"We can hope," said Mrs. Leuca, who has done her share by demonstrating through her work how heritage training can be re-introduced.

* * * * * * * * * *

After the Romanian story appeared, Walter and Mary Leuca called with compliments. They received calls from friends too, they said.

Artwork by: Tom Floyd

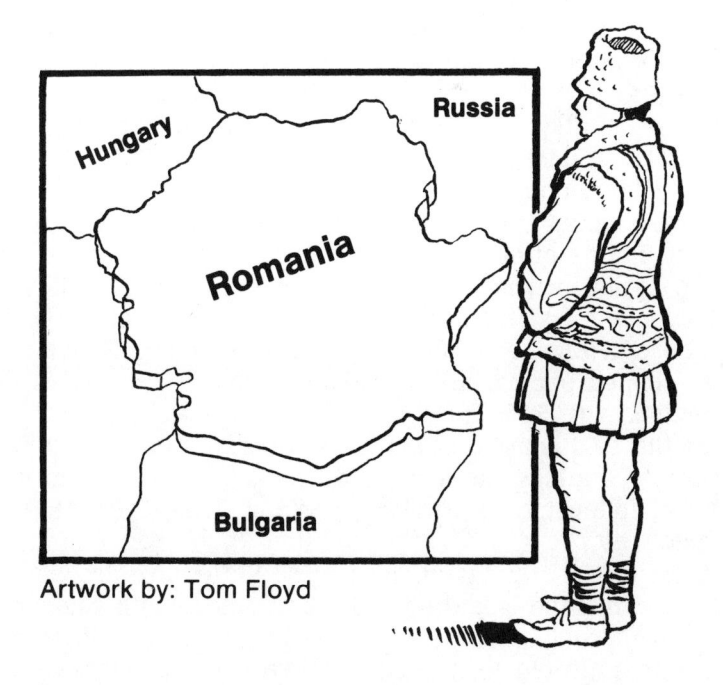

7. Italians

"If you're not proud of what you are, how can you live with yourself?" — **Peter Calacci**

With pride and passion, the Justinian Society, a band of 50 young Italian-American lawyers, is digging into its ethnic roots.

"It's back to roots," said Tony Trapane, whose grandfather, Sam Trapane, migrated from Pioppi — near Palermo, Sicily — at the turn of the century, and whose grandmother, Grace, founded Maria Principessa Dipiemonte Lodge.

Perhaps influenced by Alex Haley's book and television special "Roots," or the 1980s spirit of ethnic pride, young people, three and four generations after their immigrant grandfathers, are expressing interest in old-country customs. Attorney groups such as the Hispanic Bar, Hellenic Bar and Polish Advocates have been formed.

For the Justinians, with John Sorbello of Crown Point as president, it's a task. Only three or four can speak an Italian dialect. Fewer can name the 19 regions of Italy.

The Roman Catholic faith remains strong in the new generation, which savors the pastas and serenades of the mother country, which has given the world Christopher Columbus, Sophia Loren, Luciano Pavarotti, Mario Andretti and Rocky Marciano.

Yet, deep as Italian roots are — reaching back to antiquity, to the Latins of 800 B.C., who were conquered by the Etruscans from Lydia in what is now western Turkey, to the Greeks, the Phoenicians and the Roman Empire — the effort is being made.

There are some 70 million Italians, including 58 million in the boot-shaped peninsula. More than 100,000 live in metropolitan Chicago, with 5,000 families in Northwest Indiana.

In the 1980 census, 12,183,692 Americans claimed Italian ancestry, making them the sixth largest ethnic group in the nation, following the English, German, Irish, Afro-American and French.

Most of the Italians in the United States are descendants of people from the island of Sicily and other south regions of Campania and Calabria. Between 1880 and 1920, about 5 million Italians migrated to America. There were a few northern Italians, from Venice and Genoa areas, who settled in New York, Virginia, Rhode Island, Connecticut, Maryland and Georgia in the 17th century.

One Justinian Society member, state Sen. John Bushemi, and his brother, Jim, in 1977 took on the roots endeavor with typical Italian passion. They traced their ancestry to the 1700s, digging into courthouse records and interviewing paesanos in Palermo, Villa Rosa, Buscemi and Cala Scibetta, where their grandfather, Pietro Buscemi, lived until he migrated to America in 1909 at the age of 29. Buscemi's wife arrived later with the two oldest children, Margaret (now Mrs. Polizzotto) and Marion, who later became a state representative from Gary and died in 1976.

It was Marion and his brothers who changed the surname to Bushemi, distinguishing the progeny of Pietro Buscemi from those of his five brothers, who also came to America.

John Bushemi discovered there are 400 Bushemi or Buscemi heads of household in the United States.

Among those first Italians in Northwest Indiana were Peter Calacci's father, who worked for the railroads; Guy Carruba, 93, of East Chicago, who came in 1907 from Palermo and also worked for the railroads; and Frank Venturella of Lake Station, from Lascari, up the hill from Campo Felice, where Tony Muffoletto, 88, of Crown Point, was a cobbler.

Muffoletto arrived in Gary in 1911, opened a shop, and taught his sons, Tony of Gary, Paul of Merrillville, and Joe of Michigan how to work with leather and glue.

A daughter, Tina, also learned. Later, her daughter, Rosemarie Vaccaro, married a Frenchman, Gary de St. Jean, who now runs the Cobbler Shop in Portage.

Guided perhaps by grandmother Emilia, the Muffolettos have maintained their Italian tradition. She's proud that "all my children married Italians, I talk to my children in Italian." Paul Muffoletto is the president of the Dante Alighierie Lodge of Sons of Italy.

Another pioneer was Antonio Greco (1885-1974), who arrived in Duquesne, Pa., in 1900 from Naples, following his father, Leonardo, who made his first voyage in 1880. Tony Greco at 21 was one of the first riggers of U.S. Steel in Gary in 1906, married Lucia d'Foggia in 1911, settled at 13th and Georgia, managed a grocery store at 18th and Broadway, and then became a land developer in Glen Park. He owned the land at 35th and Indiana, now King Drive, that later was sold and donated to Indiana Vocational Technical College, recalled one of his six children, Michael J. Greco of Merrillville.

In East Chicago, among the early Italians were the Rev. Michelangelo Campagna, who with his parishioners built Immaculate Conception Church with bricks from Forsythe Avenue, now Indianapolis. His neighbors were the broommaking

Bianchi family from Ferentino, near Rome. Mary Bianchi spent her early school years in Ferentino and later married her brother James O. Bianchi's former soccer-playing buddy, Peter Calacci.

Calacci, who arrived in America in 1930, moved to East Chicago in 1936 from Chicago Heights, Ill. He was one of the first organizers of United Steelworkers during the 1937 strike, became the union's subdistrict director and recently retired to full-time volunteer community work.

Calacci and his wife speak fluent Roman-Italian, Italy's national language.

Carruba, on the other hand, has let the years erase his Sicilian dialect. Too much work, he explained.

"Ten hours a day at $1.25 a day, driving spikes," he said.

Carruba said he left everything behind in Italy. He rarely speaks Sicilian. Their four children married non-Italians, as did their grandchildren. "We are English-speaking Italian Americans," said Mrs. Carruba, whose maiden name was Spitale.

She has no desire to see Italia again, but her daughter Dorothy's son, John Szczepanski, says he fell in love with the Latins when he and his wife went to Europe.

In Gary, the early Italians included Carmelo Pullara, who first arrived in 1901, and Giusseppa Traina, who came in 1903.

With others from Bivona — Vasile, Spata, Taormino, Mortellaro, Cina, Lazzarro, Pinto, Cassarino, Militello, Delia, Spota, Quaranda and Lamela among them — they formed the Italian American Society Brotherhood of Bivona. As time went on, and more non-Sicilians arrived, the second generation took over. Angelo Grecco, Bernard Lazzaro, Roy de Gaetano, Salvatore Cimino, Frank Traina and Charles Caravana each served as president. In 1949, the club was renamed American Italian Benevolent Society. It provides health insurance for members.

The society, which built Michaelangelo Hall, sponsored wine festivals and beauty contests. Among the beauty queens were Angeline Cacciatore, Ann Chiappazza, Marion Trainer, Rosemary Naccarato, Josephine Cammarata and Antoinette Paxhia.

Akin to the Bushemis were the Giorgi and Cesare families. Dr. Antonio Giorgi, from Rome, was 49 when he settled in Gary in 1909, built St. Anthony Clinic at 19th and Jefferson, and founded Francesco Crispi Lodge. His daughter, Angelina, married another Gary pioneer, Jim Cesare, one of the first supervisors of construction of U.S. Steel. Their daughter,

Victoria, became Vicky Caesar, a state representative.

Former Lake County Criminal Court Judge Andrew Giorgi and his brother Paul, a lawyer, are grandsons of Dr. Giorgi.

Four other Italians have become judges in the area — Darlene Wanda Mears, Lake County Juvenile Court; Nicholas Schiralli, Lake County Small Claims Court; Anthony J. Cefali, Hobart City Court; and Joseph P. Allegretti, Hammond City Court.

Among the Italian professionals are state Sen. Ralph Potesta, Hammond; state Sen. John Bushemi, whose father, Sam, served 20 years as state representative and county assessor; Dr. Albert T. Willardo, former county coroner; Dr. John B. Nicosia, former East Chicago mayor; Joe Germano, retired from USW District 31; Lewis Ciminillo, Indiana University Northwest professor; Vince Panapinto, Northwest Indiana Building Trades; M.J. Pampalone and A.A. Grecco, insurance; Bernard Lazzaro, plastic and glass; Dave Colosimo II, actor; and Jean Borsattino, public relations.

To be Italian is to be proud, with passion, said Calacci.

It's to recognize history of the peninsula — the Caesars, the fall of the Roman Empire in 476 A.D., Charlemagne, the popes, the Renaissance, Napoleon — even though it was not until 1848 that Italian city states were unified through the revolt in Sicily led by Garibaldi. It was 1861 when King Victor Emmanuel II was crowned. Venetia joined Italy in 1866, followed by Latia (Rome) in 1871.

Italians are proud of their culinary arts — pastas, spaghetti, macaroni, lasagna, ravioli, vermicelli, Bologna sausage, Parma ham, Milan minestrone, and capi collo spiced meat, cannoli pastry with cream cheese, and provolone cheese.

They're prouder still of their artists, — not just Dean Martin, Frank Sinatra and Sergio Franchi, but classicists such as Ezio Pinza, Mario Lanza, Enrico Caruso, Luciano Pavarotti, Arturo Toscanini, St. Francis of Assisi, Dante Alighieri, Petrarch, Boccaccio, Nicolo Machiavelli, Michelangelo, Raphael, da Vinci and Titian.

And, of course, Christopher Columbus. Aren't all Americans Italians on Columbus Day?

They boast of their cities — Rome, Florence, Venice, Milan and Naples.

And of the Sicilians' capacity for endurance — forged by being conquered in time by the Greeks, Phoenicians, Carthagenians, Huns, Romans, Vandals, Visigoths, Saracens, French and Spanish, then maligned in their new country because of Al Capone and the Mafia.

Italians claim Napoleon Bonaparte as a paesano. His real name was Buonoparte and he was born to an Italian noble in Corsica before that island was ceded to France, along with the ethnic Italian communities of Nice and Savoy.

"When he became emperor of all of Europe, he designated himself king of Italy," stressed Calacci, a history buff.

Andrew F. Rolle in his book, "The Italian Americans," wrote that " . . . the Italians were rarely chiusi or closed, critical, or superior in attitude. Most felt bound to adopt American values at least until they had achieved more than marginal success. Then they would return to their own ways either in America or in Italy. Their assimilation, however, was often so complete that it was impossible to return to the old style of life."

To Italians, the concept of nation is relatively new, Calacci said. The Italians are closer to their paesanow, the people from their home towns.

But first of all, each Italian's love and loyalty is to the family. The family first and always, he said.

* * * * * * * * *

Artwork by: Chuck Lazar

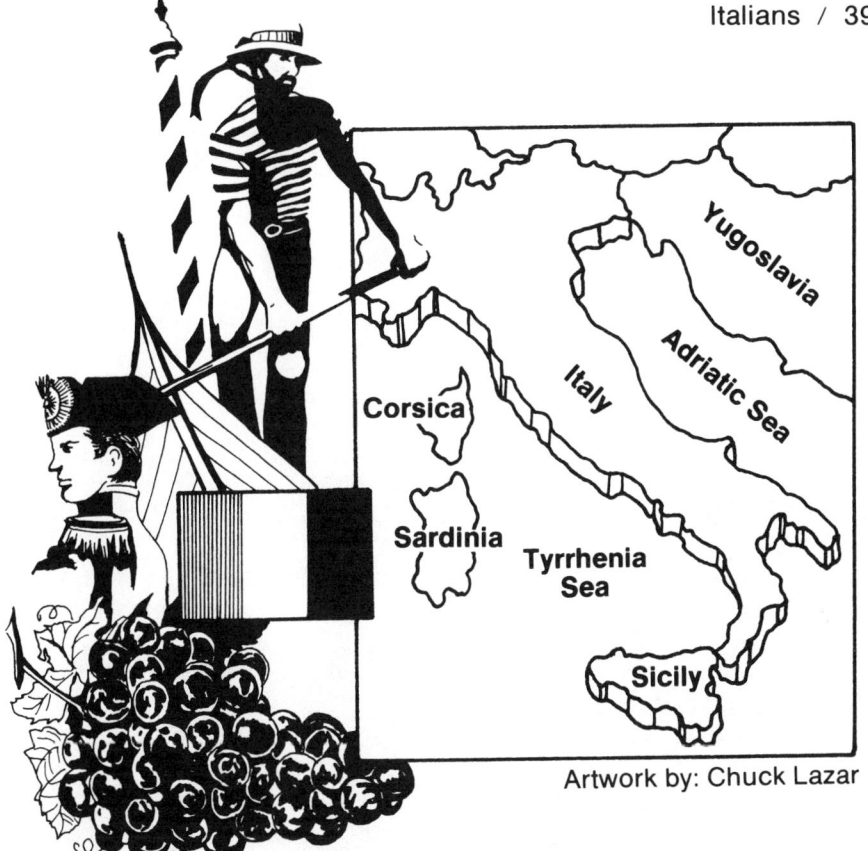

Chris Isidore, newly hired reporter of the Post-Tribune, said he's Italian. Isidore was his immigrant great-grandfather's first name, Isidore Villante, who in the 1800s was known as the "Robin Hood of Italy." But, at Ellis Island, immigration authorities misunderstood him, and thought Isidore was his last name.

Mabel Largura Joseph, Irma Gerometta and Josephine Rondinelli Dolatowski wrote letters to the editor pointing out that Northern Italians, too, contributed to the growth of Northwest Indiana. People from Piedmont, Lombardy, Venice and Fruili brought their cosmopolitan skills. Mrs. Dolatowski traced her father's roots to Florence.

Bennie Lazzaro invited the family to attend the Italian Festival. "Be my guest, bring a couple," he said with typical Italian hospitality.

Mario Tomsich, 83, one-fourth Italian, three-fourths Croatian, said Alpian Italians, speaking the Saxon Italian language, were among Gary's pioneers, such as Gariup and Chiabai.

Ann Fenton, 77, said "you missed Papa Mirando in the Italian story . . . he taught music to the kids at 19th and Broadway, and Mama Mirando used to give us a big pan of spaghetti. We used to steal tomatoes from her garden."

8.
Lithuanians

"Our main goal is that the Lithuanian name will not be forgotten." — **Birute Vilutis**

With perseverence and prayer, the Lithuanians believe, nothing is impossible.

Even freedom, says Birute Vilutis of Schererville, whose fervent hope is that someday Lithuania, now a part of the Soviet Union, again will be independent.

Her childhood freedom was shattered in 1940 when her home town of Messkuiciai, where her father was mayor, was invaded by Soviet troops. The Soviets on the night of June 14, 1941, swept the country and took 34,260 men, women and children to Siberia — never to be seen again.

Thus, it was with mixed feelings of fear and relief that Lithuanians welcomed invading Germans later that year.

"We looked at them as liberators, after the Russians," said Mrs. Vilutis. "We didn't know they would be brutal too, or that we would be sold out to the Russians in 1944."

The Allied powers at the Yalta Conference at the end of World War II decided to turn over German-occupied Lithuania to the USSR.

"Free Lithuania" is a prayer and a battle cry for these fair-skinned, fair-haired, tall, graceful, generous and musical people who speak an Indo-European language akin to the ancient Sanskrit spoken by the Aryans of India and who claim descendence from the historically-shrouded Samogitians, a fierce people who in 1241 stopped the westerly onslaught of the Mongol empire of Genghis Khan.

There are 4 million Lithuanians, including 250,000 in three counties in Poland, and about 1 million in 40 Western countries. The 1980 U.S. Census records 742,776 Americans claiming Lithuanian ancestry.

More than 100,000 of them are in the Chicago area, with 13 Catholic parishes. The Rev. Ignatius Urbonas, pastor of St. Casimir Church in Gary for the past 17 years, said about 10,000 live in Northwest Indiana. Many, he said, attend St. Casimir or St. Francis Church at 3905 Fir St., East Chicago, where the Rev. John Daniels is pastor.

From 1907 to 1925, most of the Lithuanians lived in the vicinity of the two churches. Now, they have spread out to

Schererville, Hebron, St. John, Portage, DeMotte and Beverly Shores as well.

Lithuanians were in Chicago as early as 1860, in East Chicago by 1885 and in Gary by 1907. The first attempts to build a Lithuanian church in Gary were made in 1910, but it wasn't until 1916 that St. Casimir's was built. At that time, it served about 200 Lithuanian families.

Mrs. Vilutis, who arrived in America in 1952, lived through World War II in Lithuania, then fled with her family to Germany in 1944 and spent the next three years in a displaced persons camp, "going to school and just waiting for a place to go."

The family found that place in England, where she met her husband, Antanas Vilutis, an engineer. They were married there, migrated to America in 1952 and had two sons. Now, she's a laboratory technician at St. Margaret Hospital in Hammond.

The couple were part of the "second wave" of 30,000 Lithuanian dipukai who arrived in America in the 1940s and 1950s. Another such immigrant was Alfonsas Vidutis, from the Baltic coast town of Klaipeda.

Vidutis worked at U.S. Steel, then retired to St. Petersburg, Fla., where retired Lithuanians from all over the United States are converging. They have their own hall, bakery, radio station and Lithuanian officials.

"They don't speak much English there anymore," said Vidutis' son, Richard, 38, a University of Michigan doctoral candidate studying the architectural work of the Finns in the Keweenaw Peninsula in Upper Michigan.

The younger Vidutis, a summer ranger at Indiana Dunes National Lakeshore, is American-born and speaks Lithuanian, much to the delight of one of the "oldtimers" — Antoinette Nenios, 82, who came from Vilnius in 1925, at a time (1918 to 1940) when Lithuania was an independent nation.

Mrs. Nenios visited an uncle in Chicago, she said, and married Izidor Nenios, who migrated in about 1900 when Lithuania was under Czarist Russia. They raised their family at a home at 15th and Madison in Gary.

Mrs. Nenios, a school crossing guard for Tolleston and Beveridge School children for 40 years and the winner of The Post-Tribune's 1980 Humanitarian Award, is proud that her children, Elizabeth Cinkus and Marie Ruzga, married Lithuanians and have taught their children the Lithuanian language and culture.

And she was thrilled when her daughter Marie's daughter,

Rita Jurgis, gave birth to a fourth-generation Lithuanian American, Justinas, in 1983.

Justinas' baptismal day was a time for celebration, with virtiniai meat dumplings, zemaitiskas siupinys hash, koseliena jellied pigs' feet, kumpio vyniotiniai ham roll-ups, kopustu sriuba sauerkraut soup, desros sausage, and Napaleones torte, and the wearing of gintaras, national coral jewelry from the Baltic Sea.

Lithuanians from 40 Western nations are in Chicago in 1983 for the Second Lithuanian World Festival, featuring a youth congress and sports tournament; a song festival with 1,500 singers and a 60-piece orchestra; cultural exhibits and presentation of the opera, "I Lituani," by the Lithunian Opera Company of Chicago; and the very serious Sixth Lithuanian World Community Congress to discuss the fate of the homeland.

"Our most important aim is to see Lithuania free again. We must keep the pressure on," said Mrs. Vilutis, secretary of the American Lithunian Council of Lake and Porter counties and president of the American Lithunian Community Inc. of East Chicago.

The two organizations, the two Catholic parishes and Hunters' and Fishermen's Club of East Chicago are the cultural-social centers of Lithuanian Americans in Indiana.

Albert G. Vinick, retired East Chicago water superintendent, is president of the Lithuanian Council, the earliest of the organizations. His father migrated during the first wave of 300,000 Lithuanians from 1860 to 1914.

Vinick has not lived under Communist government, but shares his fellow Lithuanians' concern.

"The Soviet Union is not a union; it's a Russian empire," he said, noting that Lithuania was annexed to the USSR by force — along with Ukraine, Latvia and Estonia — without U.S. recognition.

There's an underground movement in Lithuania, he said, and a flickering hope, kindled by support of Lithuanians in the West.

Last October, thousands of demonstrators marched in Vilnius, singing nationalistic songs.

"I think Russia will crumble. People are getting poorer, depressed," said Vilutis. "It's an empire. You know what happens to empires, eventually."

Lithuanians take pride that their ancestors on the Baltic coast, the Samogitians, repelled an empire — that of Genghis Khan, whose eldest son, Jochi, with 20,000 Mongol horsemen, was killed in 1227 by King Ryngold.

A decade later; Jochi's son, Batu, claimed most of Europe up to the Atlantic shore. His cavalry sacked Chernigov Kiev and Cracow and approached Vienna. But in December 1241, the Samogitians in the battle of Shaybek Field at Lyda annihilated the troops of Shaybek Khan, brother of Batu, and turned the tide of the Mongol conquest, according to Charles L.T. Pichel in the book, "Samogitia."

Ryngold was succeeded by Lithuania's first great ruler, King Mingdaugas, in 1251. Lithuanians celebrate that year as the birth of their nation and 1386 as the year of their conversion to the Christian faith.

Lithuania and Poland were joined in commonwealth from 1569 to 1795, when Russia occupied Lithuania, a situation that continued until 1915. During that year, the Germans invaded.

But from Feb. 16, 1918, to the Soviet invasion of June 1940, Lithuania was independent.

"We proved we could govern," said Vilutis. "People became free again, to be educated, to openly speak our language."

Mrs. Nenios was in Lithuania in 1918 when that freedom began.

"People were so happy, we sang in the streets. We went to the forests and cut pine branches and covered the streets with them," she said "I was crying with tears of joy."

Lithuanians of today have little or no desire to return to their Baltic land, although they wish it were free.

They have made their mark in America in various fields. Valdius Adamkus is Region 5 administrator of the U.S. Environmental Protection Agency. Frederick Kowsky is police chief of Gary. Dick Butkus became a football hero, following Johnny Unitas. Vitas Gerulaitis is a star in tennis, Charles Bronson and Ann Jillian in the movies.

Local Lithuanians in the professional field are many, such as Richard Mason, a one-time basketball star in East Chicago who teaches in Portage. His brother, Ted, is East Chicago librarian. Their parents, Ted and Catherine, operated businesses in Indiana Harbor.

Also well known are physicians Dr. Kazys Ambrozaitis at Methodist Hospitals and Dr. Vytantas Urba at Dyer Mercy Hospital, and veterinarian Dr. Pranas Jaras; and professors holding Ph.D.'s, Vytenis Damusis and Gintaras Reklaitis, at Purdue University, and Jenina Reklaitis, formerly at the University of Illinois-Chicago, who teaches Lithuanian at St. Casimir School, and businessmen such as Joe Neverauskas, Sol Valeiko and Kazys Valeiko.

Among the Lithuanian-American youth is Raymond Makiejus, football star in Lake Central High School, now on scholarship at

Notre Dame.

Charlie Bell, a night watchman at Merrillville's Twin Towers, who retired from Inland Steel three years ago, said "Life has been good to us Lithuanians in America."

He had never thought of returning to his father's land, but prays it will get better there, he said.

* * * * * * * * * *

Artwork by: Wendy O'Brien

There was a Lithuanian community here, but no Estonians or Latvians. But the wife of Max Lynch, principal at Gary's Riley School, is Estonian, whose grandfather came from Finland.

Len Sullivan, who retired in 1973 as food stamp director in Lake County, inquired about Lithuanian Jews, possibly his relatives. Then he learned of one, Larry Bretts of the Post-Tribune.

9.
Greeks

Onward and upward; that's the story of the Hellenes in America.

The Greeks have moved into the mainstream of American life, to the middle and upper classes, while steadily maintaining their ethnic identity as a people with a 6,000-year history and founders of Western democracy.

Appropriately, as the United States celebrates its 207th year of independence, Greek Americans like to celebrate also.

It's a time for young immigrants like Sula Tsaparikos, 25, who became from Samos Island in 1969, to savor the liberty that America inherited, a commodity rare in her homeland during the 1967-74 rule of the military junta.

"What do I like best about America?" she repeated. "The freedom, to say what you want, do what you want."

Since she left, democracy has returned to Greece, and the Rev. Evagorbas Constantinides, pastor of Saints Constantine and Helen Greek Orthodox Church in Merrillville, said Greece today has "unfettered liberty," like no other nation.

Sula's father, Mike Tsaparikos, owner of Stepping Stone Restaurant in Lake Station, arrived a year earlier, 1968, and worked briefly at the steel mills. Like many other Greeks before him, he became an entrepreneur.

Today, there are some 11 million Greeks who speak the language of Socrates, 9.8 million in present-day Greece, the rest around the world.

The 1980 Census records 959,856 Americans claiming Greek ancestry. Chicago, with 21 Greek Orthodox parishes and the nation's largest Greektown, accounts for close to 200,000. Indiana has seven parishes, four in the Calumet area — with 1,300 families affiliated with St. Constantine and Helen Church, 400 with St. Demetrios Church in Hammond, 80 with the new St. Iakovos Church in Valparaiso, and 300 with St. George Church in East Chicago, which is moving this week to Schererville.

Although there were Greeks on the crew of Christopher Columbus, and 500 Greeks settled in Florida in 1767, and Greek seamen built the first Greek Orthodox Church in 1864 in New Orleans, most of today's Greek Americans are descendants of poor shepherds and farmers who migrated between 1890 and 1920.

The census reports 675,158 Greeks entered from 1820 to 1980, most before 1914.

Like other immigrants, they came with hope, and little else. A 1911 U.S. Senate report showed 26.7 percent of the 8.4 million immigrants over 14, from 1899 to 1910, couldn't read or write. They included 55,089 of 208,608 Greeks.

But the Greek newcomers had a passion for education, for their children, who quickly moved up the business and professional ranks. Now, they're in the middle band upper classes, reports the Harvard Encyclopedia of American Ethnic Groups.

Among the Greek professionals are publicists Michael Kapnas and Fay Magnisalis Donovan, lawyers such as Nick Thiros, physicians such as Dr. John G. Kolettis and Dr. Ed T. Pappas, educators such as Kosmas Kayes, businessmen such as Lou Karras and Perry Costidakis, engineers such as George N. Halkias, contractors such as Nick Pangere and Nick Logan.

Indeed, the roster of prominent Greeks is expansive — Chapas, Christakis, Christoff, Cost, Demenegas, Demetrakis, Eliopoulos, Galanos, Kyres, Kurtis, Mammas, Pappas, Parianos, Petalis, Platis, Retson, Sacketos, Stath, Stroguiludis, Thomas, Tsangaris, Vazanellis, Volan and Zonakis.

At St. Constantine and Helen, where the Rev. Michael A. Kouremetis is associate pastor, visitors at the five-day Greekfest will have roast lamb and gyros and feta cheese and pastitso and dolmaddes and spanakopita and loukoumades, along with baklava, while enjoying the company of the gregarious, enthusiastic, freedom-loving, ethnically proud people from ancient Athens, Kalymnos, Sparta, Patras, Salonika, Chios, Crete, Cyprus and Aegean Sea islands off Asia Minor.

The Greeks, who like to dance to clarinets and bouzoukia, will engage in lively discourse, as is their custom, talking of politics and old times and places, as in coffee houses of the past — speaking in Greek, mostly.

Even the American-born and third- and fourth-generation Greeks know their language and culture, learned on their mothers' knees and through the church schools.

Their "Greekness" is maintained through social-fraternal groups as well, keeping them together. They include Ahepa, GOYA (Greek Orthodox Youth of America), Sons of Pericles, Daughters of Penelope, Maids of Athena, and regional clubs such as Kalymnian, Chion, Macedonian societies and Greek American Brotherhood.

Greek youngsters attended classes at the church after school and on weekends, and learned about their history, from 4,000 BC through Minoan and Mycenean civilizations, the great city-states, Greek expansion from 600 to 300 BC, the Roman Conquest, Byzantine Empire, the Turkish occupation from 1453 to 1821 and modern times.

Carol Sotos, whose father came from Icaria, didn't visit Greece until 1981, when she was already a mother of two teenagers. "It was a dream come true," she said, proud that the mainland Greeks could easily understand her American-learned Greek.

U.S.-born Cathy Manes, whose father, Nick Pannos, left the farms near Sparta in 1908, is equally fluent. But it took work. She remembers her after-school Greek classes with nostalgia.

"The other kids were playing while we were studying," she said.

Pannos was among the first in Gary, along with Faye Bikos, 74, whose father, George Chapas, came from Langadhas in 1906, lived at 11th and Polk and became a contractor. His seven children married Greeks, and Mrs. Bikos, the oldest, said, "well, we believe in that."

She married James Bikos, cousin of the Nick-Dan-Pete Bikos brothers, who went into the theater business and built the Roxy, 3764 Broadway, now Andros Furniture in 1927. A Bikos cousin, John, owned a hotel at 7th and Washington, and his daughter, Sophie, married Frank Orphanides. Their daughter, Maria Orphan, taught at Emerson School until 10 years ago when she migrated to Athens.

Mrs. Bikos noted that her own daughter, Christine Damaskos, has a fourth-generation son, Demetrios, 21, and "he speaks Greek as well as we do."

Another pioneer was Tom Magrames, who came to Gary in 1906 with his brother, Chris, and cousin, Jim, and sold gloves and fruits from a mule-drawn cart at 4th and Broadway. Later, he opened Candy Kitchen, the place to be, at 7th and Broadway, said Jim's daughter, Demetria Floros, a Gary teacher.

Tom Magrames' widow, Bessie, 87, said she watched Gary grow. She knew the city's first mayor, Tom Knotts. She lived for seven years at 817 Jefferson St. and 56 years at 5th and Buchanan, in a house her husband built. He was a co-founder of the first Greek church.

Vasiliki Magrames also came from Tripoli on the mainland, in 1929 after her marriage to Labros Megrames. They lived in Indiana Harbor and moved to Gary in 1947 and had three children. One of them became a radiologist, Dr. Theodore Magrames, in Bloomington, Ind.

In Hammond, Alex Dremonas, 64, spoke of his 98-year-old

mother, who arrived as a bride in 1910 and had seven sons.

Her husband, George, built the Indiana Hotel in Hammond and founded Jersey Maid Ice Cream Co.

Mary Biegel's mother, Bessie Theoharis, 85, came to the United States in 1909 at the age of 12, from Constanza on the Black Sea, joining her father, who was a carpenter and bricklayer. She and her husband, George Theoharis, operated Boston Restaurant at 8th and Broadway, and then the Rainbow, at 464 Broadway.

Another restauranteur was Gus Magnisalis, whose story, as told to his daughter, Fay Donovan, is sparkling.

Magnisalis, who died in 1973 at the age of 83, was born on the island of Anglesonisi, in the Bay of Smyrna, (Izmir), off the Turkish mainland. The island was settled by Greeks centuries ago.

He left in 1911 to avoid being drafted into the Turkish army (to fight against Greeks), lived in Alexandria, Egypt, for a year, then New Hampshire, then to Gary in 1917.

He returned to Smyrna Bay to take his three sisters to America in 1922, and just in time. The Turks dealt Greeks a crushing defeat in Asia Minor, and the Magnisalis family fled west in fishing boats to Chios, while across the bay they saw Izmir in flames.

In the Treaty of Lausanne that followed, 1,250,000 Greeks in Turkey were repatriated in Greek territory which contained six million people.

In Gary later, after making one more voyage to obtain a bride in 1928, Magnisalis worked at the Sheet and Tin Mill, then joined relatives at Parkway Restaurant across from Froebel School. He later owned Princess Confectionery at 8th and Broadway, and became a partner at Crystal Tap.

Mrs. Donovan recently went to Turkey and her family's ancestral island home of Anglesonisi, and found it uninhabited.

Her godfather — a most important role in a Greek's life — was the late Dr. George Karras, father of football heroes Lou and Ted and Alex Karras, whose mother is from Nova Scotia, Canada.

Alex Karras gained national prominence through sports, like baseball's Alex Grammas and Milt Pappas and wrestler Jimmy Londos. Popular in the theater are Elia Kazan, John Cassavetes, Telly Savalas and George Chakiris. Modern classicists are opera singer Maria Callas and conductor Dimitri Mitropoulos, both deceased.

John Brademas of South Bend, now president of New York University, was the first Greek-American congressman, and Paul Tsongas of Massachusetts and Paul Sarbanes of Maryland were the first Greeks in the U.S. Senate. Spiro T. Agnew, governor of Maryland, became U.S. vice president; Michael Dukakis became governor of Massachusetts.

Just as the Greeks are proud of the Western World's first great historians, scientists and philosphers — Socrates, Plato, Aristotle, Homer, Euclid, Hipparchus, Archimedes, Pythagoras — they relish the ancient glories of Athens, Rhodes, Corinth, Troy and Knossos and they rely on the Orthodox religion, their heritage from St. Constantine (274-337), the emperor of Rome who protected Christianity, and his mother, St. Helen, who sought and found the cross on which Christ died. May 21 is observed as the two patron saints' day.

Gary's first Greeks, arriving in 1906, started building their church in 1911. It was dedicated in 1919, at 13th and Jackson.

The church moved to its 37½-acre site in Merrillville in 1971.

For 20 years, 1931-51, the pastor was Irineos Cassimatis, who became a bishop in South America and died in Athens in 1961.

Constantinides became pastor in 1969.

* * * * * * * * * *

Artwork by: Maryann Bartman

A story about an International Institute project, "Pass the Culture, Please," led a Greek lady to say her father wasn't a sheepherder in southern Greece. He was a landowner who also had sheep.

10. Polish

> "How could I do it?" I asked myself." —
> **Martha Jaskulski, 1982**

> "No mother could be happier. How I hugged her, my Ashka."
> — **Martha Jaskulski, 1983**

> "Mother, never leave me again."
> — **Joanne Jaskulski, 5**

A Polish mother's choice, unlike Sophie's, has had a happy ending in Independence Hill.

Martha Jaskulski, 28, and her husband, Andrew, 30, are ecstatic and thankful. Their prayers, indeed, have been answered, as they embark on a new life — with Joanna, their 5-year-old daughter.

The couple — she was a nurse and he was an airplane instructor — fled their Communist-controlled homeland in the summer of 1981, and left Joanna, then 3, behind.

There were agonizing months, said Mrs. Jaskulski, as she wondered if she'd ever see the child again. The couple waited three months in a refugee camp in Austria before coming to America in September.

More than a year later, as if from heaven, a telegram last June 11 told them Joanna would be at Chicago O'Hare Airport the following evening.

"I don't know if any mother could be happier," said Mrs. Jaskulski in almost-perfect English, which she learned since October 1981.

And when, at O'Hare, she hugged the beautiful blond child ever so tightly, she said she couldn't laugh or cry. Her husband was speechless too.

"Never leave me again," blurted Joanna, who was born Jan. 18, 1978, and is endearingly called "Ashka."

The couple, convinced that the political situation in Poland was getting intolerable, decided to make a bolt for freedom, and escape. They applied for passports to go on a family vacation to France, with Joanna.

But when the passports arrived — after they had disposed of their belongings and had said secret goodbyes to close relatives — there was none for the little girl.

They decided then to flee anyway, and left the child with Jaskulski's brother. They told her they were just going for a ride.

"We went to the airport and, instead of taking the plane to Paris, we went to Vienna," said Jaskulski.

The Jaskulskis — now she's a dialysis technician at St. Anthony Medical Center, where he is a maintenance man — are among 50,000 immigrants, like Tad and Grace Krolik of Wroclawa, who have found new homes in America since martial law was declared in Communist Poland on Dec. 13, 1981.

Krolik, now in Highland, teaches computer science at Indiana Vocational Technical College in Gary and Valparaiso.

"Please tell everyone — St. Andrew's Church, Catholic Charities, Helen Rzepka — how thankful we are," said Jaskulski.

The two dozen "new wave" Polish immigrants are on home turf in Northwest Indiana, with about 50,000 Poles. Chicago with close to a million is the largest community of Poles outside Poland, second only to Warsaw's 1.5 million.

The Polish People's Republic, about the size of New Mexico, has 36.3 million people. There are about 12 million outside Poland; the 1980 U.S. Census reported that 8,228,037 Americans claimed Polish ancestry, the eighth largest ethnic group in the nation.

Harvard Encyclopedia of American Ethnic Groups reports four periods of Polish migration, 1608:1800, 1800-1860, 1860-1914, and post World War II, including the latest wave.

Poles were reported to be on the Vikings' ventures to America and on Christopher Columbus' crew. They were among the first settlers in Jamestown in 1608. Poles participated in the American Revolution, notably Count Casimir Pulaski, "Father of the American Cavalry," who died in the siege of Savannah in 1779, and Gen. Thaddeus Kosciuszko, the military engineer at Ticonderoga and Saratoga, who returned to Poland and led the insurrection in 1794.

Before departing, he willed his American properties for the purchase of freeing and educating Negro slaves.

Tawronia Koscielniak, great-grandmother of Joseph Piekarczyk Sr., 76, of Hammond, was in that large 1860-1914 immigration wave, coming from Prussia-controlled Poland around 1880 following her sons, Adam, Frank and Wincenty. She was buried in 1914 in St. Michael's Cemetery.

Piekarczyk's father, Andrew, who arrived in 1893, married Wincenty's daughter and worked at the chemical plant which later became duPont.

Now, there are American Poles five or six generations away from their immigrant grandparents. They don't speak Polish anymore, Piekarczyk noted.

But Polish tradition persists, particularly the religion and the customs and the foods.

Devotedly Roman Catholic, proud of Pope John Paul II, from Wadowice, they devour news about his trip to his homeland last month.

"Mostly, Polish people are kind," said Steffie Harrill, 68, whose father, Steve Urycki, came from Warsaw in 1908. A widow, mother of 10 children, she was married to an Oklahoman. "I wish I had married Polish," she said.

The Poles are known for industriousness, hospitality, devotion to America, their outspoken pride in being Polish, and their spectacular festivities.

Celebrations are times for prayers in solidarity as well as feasting on kielbasa and kiska Polish sausage, czarnina duck soup, pierogi dumplings and dancing the polka and mazurka.

Prayer particularly. These are trying times. Their land is beleaguered by 57 Soviet divisions in East Germany, Czechoslovakia and the Soviet Union, reports National Geographic. Jobs and food and clothing are scarce.

Joseph Raczynski, of Polonia gift shop in Crown Point, agrees with Pope John II's message to remain peaceful, stay healthy, and try to make the country productive — for the sake of the younger generation.

"Poland must survive," he said.

Raczynski, who came to Gary from England in 1952, grew up in Wadowice, hometown of the pope, at the time when Poland was free (1918-1939) after 123 years of political partition and servitude.

He was lucky. He was able to flee Poland in 1939, before Hitler's invasion. One of every six Poles perished in World War II, victims of Germans, then the Soviets from the east in October that year.

Not so lucky was Lucian Markiewicz, who was a Polish soldier in 1932, and was held prisoner by the Germans from 1939 to 1945. He survived, was put in a Displaced Person camp, and came to America in 1949.

Frank B. Roman of Gary, formerly George Witowski, whose parents Adalbert and Ada Witowski came from Krakow in 1910, was a Holy Cross Brother, helping to set up a boarding school for poor children, when he was caught by the war in Poland in 1939. He was imprisoned by the Soviets until 1940, when he returned to the United States.

He remained a clergyman until 1955, when he returned to civilian life and Gary, where he grew up and learned Polish at the parish school.

Home was 1801 Maryland St., in the Polish neighborhood near St. Hedwig Church, 17th and Connecticut.

Helen Zielinski of Merrillville, national president of Polish Women's Alliance, and Helen Rzepka, 72, lived in that same area, between 15th and 20th, Broadway and Georgia.

"Everyone spoke Polish there, even the black kids," Roman recalled. In 1920, Gary had about 2,000 Poles. By 1960, the Poles in Gary exceeded 20,000.

Polish people had migrated to Indiana and Illinois as early as 1834, when 235 insurrectionists were deported by the Austrians. By 1867, the first Polish church, St. Stanislaus Koska, was built at Noble and Bradley in Chicago.

In Indiana, Polish farmers and tradesmen built their first Catholic Church, St. Mary's, in Otis, LaPorte County, in 1873.

It was followed by St. Hedwig's in South Bend in 1877, St. Casimir's in Hammond in 1890, St. Stanislaus Kostka in Michigan City in 1891, St. Michael's in East Chicago in 1896 (which was renamed and relocated as St. Stanislaus' in 1901), St. Adalbert's in Whiting in 1902, St. John Cantius in East Chicago in 1906, St. Hedwig's in Gary in 1908, Sacred Heart in Gary's Tolleston in 1913, St. Joseph's in East Chicago in 1916, Assumption in New Chicago in 1917, and Holy Family in Gary in 1926.

Helen Rzepka, whom Mrs. Jaskulski called a guardian angel, was born to Karol and Mary Rzepka, who settled in Chicago from Krakow before 1906, said the Polish families started talking about building a church planning for a church when Gary was incorporated in 1906. It was difficult to travel to Indiana Harbor to go to mass on Sundays, she said.

Twenty-five families organized the church in 1907, led by Frank Zawadski, Anton Bankus, Val Fabjanski, John Wasielewski, Valentine Nowak and the Rev. Anthony J. Stachowiak.

Some Poles belong to the Polish National Catholic Church established in 1897. Its affiliate, Church of Divine Providence, opened in Merrillville in 1970.

Following the churches were the fraternal and veteran organizations, more than 50, from the umbrella group, Polish American Congress with Steve Tokarski as president, to new-immigrant clubs.

The main groups are Polish Women's Alliance, Polish National Alliance, Polish Roman Catholic Union, Polish Singers Alliance (Chopin Chorus), Polish Army Veterans, Polish American Democratic Club, Polish Falcons, Silver Bell Club, Polish Immigrants Club and Polish Home Dom Polski.

Polish Musical Varieties, Eddie Oskierko's radio program, started in 1930. Today, with Lottie Kubiak, the Sunday programs continue on local radio.

Maintaining Polish culture too are the religious orders, the Carmelite monks in Munster since 1952, and the Salvatorian priests from Krakow since 1938.

Catholic education has been provided by the nuns, in the parish schools — the Franciscans, Sisters of St. Francis, known as "Josefinki," and Sisters of the Holy Family of Nazareth.

Poles take pride in their Catholic millenium, 1,000 years of Christianity, dating back to 966 when the first Polish king of the Piast Dynasty, Miezko I (960-992) converted his people and planted the cross deep into Polish soil. Through 40 monarchs, ended in 1772, Polish faith was strengthened.

But 1772 to 1918 were years of subjugation as Poland was partitioned by Prussia, Russia and Austria — until post World War I, 1918, when noted pianist Paderewski served as prime minister.

Polish Freedom was again snuffed by the German attack on Sept. 1, 1939, followed by the Soviet invasion from the east three weeks later. Germans massacred six million Poles, half of them Polish Jews, at Auschwitz-Birkenau and other camps, and the Russians executed 15,000 Polish officers at Katyn Forest.

Raczynski returned to Poland in 1975 and toured Auschwitz. He decided then to dedicate himself to the study of the Holocaust, to remind others of the horrors that wars bring.

While Poles revel in military glories of the past, like Casimir the Great (1333-1370) who expanded the Polish kingdom, they are prouder of religious accomplishments, such as the first Polish pope, John Paul II; the canonization of St. Stanislaus, Bishop of Crakow, in 1253; the Union of Brzesc, uniting the Orthodox Bishops of Poland and Lithuania with Rome in 1596; the Black Madonna of Czestochowa, credited with saving Jasna Gora monastery from the Swedish invasion in 1655; and Maximilian Kolbe, canonized a saint Oct. 10, 1982, for offering his life to save a Polish Army sergeant, Francis Gajowniczek, imprisoned by Nazi Gestapo.

To be Polish is to brag of great figures in culture and history — Copernicus the astronomer, Chopin the composer, Josef Conrad the author, Madame Curie, who researched radium — and popular Poles, Loretta Swit on television, Gloria Swanson on screen, the late drummer Gene Krupa, Bobby Vinton and Liberace (part Polish) on stage.

Joe Piekarczyk Sr., a baseball fan for 60 years, even as a Polish All-Star All-Time Team, based on 180 professional

Polish / 55

players.

He would start Stan Coveleski, who won three games for Cleveland in the 1920 World Series, as pitcher, with Frankie Ptylak as catcher, Stan Musial at 1st, Bill Mazeroski at 2nd, Tony Kubek at short stop, Whitey Kurowski at 3rd, Al Simmons at left field, Carl Yastrzemski at center, and Gene Hermanski at right, he said.

Outstanding Poles of Northwest Indiana make up a whole directory.

Included are Banasiak, Baran, Breclaw, Budnik, Buczyna, Dobis, Dziuba, Forzst, Kahelek, Kaul, Kowalczyk, Krysinski, Kubiak, Krupa, Lazarz, Lis, Lisek, Maciejewski, Mackowiak, Markiewicz, Mroz, Mysliwiec, Naspinski, Nawrocki, Ostrowski, Piasecki, Pikula, Pinkowski, Plecinski, Piekarz, Ryper, Sambor, Tokarski, Tolpa, Tomaszewski, Trela, Wasielewski, Wilusz, Wroblewski, Wyszynski, Zaleski, Zajac, Zielinski, Ziemba, Zotkiewicz, and more.

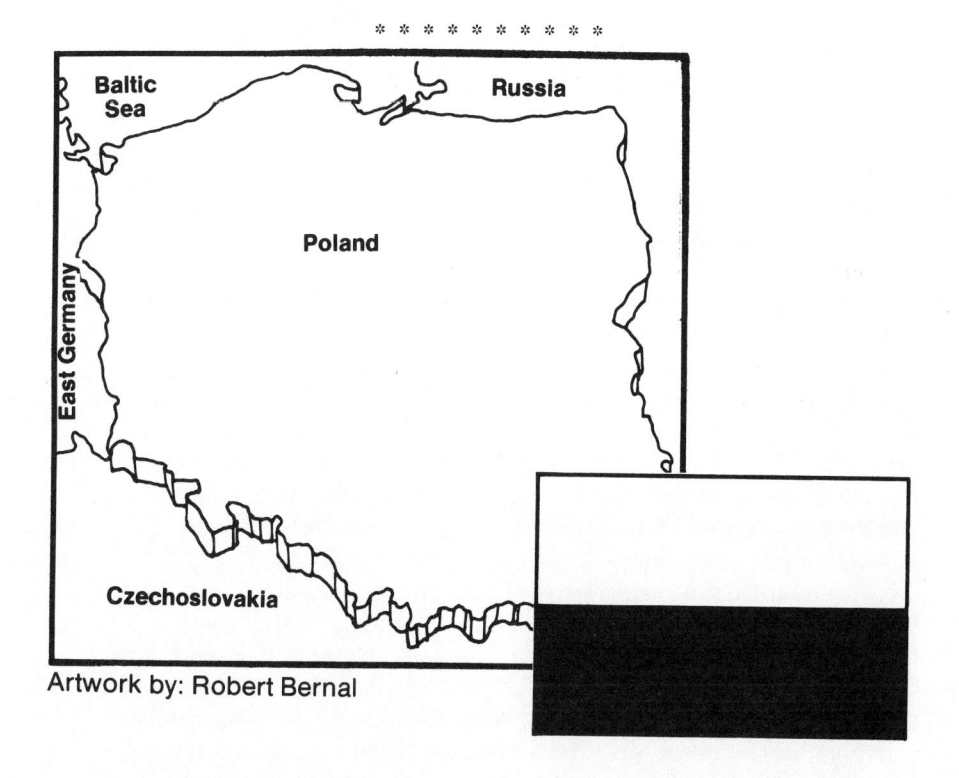

* * * * * * * * * *

Artwork by: Robert Bernal

Polish people are outspoken. Moments after Helen Lis walked into the room filled with Polish leaders being interviewed, she and John Ziemba disagreed on the identity of the first Polish midwife in Gary. The discussion ended.

11. Filipinos

> "America, we stand beside you,
> Loyal sons forever true and brave,
> Ready to fight for the Red, White and Blue,
> And Stars and Stripes forever wave."
> — *Jose M. Hernandez*
> *Dec. 7, 1941*

Dec. 7, 1941.

I love America.

As a first-generation, American-born, war-veteran, Filipino pioneer, I am an immigrant ... a Double American, as many, many others, happy to be living in a country like ours, unashamed of the foreign culture we have brought to it.

Proud of the American flag, town board and city council and state legislature and Congress, the small-claims court and the Supreme Court, the bookstores, newspapers and magazines, supermarkets, drive-ins, superhighways, shopping malls, neighborhood bars, baseball, apple pie, Chevrolet.

At the same time, like my fellow Pinoys, I like to speak Tagalog, eat steamed rice, dinuguan blood stew, balut duck egg, pancit noodles, bibingka and puto and kutsinta rice cakes, kamote sweet potatoes, lechon roasted suckling pig, halo-halo mixed sweets, tinapa smoked fish, and watch our native dances like tinkling and pandanggo sa ilaw, talk about our own 20 aboriginal minorities —Negrito, Igorot, Dumagat, Tagbuana, Magindanao, Tasaday, and recall our own experiences and war stories in the quest for freedom and a better life.

While there are many of us in the United States today - 795,275 according to the 1980 Census, more than Serbians, Belgians, Cubans, Finns, Lithuanians, Slovaks and French-Canadians — 80 percent of us arrived in the last 10 years, after the 1965 Hart-Celler Immigration Act abolished national-origin priorities and opened the gates to Asian-Pacific immigration.

Before 1900, there were fewer than 100 Filipinos in America. Frank B. Roman of Gary and I knew one of them, Pastor Villaflor, an embroiderer and handyman at the University of Notre Dame, who arrived in 1899, adopted by the Holy Cross Fathers. He was there when Roman was a lay brother at Notre Dame, and my father, Jose M. Hernandez (1904-1982) was a graduate student, in the 1930s. I was born in South Bend in 1931, then taken to the Philippines. When I returned to Notre Dame after World War II, I met Pastor Villaflor who told me his life story.

The 1910 Census noted 2,767 Filipinos in America. There were 5,603 in 1920, when workers were recruited for the farms of Salinas and San Fernando Valley, even while Filipinos were hired to harvest sugar and pineapple crops in Hawaii. By 1931, 113,000 had arrived, but only 55,000 stayed; 39,000 returned, and 18,600 moved on to the mainland. In 1930, there were 45,000 in the mainland, consisting of cropworkers, hotel boys and salmon cannery crews and domestics.

The U.S. Navy recruited, too, and promised U.S. citizenship. By 1970, 14,000 U.S. sailors were Philippine nationals, and many were cooks in the galley.

In Indiana, a Filipino was scarce. But now, the 1980 U.S. Census accounts for 3,507. Philippine Professionals Association, with Dr. Manuel Z. Rosario of Munster as president, has 365 members, physicians making up 65 percent. Dr. Adriano A. Agana of Gary is president of the 400-member Indiana Philippinne Medical Association founded 10 years ago in Scottsburg by Dr. Jesus Bacala.

Another group, Philippine American Association of Lake County, with Vic Rondez as president, is active in the area.

PPA serves as the cultural base for Northwest Indiana Philippine Americans. Its annual picnic was held in 1983 at the estate of Dr. and Mrs. Filemon Lopez in Cedar Lake, and 1983'sPhilippinefest featured a rice festival with a fair, style show, movies, folk dances and food at St. Thomas More Church gymnasium in Munster.

There, along with the program coordinated by Trinidad Tabayoyong Moore, a teacher at Gary's Chase and Bethune schools, the anthem my father wrote, "America, We Stand Beside You," which drew commendation from President Eisenhower, was sung by the PPA Choir led by Lorie Cuevas, accompanied by he PPA Band directed by Guillermo Rivera.

My father, who wrote the Jose Rizal history and English for Filipinos series of textbooks for Philippine schools in the 1950s and 1960s, was a major and dean of arts and sciences at the Philippine Military Academy in Baguio when he wrote the lyrics of the song, which was dedicated Dec. 7, 1941, the day before Baguio, Manila, Nichols, Cavite and other U.S. and Philippine installations were bombed by Japanese invaders.

The song became a guerilla theme after Bataan and Corregidor and the 1942 defeat of the Philippines. After the war,school children sang it until 1946, when the U.S. granted independence.

But it wasn't until June 1960, when Eisenhower visited the Philippines, that he heard it. On Aug. 6, he wrote to my father: "I have only recently discovered that you wrote the lyrics to "America, We Stand Beside You" — the song that so moved me when I was in Manila in mid-June. I congratulate you on your effort, and assure you of my own deep appreciation of the sentiments expressed in the lyrics."

History has recorded how wellthey stood — and fought, and died — together, Filipinos and Americans.

More than a million Americans from all walks of life, Army, Navy, Air Force, Marines, more than a dozen divisions, served in the Philippines during and after World War II, and they have recollections of Baguio, Manila, Cebu, Mindanao, Leyte Samaar, Pangasinan, Lingayen Gulf, Bataan, Corregido, Batangas — where they and their chocolate bars were welcomed with wide smiles and "Hello, Joe."

James Baker of Gary, United Steelworkers District 31 safety-health coordinator, was one of them. Ed Seykowski of Valparaiso, as a Navy Reserve flyer, goes on maneuvers at Subic Bay every year. Ron Hayes, who serves lumpia at Patron West, 11th and Chase, did five tours of duty in the Philippines during his 20-year stint in the Navy. "I learned to cook from Filipinos in Personnel," he said.

'In 1981, I vacationed in the Philippines for the first time in 30 years and visted the 152-acre American Cemetery at Camp Bonifacio near Manila, where it was impossble not to weep at seeing the white-marble crosses as far as the eye can reach, and reading the 36,279 names of Americans missing and presumed killed in action from 1941 to 1945.

I remembered guys like Ray Martinez and "Scotty" and "Henderson," 37th Infantry Division GIs, who in March 1945 slept on our lawn in Manila as they prepared to attack Japanese holdouts in the walled city of Intramuros. They never returned.

One of Gary's Filipinos, Ernie Gabriel, 64, fiscal analyst for Gary Manpower Administration, survived the 65-mile Bataan Death March of 78,100 American and Filipino prisoners in April 1942, which military write Stanley L. Falk called one of the most atrocious chapters in history.

Another survivor was former Indiana Gov. Edgar D. Whitcomb, who wrote about it in a book, "Escape from Corregidor," in 1967.

Gabriel, 23, was more than halfway through the march, when

he escaped on the second try.

He spent the next three years as a guerrilla fighter with the American Dominion Forces under Col. Magtanggol Hernandez, until the unit was attached to the 37th U.S. Infantry Division in the siege of Manila.

Gabriel retired as a Philippine Army lieutenant in 1963, then worked in Vietnam from 1966 to 1971 with an engineering firm on contract with the U.S. Navy.

That tour over, he migrated to Gary in 1972, and his family followed. Now, eight of his nine children are in Indiana, and three of them, Myrna Sison, Edna Gonzalez and Tessie Biscocho, are nurses at St. Mary Medical Center. Two other daughters are nurse-students.

Humble, mild-mannered and polite, like most Filipinos, Gabriel said "please don't play it up, there were many others before me.

And many have distinguished themselves in the professional world, including heart specialist, Dr. Felipe Chua, and an assortment of physicians in every hospital in Indiana — Mangahas, Rivera, Lopez, Blando, Jao, Carlos, SantaMaria, Angeles, Dy, Verde, Madlang, Agana, to name a few.

Before Ernie Gabriel in Indiana was Mrs. Lily Shreve, who arrived in Michigan City in 1952, brought over by her husband, Kenneth, who met her near Subic Bay when he was a civilian workee there, 1946-52.

"As far as I know, there were no other Filipinos here," said Shreve. Their children don't understand a word of Tagalog.

I met the Shreves in 1957 when I worked for the News-Dispatch. There was one other Filipino family then, Dr. Ben Balingit (now deceased), medical director at the state prison, who transferred from Inland Steel.

In 1958, we were the Indiana pioneers, along with Drs. Monico Valencia, Robert Golding, and Sylvia Kern, Patsy Patton, Betty Radinsky and Dr. Agana, whose wife was known as the movie star Linda Estrella in pre-war Philippines. Their child-star daughter, Tessie Agana, later married Dr. Rodolfo Jao, and now has nine children, and the eldest, Marita, was salutatorian at the 1983 Class at Andrean High School.

Marita exemplifies the latest wave of Filipino immigrant, from educated and well-to-do families usually a specialist in a medical field.

Another Filipino whiz kid is Norman M. Dy, son of Dr. and Mrs James T. Dy of Portage, salutatorian at Culver Military Academy.

The list grew: Rodolfo Madlang, Uldarico Angeles Roberto

60 / Filipino

Madrilejo, Chris Abasolo, Arturo Capuli, Ponciano Olayta, Trining Tabayoyong.

Then, as the 1965 Act brought on the ethnic explosion, more arrived. In Los Angeles, Time magazine reported last month that Koreans, Vietnamese, Asia Indians and Arabs multiplied in numbers since 1970. There were 33,500 Filipinos for instance; now, 150,000 concentrated near Glendale.

"We're on our way," said Dr. Manuel Z. Rosario, PPA president, whose clinics are in Miller and Downtown Gary.

One of his first pet projects to give back to the community: He enlisted Filipino doctors to offer their expertise at free diagnostic clinics for the poor.

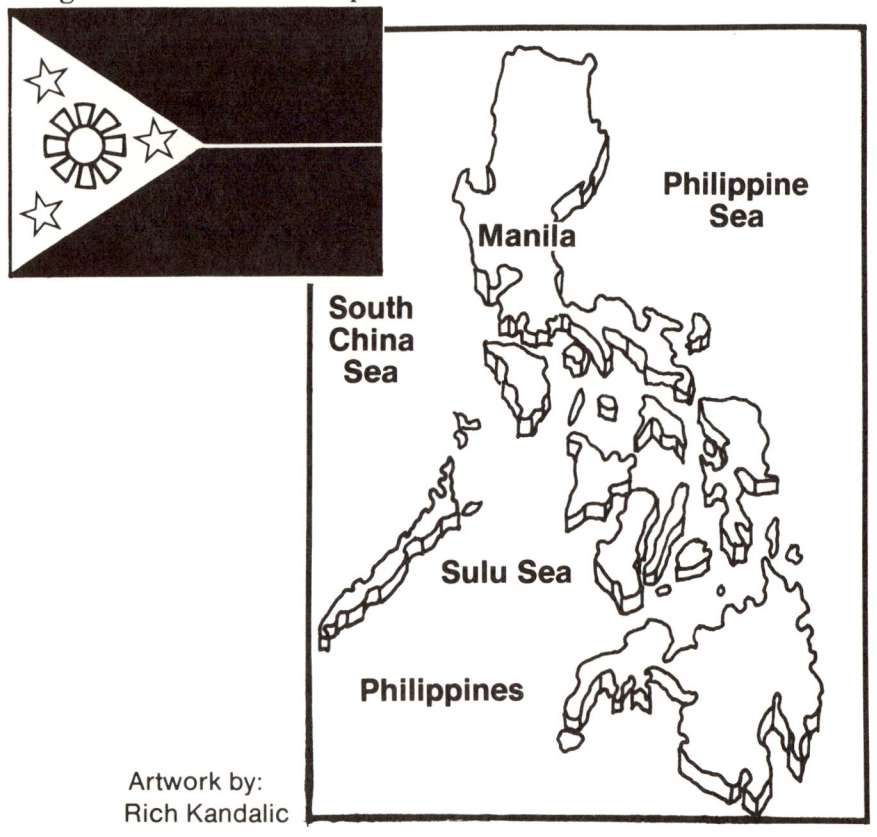

Artwork by: Rich Kandalic

Betty Radinsky, whose husband is Lithuanian American, wrote a long letter about the first Filipinos she knew in Indiana, after World War II. She was in the Philippines before the war, married to Aaron Feinstein, who was killed.

Raymond Vince of East Chicago wrote that the Philippine story "brought tears into my eyes, along with sad memories." He was among thousands of Americans in the Philippines in World War II, and served with the 40th Infantry Division.

12.
Assyrians

> "If one has no respect for his own heritage, he'll have no respect for the heritage of others." — **Woodrow Wilson**

Assyrians — America's link to antiquity.

There are less than a million Assyrians in the world today, and only 75,000 in the United States, 60,000 of them in the Chicago area, three dozen families in Northwest Indiana.

But through their illustrious sons — like the late U.S. Rep. Adam Benjamin Jr. — and the healthy political climate in America, "our heritage will survive," says Malcolm Karam, a former Gary resident now of Skokie, Ill.

Karam, who migrated from Tabriz, Iran, in the 1920s, is a former president of the Northwest Indiana International Institute and a former editor of the Assyrian Star, the Assyrians' magazine circulated in 26 nations around the world.

Nurtured in America, free of religious suppression, the ancient Aramaic spoken by Christ and the culture that dates back to Nineveh can be maintained, said Karam.

Prosperity and freedom, rather than poverty and persecution, have become silent enemies of that goal. Free to move about, free to explore other ways, free to meet and marry mates from other ethnic groups, the Assyrians — like other Americans — are being challenged to assimilate, to blend into the melting pot.

"We've been without a nation for thousands of years. Wherever our people went, they tried to assimilate us, or annihilate us," he noted. "We are still Assyrians."

Assyrians, who established one of the earliest of the 21 civilizations that have existed on earth, lived in Mesopotamia, between the Tigris and the Euphrates rivers in what is now Iraq, as early as 9000 BC.

Those early men domesticated animals, grew plants, developed the cuneiform alphabet. Their cities were Jericho in 8350 to 7350 B.C., Catal Huyuk in 6250 to 5500 B.C., and the people were the Sumerians, Akkadians, Babylonians and Assyrians, who reigned from 1800 to 1300 B.C. as the first military power known to man.

From 824 to 624 B.C., their zenith of power, Assyrians ruled their part of the world, Egypt down to the Red Sea, Jerusalem and Phoenicia. Cyprus, the land now known as Syria, Eastern

Turkey, Iran and Iraq.

But the empire fell to the Medes from the East and the Babylonians from the South in 612 B.C., never to rise again — even as new civilizations were emerging elsewhere, along the Indus River in West Pakistan in 2500 B.C., the Aryans in 1500 B.C., the Shang Dynasty in North Central China in 1500 B.C., the Aegean, Minoans, Myceneans in 3000 B.C., followed by the Hellenes in 400 B.C. and the Romans until 476 A.D.

Ben S. Benjamin, an uncle of Gary-born Post-Tribune sportswriter Marty Shahbaz, wrote the story of his life and escape from Turkish persecution in 1917-21 and placed today's Assyrians in historical perspective.

He came to America about the same time many other Assyrians did — after World War I.

Karam recalled that they came to Gary as carpenters, bricklayers, painters, decoratoors, grocery owners, millworkers.

They settled between 4th and 8th avenues along Monroe Street, close to work and their children's schools. They established the Assyrian American Association of Northwest Indiana.

They built the Assyrian Presbyterian Church at 456 Monroe St. in 1926, with 300 members. Later, the Assyrian St. Peter's Church of the East was built at 35th and Delaware.

Shahbaz' Uncle Ben was a Warda, the family's name in Ardeshai, the Iranian town near Lake Urmia. He took on the name of Benjamin, but he's not related, except ethnically, to Adam Benjamin Sr., who came from Turkey and married an Armenian woman.

The Armenians are Christians like the Assyrians, whose ancestors were converted to Christianity by St. Thaddeus in 78 A.D. "We were the first nation to become Christians," said Karam.

Ben Benjamin, retired in Clearwater Beach, Fla., was 10 when persecution of Assyrians, the San Qal'ah Massacre, was started by the Turks in 1917.

In the past, the Christian Assyrians were protected by Czarist Russians, but Russia was embroiled in the Bolshevik Revolution then, and Czarist troops were sent home.

During the evacuation of Ardeshai and the panic that followed, Ben Benjamin, sick with malaria, was separated from his family. He recalls in his autobiography that he saw a soldier bayonet a young girl, and how, miraculously, he was saved when 10,000 were massacred.

By luck, he was reunited with his family near ancient Nineveh, and they proceeded on a 13,655-mile journey to

Baghdad, the Tigris River, Basra, the Indian Ocean, Bombay, Marseilles, Barcelona, and finally Providence, R.I., on Jan. 9, 1922.

Karam, a physician's son, came to America by way of Beirut, where he had studied.

A later arrival was Elizebeth Abraham Rainford, who was born in Baghdad and grew up in Basrah on the Persian Gulf.

She arrived in Gary in 1962, after visiting relatives in Skokie. The Assyrians then were caught in the Kurdo-Iraqi War.

"There was a big revolution in Iraq in 1958, and Muslims took over the government," she said. "My father said to me, 'Go, we (Christian Assyrians) will suffer in this country as many have suffered for centuries.'"

She met and married Clyde Rainford, a teacher at Black Oak School. Later she became a U.S. citizen, and her mother arrived in 1967 and her sister, Victoria, in 1968.

The Assyrians brought with them the customs of their ancestors — such as the purple, white and crimson flag for royalty, constancy and blood in the preservation of national identity. It has three stars representing Babylon, Chaldea and Assyria, together the once-great empire.

The customs will not die. They're too stimulating — the janimar and towlama and tanzara dances, the zurrna dowule drum and bagpipes, the sabakhta gift-giving at weddings, the kaloo sulaka festival 40 days after Easter.

Then, religiously, there's Shara, in April and November, to celebrate the miracles of St. George, and Dookhrana, a special gift-giving as thanks to God for good fortune, the healing of the sick, escape from danger, or as prayer for a male sibling.

Mrs. Rainford said one custom could have been left in Iraq, and that is the strong dominance of the male over the female.

Traditional foods will prevail, even if Assyrians marry non-Assyrians. A family gathering invariably will have rizza, a rice cake; bushala with yogurt and spinach; chada cake; dulma stuffed grape leaves; reesh-eklee with tripe and beef feet; haressa with wheat and chicken; mashi kidney beans and lamb; and chipti lamb meat balls.

These should be enjoyable to the families of Shahbaz, Yonan, Yacoub, Joseph, Baboo, Ismael, Solomon, Warda, Odishoo and others in the local Assyrian directory.

Many of the Assyrians arrived poor in the 1920s, but their progeny have reached success.

Karam pointed to notables such as Walter B. Elisha, a Harvard graduate; Norman Pera at Inland Steel; Robert Canon, an electrical engineer; David Gilyan, a lawyer; Dr.

Philip Novzaradan, a physician; Joseph Jacob, a chemist and company president; and the children of Adam Benjamin Sr. notably Adam Jr., who was the first Assyrian elected to Congress, and his brother, Samson, a physician.

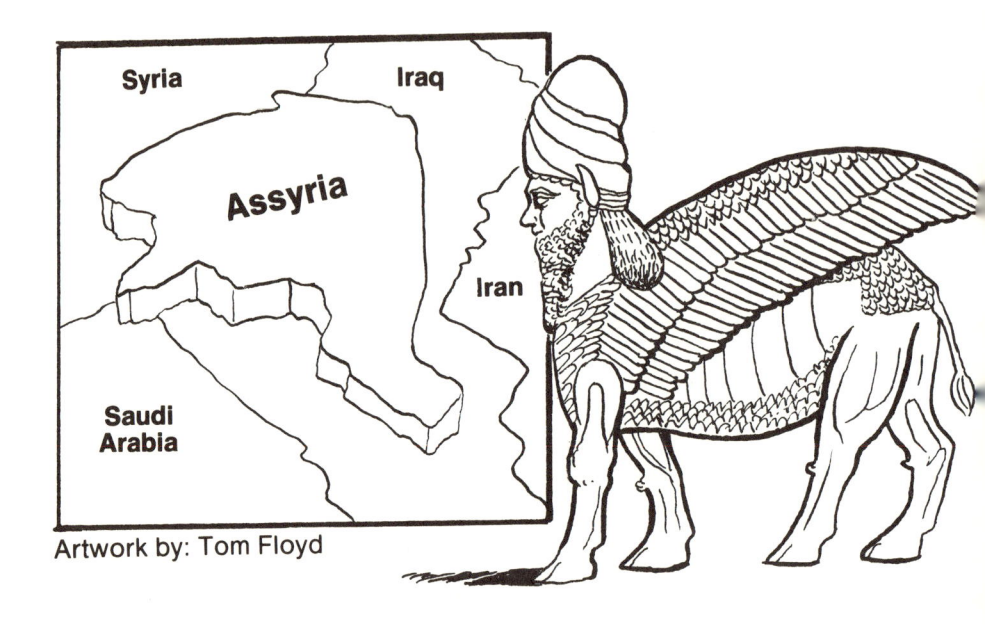

* * * * * * * * *

Artwork by: Tom Floyd

Clyde Rainford, husband of Assyrian Elizabeth Rainford, has an explanation for the ancient Assyrians' loss of power: When they were in command, they were cruel and bloodthirsty, he said.

13.
Vietnamese

> "We are community. Even though there are only 110 families, from Whiting to South Bend, we're together. If anyone needs help, we"ll have 12, 15 people there right away." — **Thuy Thi Vu Rosenfelt, Vietnamese "pioneer"**

It's not exactly true, as an old Vietnamese philosopher said, that "the reign of the emperor ends at the village gate."

But "that's close to it," said Luu Viet Nguyen, 29, a Purdue University electrical-engineering student, who has emerged as one of the leaders of Northwest Indiana's Vietnamese community.

Nguyen, of Valparaiso, is a former Vietnamese Marine lieutenant who escaped in a fishing boat from Communist Vietnam in 1975. He said "we are like one family here, like in Vietnam."

It's the practice in Vietnam, he said, for the grandfather and grandmother to live under the same roof with their sons, daughters-in-law, grandchildren and unmarried daughters — while other relatives live next door in the same village. That essentially is their world.

Thuy Thi Vu Rosenfelt, Northwest Indiana's Vietnamese "pioneer," arrived in 1970 and has become her people's counselor, translator and house mother as head of the Refugee Assistance Program of Gary Catholic Diocese. She said the Vietnamese have made adjustments.

Now every Vietnamese, from Saigon or Danang Chu Lai or Bong San, Quang Tri, Pleiku, Nha Trang, etc., is family.

That was emphasized when four Vietnamese students from Chicago were killed in a car crash on Interstate 65 near Lowell. The entire Northwest Indiana Vietnamese community responded.

Mrs. Rosenfelt, who grew up in Saigon (now called Ho Chi Minh City), was the first to arrive in Gary, in 1970.

Today, there are about 110 Vietnamese families here, including the Le, Nguyen, Hue, Binh and Tran families, Ba Johns. One of the most recent additions to the community of nearly 350 Vietnamese here was Phat Thanh Nguyen, 22, who arrived last February, sponsored by Mrs. Rosenfelt.

The 1980 census reported 2,137 Vietnamese in Indiana, and 215,184 in the nation.

66 / Vietnamese

The Vietnamese, their history dating back 20 centuries when Viet tribes were forced to migrate south from their original homeland in Southern China, are among the latest arrivals to the United States.

They began coming to this country in 1975 when the United States pulled out of that Southeast Asia country. A total of 2.7 million Americans (about 50,000 from Northwest Indiana) served in Vietnam from 1959 to 1975, and 57,939 died.

The U.S. census of 1980 reported 215,184 Vietnamese Americans, a fast-growing group, now exceeding Armenians, Slovenes, Syrians and Serbians.

Time magazine reported that Vietnamese in Los Angeles, "the new Ellis Island," increased from less than 2,000 in 1970 to 40,000 today.

Mrs. Rosenfelt, who joined her husband, Robert, in California, said Westminster, in Orange County, where they will live is virtually a Saigon. It has 70,000 Vietnamese, with their music shops and restaurants where nhoc mam sauce and fried meat egg rolls and blended green vegetable juice are commonly served.

There could have been more Vietnamese in the area, but Mrs. Rosenfelt said they gravitated to warm costal areas near New Orleans and San Diego as soon as they could.

Rosenfelt, formerly with Correct Maintenance Inc. of Portage, has an executive job with a Los Angeles firm. The family, with four boys, decided to live in Vietnamese Westminster.

Luu Nguyen, who arrived in Indiana in September 1975, sponsored by Hope Lutheran Church of Portage, was one of the "boat people."

He was a South Vietnamese Marine lieutenant when North Vietnamese Communists took over his country.

"We went, in spite of the danger. It's better to be a ghost at sea than die slowly under Viet Cong," he said.

On May 1, 1975, with 52 men, women and children, he boarded a fishing boat at Phan Rang, headed eastward to the China Sea, where U.S. ships were at anchor or cruising.

But on the second day, the boat's motor conked out and a tropical storm came. When it subsided three days later, the boat drifted for another seven days as food and water supplies were depleted and the sweltering sun burned the flesh. An old man and two small children died.

"It was heart-breaking — we had to tear the dead children away from their mothers' arms, so that we could bury them at sea," said Nguyen.

Meanwhile, their "hope," the American ships, had left

Vietnam waters.

On the 10th day, all supplies used up, five more died.

"I thought of my beloved parents whom I left behind, and my defeated homeland, and I prayed to God with what little strength I had left," he wrote. "We were totally exhausted, our spirit broken. In delirium, we lost all scope of time."

But, like a miracle, they were saved.

First came the faint moan of a motor, then the vision: Their savior, a fishing boat.

The Thai men aboard gave them food and water and towed the boat from Phan Rang to Thailand.

Soon, Ngyyen was in a crowded refugee camp, then America, then a home provided by Hope Lutheran Church, clothes, food, lessons in English, a job at Bethlehem Steel, and U.S. citizenship.

Last year, as his language skills improved, and his part-time business as a kung fu instructor developed, Nguyen quit his job at the mill to become a full-time student. At Purdue North Central, his English professor Barbara J. Lootens, encouraged him. He later enrolled at Purdue in West Lafayette.

"Someday, I want to go back and rebuild my country, if it's not communist," said Nguyen.

Meanwhile, he's helping fellow Vietnamese immigrants, like Phat Thanh Nguyen, from Song Be, who arrived last February from a refugee camp in Bataan, Philippines. Phat was drafted by the Communist government and sent to fight in Cambodia in 1981.

One night, near the Thai border, he hid from his companions and found his way to freedom. He was in a Thai refugee camp for eight months.

Phat is learning English from Nguyen, while others — dozens of Vietnamese — are being taught by Louise Tomasko of the Adult Education Program in the Lake Ridge Schools.

They are learning American ways, and they, like many other immigrants, will eventually be assimilated. But like the Assyrians, an ancient nationless people, the Vietnamese will probably retain their cultural identity come what may.

68 / Vietnamese

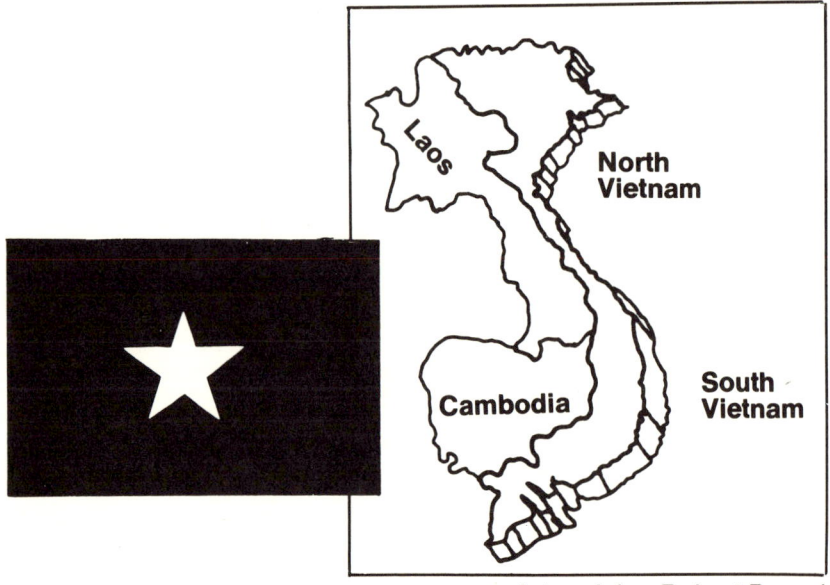

Artwork by: Robert Bernal

14.
Hungarians

"This is my country," said Ilona Horzsa, 23. "But I and my children will always be Hungarian."

In the modern era of mixed ethnic marriages, as the American melting pot continues to be blended, a Hungarian-Hungarian wedding in America is rare.

But recently, it became the real thing, as in "the old country" for Ilona Horzsa and Laszlo Nemes. They're pure Hungarians, Ilona's parents coming from Szalafo in Vas County near Hungary's border with Austria, and Nemes' family from the area near Budapest.

Ilona's father, Tivadar Horzsa, is particularly pleased. Among Northwest Indiana's 2,000 Hungarian families, and as an active member of Hungarian Independent Freedom Fighters Association, he's a stickler at keeping the Hungarian language and culture alive. The bridegroom, American-born like Ilona, is fluent in Magyar, too.

It's a time for gaiety, for goulash and paprika-spiced foods, laci recsenye deep-fried pork and all the delicacies Ilona, her sister, Kati, and friends have prepared for weeks.

It came just a week before the traditional St. Stephen's Day picnic on Aug. 14, at Black Oak Grove. St. Stephen was the king who united Hungarians in the year 1000 and converted them to Christianity.

Among local Hungarians, Horzsa belongs to a later wave of immigrants, 60,000, the Freedom Fighters of 1956, who left their homeland when Soviet tanks and troops snatched success from rebels who had reclaimed Hungary for freedom.

Most well-known among the post-World War II Hungarian immigrants are Eva, Magda and Zsa Zsa Gabor.

The first wave of 458,000 came between 1899 to 1914, to the coal mines of Pennsylvania, Ohio, Virginia, Illinois and Indiana. Today, their descendants are among the 1,776,902 Americans, polled by the 1980 U.S. Census, who say they're of Hungarian descent.

Even before 1899, during the time when Hungary was a free nation, there were reported to be Hungarians in America. One traveled with Leif Ericson in the year 1000. Mihaly Kovats de Fabricacy (1724-1779) died fighting for the American Revolution in the Battle of Charleston. Agoston Haraszthy (1821-1869) introduced Tokay grapes to California. Joseph Pulitzer (1847-1911) is credited with founding modern journalism.

Holy Trinity Church in East Chicago started in 1906 and St. Emeric's Church was established at 15th and Harrison in Gary in 1910, followed by Grace Reformed Church at 13th and Jackson.

The father of Michael Ponczak of Merrillville, also named Mike, came to Gary after 1906. His mother, Julia, now 91, still recalls Magyar Haz, the Hungarian boarding house at 11th and Harrison.

The Calumet Region Historical Guide, published by the Gary School Board in 1939, noted the Hungarians' penchant for organizations, such as the Verhouvay Aid Association, Hungarian Reformed Federation, Hungarian Educational and Entertainment Club, and five other clubs.

Today, the Hungarian Freedom Fighters Federation, Gary Area Chapter, is the predominant unifying factor, along with Holy Trinity Church in East Chicago, where the Rev. Alphonse Skerl is pastor. St. Emeric's closed a decade ago.

Jozsef Cardinal Mindszenty (1892-75), an inspiration to Hungarians for his opposition to Naziism and communism, visited St. Emeric's in 1947, recalls Poncsak.

He returned in 1974 and Kati Horzsa, 17, recalls it with pride. She received her First Communion from him.

Between those dates were years of strife, for the cardinal and for freedom-loving Hungarians.

Kati's father was a slave-labor prisoner of war of the Soviets for 39 months, from 1945 to Aug. 17, 1948. He worked day and night in a coal mine in Kazakstan.

He remembers those months all too well. "No food, no water," he said.

It was a thrill for him a few years ago, when attending a Freedom Fighters picnic in Black Oak, he met a man who worked with him in the same coal mine, No. 72 shaft, in Bogorodec.

The man, Bela Janko of Oak Forest, Ill., told a newsman, "That was a long, long time ago," and he said he preferred not to talk about it.

Horzsa was released in 1948, got married and settled down in his old hometown as a forest ranger and as a distillery employee.

But 1950 to 1956 were "bad years," he said. Secret police made life miserable. Student demonstrations started. Then, the revolution on Oct. 23, 1956. The rebels appeared to have won. Gen. Pal Maleter, ordered to quash the revolt, joined it instead.

The cardinal was freed on Oct. 30.

But 5,000 tanks and 300,000 Soviet Siberians entered Hungary on Nov. 4 and smothered the revolution.

Horzsa, his wife and two sons, 6- and 2-years-old, barely managed to escape to Austria. They were stopped by Russian soliders, but Austrian officers intervened and declared they were on Austrian soil.

On April 9, 1957, Horzsa and family arrived in New York and he settled in South Haven with his chickens, bees and rabbits. It's like Hungary before World War II, he says. The Hungarians, known for their czarda folk dances, and their colorful costumes, are a gregarious people who like the company of others.

The local Hungarians — such as Beres, Bodnar, Danko, Hatala, Horvath, Konrady, Lazar, Onda, Orosz, Yuha and Yuhasz — are descendants of Magyar tribes that settled in the Danube River basin in the 7th Century.

They are believed to have come from the East, in the land of the Assyrians, around 1000 B.C. Estonians are ethnically related to the Hungarians.

Today, compared to the 1950s and 1960s, there may be more freedom in communist Hungary, but Horzsa and many others have made roots in America. There's no other place now, he concludes.

* * * * * * * * * *

Artwork by: Maryann Bartman

The Hungarian story drew Veronica Stuecker of Ogden Dunes. She called about her father, from Budapest, who married her mother, from Vienna.

Bonnie Smith Hall of DeMotte wrote after reading the Hungarian story that her cousin, Anna St. Peter of Penfield, Ohio, is searching for roots, for Magyar people from Galicia, Cracow, or western Ukraine.

15. Saxons

> "I am a Saxon, I'm proud to say
> From old and noble Saxon roots,
> Just honest men, German and free."
> — **from old Saxon song.**

Are the Saxons an endangered species?

These Germanic people, who came from Transylvania in what is now Romania since the turn of the century, amount to about 100,000 in the United States today, according to Ernst Wagner, co-author of "The Transylvania Saxons," a 1982 book published by the Alliance of Transylvania Saxons.

But the number is deceiving. Even local Saxons admit, with not much concern, they are being assimilated into the general American, English-speaking mainstream, and the younger Saxons are calling themselves German, which they are.

The U.S. Census doesn't recognize Saxons as an ethnic classification, while reporting that 49,224,146 Americans, including 1,776,144 in Indiana, claimed German ancestry, the second largest ethnic count following the English.

The Harvard Encyclopedia of American Ethnic Groups, 1980, reported on 106 U.S. ethnic groups, but made no mention of Saxons.

But even as 1983 was celebrated as the German-American Tricentennial, with Saxons included, Northwest Indiana's ethnic history should list Saxons as separate, says Marcella Otasevich, former executive director of International Institute, and Edward Gottschling, long active with the Saxon Lodge, 5757 Massachusetts St., Merrillville.

"They've always considered themselves Saxons," said Mrs. Otasevich.

"We're a separate entity," said John Guist, 70, a former president of the lodge, who was born in Transylvania in 1913, before his parents migrated from that section, controlled by Austria-Hungary, in 1916.

Andrew Guist Sr., who died in 1975 at age 86, was among the 20,000 Transylvania Saxons who migrated to America during the first of three mass migration waves, 1886-1914. The family had eight children, with Paul, U.S.-born, former Gary city councilman and Gary National Bank vice president, as the youngest.

The oldest, Andrew, 84, lives in Detroit.

The pioneer Guist worked as a molder in Pennsylvania, then he became a machine shop operator at the Gary mills in 1929. John Guist worked at the mill too, for almost 39 years.

The Saxons, whose ancestral home in 100 A.D. was northern Germany in what is now Kiel, Hamburg, Bremen and Hanover, migrated to Transylvania, in the province of Hermannstadt, from 1142 to 1162, at the invitation of Hungarian King Geisa II.

They became known as the Transylvania Saxons, while some of their cousins who invaded Britain in the mid-400s merged with the Angles to form the English people.

For centuries, the Saxons lived in Transylvania, which was invaded by the Crusaders, the Tartars, the Turks and the Hungarians. But they were always a minority, comprising no more than 10 percent of Transylvania's population, although communities such as Seleus, Laslau Mic, Filitelnic and Cisnadioara were more than 90 percent Saxon in the 1930s.

Formerly Catholics, they accepted the Augsburg Confession in 1572.

Emigration of the Saxons from parts of Hungary and Transylvania came in three waves — 1886-1914 when they were under Austria-Hungary, 1918-1930 under the Romanian kingdom, and 1949-1955, when 5,000 came to the United States and 5,000 to Canada.

The Saxons of America, with names like Guist, Gottschling, Urschel, Schmidt, Krone, Untsch, Schiller, Helwig and Frenzel, are descended from those minority Germans.

Today, said John Guist, the lodge has only 60 members, down from about 200, and many don't speak Saxon German anymore.

The Saxon language, with Romanian and Turkish words, is slightly different from standard German.

As early as 1909, there were Saxons in Gary. They formed Branch 26 of the Alliance of Translyvania Saxons, with Carl Frenzel as president, bought land for a lodge at 15th and Grant in 1911, and later, when the women's Branch 40 was formed, purchased the Englehart Mansion at 5757 Massachusetts St.

The Saxons of America built 11 churches between 1902 and 1932, and one of them, Honterus German Evangeligal Lutheran Church with the Rev. John Teutsch as pastor, was constructed in 1924 at 10th and Fillmore, known then as a Saxon neighborhood.

The church was later sold, as members moved to Merrillville, Highland, Portage and other suburban communities and joined other Lutheran churches.

Now, what remains of the Saxon tradition is maintained chiefly by the lodge as one of 31 branches of the Alliance of

Transylvania Saxons and the newspaper, Volksblatt, printed weekly in English and German.

The paper, based in Cleveland, makes frequent appeals for aid to 150,000 Saxons left in Romania. Many of the Saxons, estimated at 65,000, migrated to West Germany between 1950 and 1980.

The Saxon organization expressed concern for those Romanian Saxons. "Will the descendants of the Saxons who developed the 800-year history of Transylvania (the Land beyond the Forests) forsake their homeland because they will succumb to the alluring call of the Golden West?" Wagner speculated.

Guist noted that American Saxons may be losing their ethnic identity. Young Saxons don't use the lodge anymore, except to pay their insurance dues; it is used primarily by the Golden Age Clubs, whose members, in their 70s and 80s, talk about the early days of Gary.

Mrs. Katherine Schiller, 87, was 18 years old in 1914 when she came to Gary from Transylvania and lived in Tolleston. She was president of Branch 40 for many years.

In those early years, in the 1920s, the Saxons spoke Saxon at their meetings, Anna Helwig said.

She recalled that when her child went to school, speaking Saxon, no one could understand her, not even the Germans in Tolleston. She quickly learned English and adapted, however.

While the Saxon children have become mainly English-speaking, and tend to marry non-Saxons, they have maintained their Lutheran faith and their preference for Saxon foods, which are Germanic with Romanian influence.

Some of the Saxon delicacies are hunklich Saxon pie, Kkrapfen bismarck, Klausenberg cabbage, szekely gulyas, kletiten pancakes, palukas mit kase corn pudding with cheese, taken with Zuika plum brandy.

Wagner in his book described the Saxons, minorities in their homes for 800 years, learned to be "prudent, deliberate and cautious" and the senior citizens at the lodge said Saxons are known to be clean, honest and religious.

"Radical behavior, the wish to stake everything on one chance, would have been ruinous to their existence as a group," noted Wagner.

John Guist, who never had a desire to visit Transylvania, although his wife did, said Saxons learned to survive, to adjust to their environment.

* * * * * * * * *

Saxons / 75

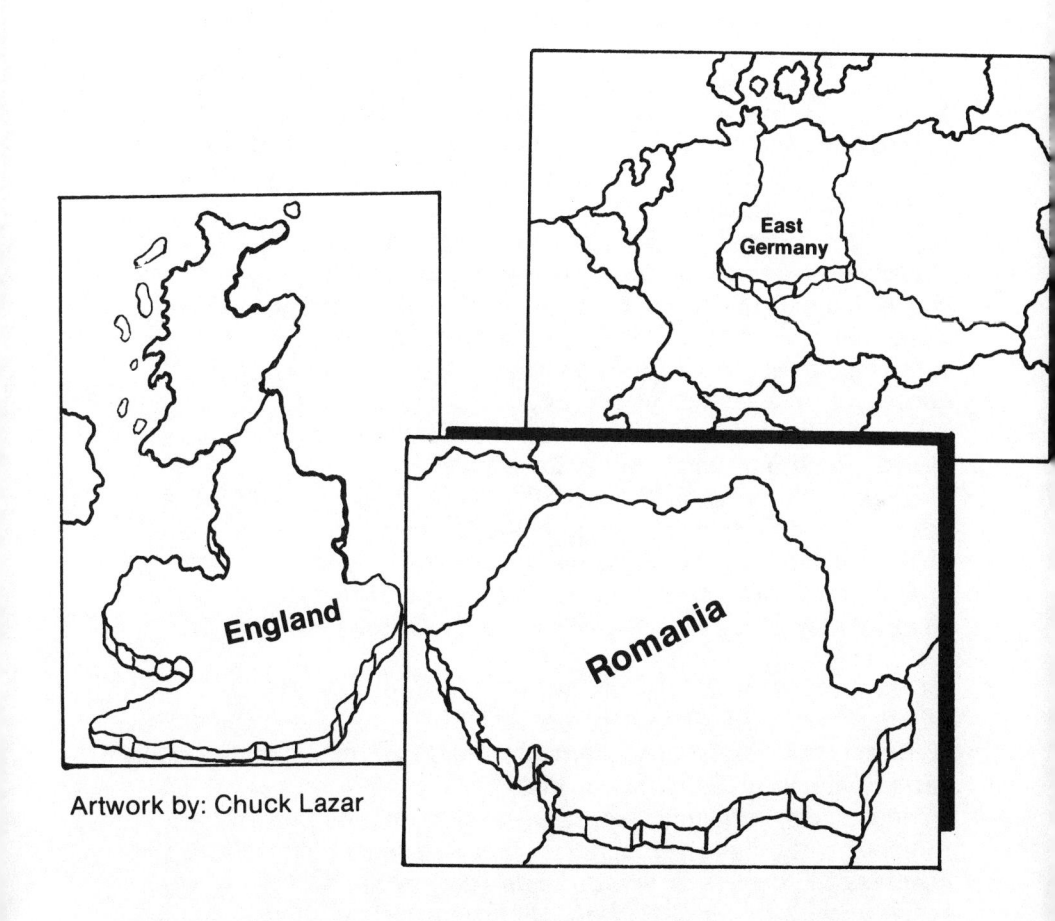

Artwork by: Chuck Lazar

There are only a few identifiable Saxons left, but Ed Gottschling said he dreaded the repercussions that would result after publication, when some aren't recognized.

16. Jewish

"I've tried to put the whole thing behind me. Still, it haunts me, I have nightmares, almost every day." — **Sol Rosner, a survivor of Auschwitz**

"Tzedakah is more than charity or philanthropy . . . it is the highest ideal of Jewish teaching . . . Judaism in action, a way of life, a way of living." — **Philip Bernstein, Director, Council of Jewish Federations**

To understand the Jew, you must know something about Tzedakah," said Barnett Labowitz, executive director of the Jewish Federation of Northwest Indiana.

"It's the fiber that identifies and unites the Jews."

The Jews, their recorded history dating back 5,000 years, are united indeed, bound by their one-god religion and its sweeping ethics, their blood ties, and documents and documents of suffering, struggle and survival — in their Middle East homeland, around the world, even in America.

For the 10 million Jews on earth, 5.7 million in the United States, Rosh Hashanah is important.

It starts the year in the Jewish Calendar — more than 5,700 years after the calendar started — indicating the lengthy past of the people who were led by the patriarch Abraham from Ur in ancient Mesopotamia, on the Tigris and Euphrates rivers in what is now Iraq, to the land of the Canaanites around 1700 B.C.

(Jews call that B.C.E., or Before the Common Era).

Some four million Jews make up 85 percent of the population of Israel, the size of New Jersey, which became an independent nation only in modern times, 1949.

Industrious, congenial, spirited, business-minded, deeply religious, they have through time contributed immensely to the progress of peoples in whose lands they lived. Northwest Indiana, with about 5,000 Jews, is no exception.

The work of one man in particular, Mandel Sensibar, is noteworthy. A Russian-born immigrant from Wheatfield, he was the contractor who excavated seven million tons of sand in 1907 in the creation of Gary.

He later moved to what is now the nation of Israel and drained swamps there. He died in 1931 at the age of 66, according to Temple Israel files.

Labowitz, 58, whose mother came from Hungary and whose father was born in Czechoslovakia near the border of the Ukraine, said Jewish history binds the people. Early in life, they learn about the Chosen People and the Promised Land, once named Canaan, which is now Israel.

They learn about the Biblical patriachs, Abraham and Isaac and Jacob, the migration to Canaan, the exodus of Moses who welded the Jews into a nation, the Ten Commandments, and Saul, the first king (1020 to 1004 B.C.)

Saul was followed by David and Solomon, whose Jewish empire in 930 B.C. spread from the Euphrates River to Egypt, who wrote the Book of Proverbs and built the First Temple at Jerusalem.

The history goes on through 20 Jewish kings until 722 B.C. when Assyrian King Argon II conquered the Jews and dispersed them, but the Kingdom of Judea under the lineage of David survived.

Babylonians in 587 B.C. destroyed Solomon's Temple, enslaved and exported the Jews, who felt then that in defeat, they lost Shekhina, Divine Presence too.

Jews continued in subjugation, although Cyrus the Persian drove the Babylonians out in 539 B.C. allowing the First Return of 42,000 Jews, followed by the rebuilding of the Temple at Jerusalem in 525 B.C. Jews increased in number through Greek and Latin reigns, until in 70 A.D., the Roman commander destroyed Jerusalem and the Temple and the "Diaspora" — the worldwide dispersion of the Jews — began. Of the three million Jews then, a million died. Many consider it the first Holocaust, bypassed in modern times by Hitler and Eichmann, who in 1939-45 engineered the extermination of six million of the 16 million Jews in existence.

One hundred thousand survived the modern Holocaust, and at least two of them eventually settled in Indiana. Sol Goldstein of Munster is one, a survivor of the Auschqitz-Birkenaw extermination camp in Poland.

Another is Sol Rosner, 55, who works at Milgram's Shoes in Southlake Mall.

"I have tried to put the whole thing behind me," said Rosner."I still have nightmares, almost every day."

It took many years before Rosner was able to talk about the ordeal of his youth. On May 5, 1945, when he was rescued by U.S. soldiers, he was 17 years old, and weighed 60 pounds, weak and anguished by the loss of his father, mother and three sisters at Auschwitz in Poland.

The family lived in Mukachevo, Czechoslovakia, in the

78 / Jewish

Carpathian mountains, in 1944 when they were captured by German storm troopers, he said.

That town, now part of the Ukraine, Soviet Union, was under Czechoslovakia when Germany invaded.

They were moved in people-packed cattle trains from labor camp to labor camp, for about a year, until they were taken to Auschwitz-Birkenaw.

"My mother and three sisters were immediately taken — I never saw them again," said Rosner. He and his father were spared, briefly.

But two days later, "They picked my father. It was the most devastating fear in my life. I knew I was never to see him again," he said.

Moved from camp to camp, beaten and kicked almost daily, and rarely given food, Rosner said he despaired.

"I didn't believe in God. How could He let it happen?" he said.

But years later, after his rescue, his migration to New York in 1947, after he learned English, served with the U.S. Army in Alaska, married at 35 and settled in Gary, "I became reconciled," he said.

He has never wished for revenge against the German people. "What for?" he said. "It does no good."

Recently, he enjoyed a happy sequel to his horrendous story. He enrolled his son in college.

Rosner works for one of the "pioneer" Jewish families in Northwest Indiana — the Milgrams, who founded M&B Boot Shop in Gary. Other oldtime Jewish families are Rosen, Noe, Fox, Cohen, Levy, Muscat, Goodman, Steiner, Greenbaum, Mack, Schuler, Klein, Kaplan, Rosenbloom, Braman, Given, Wechsler, Aranson, Blackstone, Lakin, Bernstein, Lazerwitz, Finkel, Gordon, Nelson, Lieberman.

As early as 1906, there were 36 Jewish families in Gary, founders of Temple Beth'el, which had its first service in 1907 at a hayloft in the home of Philip Mackatinsky near 9th and Adams. Later a wooden structure was dedicated at 8th and Connecticut, then a new structure in 1955 at 5th and Roosevelt. Much later, Beth'el was merged with Beth Israel in Hammond and now has 550 families.

Temple Israel, a Reformed congregation, started at 4th and Adams in 1910 with William Feder as the first president. Gary Angust was rabbi from 1926 to 1951, and Carl Miller from 1951 to 1979. The temple in Miller was built in 1959.

Other congregations are Temple Israel in Valparaiso, Sinai Temple in Michigan City, B'nai Judah in Whiting, and B'nai

Sholom in East Chicago.

Working with the synagogues has been the Jewish Federation, a kind of umbrella group established in 1930 as the Gary Jewish Welfare Federation. It became the Northwest Federation in 1958, and recently celebrated its 25th anniversary.

The federation is a manifestation of Tzedakah, which Jewish people define as a way of life, based on the idea that it is God's will that the poor and the traveler must be given assistance.

"It's not charity, it's justice," said Labowitz, who noted that when Jews were farmers, they designated parts of their land for the poor.

Tzedakah has different elevations, the highest being the action of a giver who provides for an unidentified recipient, with the recipient not knowing where the aid came from.

Today's United Way, evolved from Community Chest, has similar applications of Tzedakah.

"One God, Tzedakah, the Ten Commandments of Moses and the 613 Precepts — they're the keystones of the Jewish faith," said Labowitz.

The Jews are also united in their almost unqualified support of Israel and its four wars — 1947, 1956, 1967 and 1973 — of independence and preservation. The United States' annual aid to Israel is $2 billion, and the Jews of America contribute more.

American-born William Braman, whose 90-year-old father, Milton Braman, moved from Indiana Harbor to Gary in 1909 and later established a real estate and insurance business, said the strong connection to Israel is understandable.

Israel is home to people who had fled Hitler-infested Europe, survivors. "There but for the grace of God go I," said Bill Braman.

This also explains Yom Hashoah, the annual springtime remembrance of the Holocaust, when Jews arouse the world's consciousness about man's inhumanity to man.

"Out of the ashes of Holocaust was born Israel," said Labowitz.

There are other special days on the calendar. Yom Kippur, followed by Sokot, the harvest festival, and Simhat Torah. Hanukkah, the Feast of Lights, is later.

Love of music, devotion to education and family togetherness are Jewish characteristics.

Jewish foods are well known, served at home or at delicatessens.

Labowitz noted that in the 1920s and 1930s when waves of Jewish immigrants arrived from Germany and Eastern Europe, they decided to adjust to America. They didn't urge their children to learn the European tongues.

Yiddish itself is a type of Germanic slang, and a fading language. In Israel, the language is a modernized Hebrew. Labowitz said few Jewish Americans speak Yiddish.

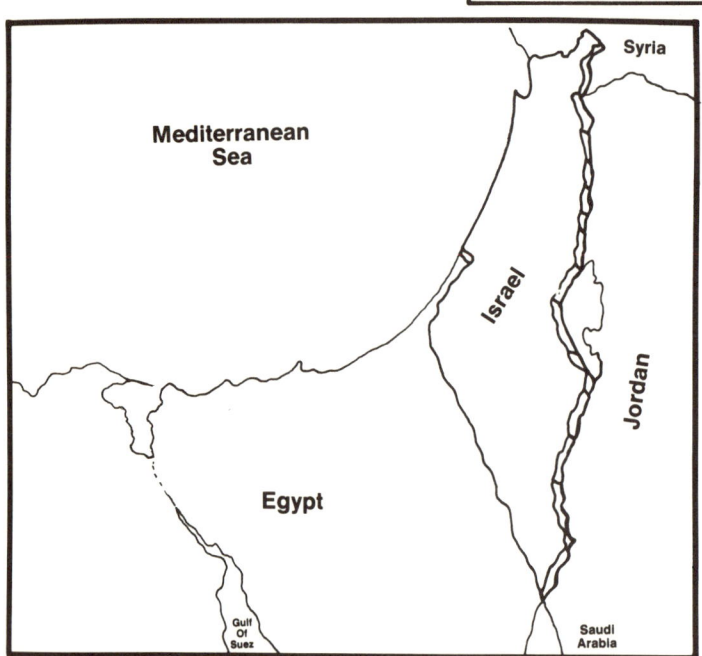

Artwork by: Rich Kandalic

17. Slovenes

What do Mayors Edward J. Raskosky, Robert J. Pastrick and John Grenchik, former United Steelworkers local presidents Henry Yurin and John M. Mayerik, and Principal Terry Levenda have in common with Bishop Andrew G. Grutka?

They're Slovaks — who gained prominence in their fields — and they're all American-born.

For the rest of the world, outside Czechoslovakia with five million and the United States with 776,806 of them, Slovak needs definition.

Slovaks are a Slavic people who settled in Slovakia, now part of Czechoslovakia, in the 6th century, who for a thousand years were ruled by Hungarians. They speak Slovak.

They are to be distinguished from:

Slovenes — the people of Slovenia, one of the states of Yugoslavia, who also are a Slavic people. Their language is similar.

Slavs — the general term for the East European people, including Slovaks, Slovenes, Croatians, Macedonians, Serbians, Polish, Ukrainians, Russians, Belorussians, Carpatho-Rusyns, Bulgarians, Czechs.

Slavonia is a region in north-eastern Yugoslavia, south of Hungary. Slavonia is near Slovenia, which is in the northwest sector of Yugoslavia, just south of Austria.

Definitions are important. Northwest Indiana is home to descendants of many of these peoples, who in the past warred with each other.

The Slovaks were among the early settlers of Gary and Northwest Indiana, arriving usually from Pennsylvania after U.S. Steel built its Gary Works on the shores of Lake Michigan.

In 1907, one of the first meat markets in Gary was run by Slovaks, John and Mary Bilkovic, reports Indiana University Northwest professor James B. Lane in his 1978 book, "City of the Century."

Today, there are about 4,000 Slovak families in Northwest Indiana, Roman Catholic Church members of St. John the Baptist parish in Hammond, Immaculate Conception parish in Whiting, Holy Trinity parish in Gary, Sacred Heart parish in East Chicago, and Assumption parish in Indiana Harbor. Some are with Holy Trinity Slovak Evangelical Lutheran Church in East Chicago and with St. Michael's Slovak's Byzantine Church in Merrillville.

While the Slovaks in the 1920s to 1950s lived near their churches, at 12th and Madison near Froebel School in Gary for instance, their children moved into the suburbs, to Merrillville, Portage, Highland and Munster.

The 1980 U.S. Census showed that roughly one-half, 361,394, of the 776,806 Slovaks in the nation, reported single ancestry, that is Slovak mother and Slovak father. The total for Indiana is 23,080.

Grutka, who celebrated his 50th anniversary as an ordained priest in 1983, has been bishop of the Gary Catholic Diocese, with 200,000 parishers in 85 parishes in Lake, Porter, LaPorte and Starke counties, since 1957. Grutka may be the most prominent Slovak in America, although Chicago hockey star Stan Mikita, football kicker George Blanda and White Sox player Tom Paciorek are as well-known among sports fans. Novelist Thomas Bell, formerly Belejcak (1903-1961) who wrote "Out of This Furnace," an immigrant steelworker's story, and Milos Mlynarovich (1887-1971), poet, lecturer and author, are as popular with Slovaks as the Slovak-American Cook Book of the First Catholic Slovak Ladies Assocation, established in 1892.

Msgr. Mlynarovich was a priest at the Seven Dolors Shrine, established by the Slovak Franciscan friars, in South Haven. His nephew is the Rev. Joseph Viater, pastor of Holy Trinity Church, where Grutka served earlier as a young priest.

Grutka's parents, Simon and Sophia Grutka, came from the village of Stara Ves, in the Tatra mountains. They actually met and got married in Pittsburgh; Simon had migrated at 15 to work as a coal miner. They moved to Joliet, Ill., where Andrew, oldest of six, was born, to work in the steel mills. Later, Andrew labored there, too, under William Gleason, who transferred to the new plant in Gary.

But instead of pursuing a career as a steelmill supervisor or as a physician, Grutka decided to become a priest. He was ordained in 1933, served in Elkhart, then East Chicago, then at Holy Trinity in Gary in 1943.

Why did he become a priest? "I thought I could do more for my people as a clergyman," he said. "I have never regretted that decision."

He became the Slovaks' parish priest; he was fluent in the language of his parents, and through Slovak, he quickly learned the other Slav tongues.

While Grutka was pursuing his religious career, other Slovaks were making history in Gary. Lane recorded the story of Henry Yurin and John M. Mayerik, young Slovak millworkers, who helped organize the United Steelworkers of America in the 1930s. Mayerik, president of USW Local 1014 from 1937 to 1944, 1946 to 1962, whose parents moved to Gary from Pennsylvania in 1910, was one of 13 who secretly met in 1933 to form the Amalgamated Association of Iron, Steel and Tin Workers, forerunner of John L. Lewis' Steel Workers Organizing Committee. Mayerik is retired in Gary.

Yurin, known as "Pennsy," who was USW 1014 president in 1945, is married to Anna Rigovsky Yurin, whose parents, John and Mary Rigovsky, took her to Gary in 1912. Mary Rigovsky lived in her 90's in Merrillville; and Mrs. Yurin, one of the first students of Holy Trinity School which was built in 1913, marveled recently at the changes in "my hometown, Gary." She lives in Glen Park, and will not move.

She raised her children in Gary. William, who went into the Navy in 1945, now teaches at Duncan School; Bernie, who fought in the Korean War, is a manager at Texas Instruments, Dallas; Henry, who served two tours in Vietnam, died 10 years ago at 28; Barbara Kvachkoff, who married a Macedonian, is financial secretary at Crown Point High School.

Mrs. Yurin has never been to her parents' home in Slovakia. "There's nothing there for me," she said. "I'm also afraid — it's communist."

Communist indeed, but Michelle Kalena, 47, who learned "Axa mate" (How are you) and "Dobre" from her grandmother, plans to go in 1984 anyway to trace her roots and to see if the music, the art, the culture she has learned as a third-generation Slovak is thriving or declining.

Her grandfather, Ignac Chernota, came from Dhuly Kubin village in 1894 and became a pipefitter at Standard Oil in Whiting.

Chernota fled from Hungarian oppression, and told her many times that he had to speak Magyar, not Slovak, in his own village.

In 1900, in Slovakia, the Slovaks expressed their protest by clandestinely writing and publishing books, codifying their language, reports the Harvard Encyclopedia of American Ethnic Groups.

One of the most cherished customs, practiced at Christmastime, was described by Carl Yurechko of Merrillville, a Pennsylvania-born coal miner's son who came to Gary at the age of 18 to work in the mills. He and his wife, Betty, are active in Slovak Club, Slovak Federation.

"On Christmas eve, at dusk, the father walks outside the house and looks to the sky, then goes inside and declares, 'I have seen the North Star.' That's the beginning. Then, the candles are lit, and oplatky Christmas wafers are distributed like Holy Communion. The father breaks it up and divides it among the participants, and it is eaten with honey," said Yurechko.

"Then it's time for wine and pagach and mushroom soup, fish, beans, sauerkraut and rozky. After the meal, there's no washing of dishes. The table is covered and the family goes on to the living room, exchanges gifts and pleasantries, and then prepares to go to Midnight Mass and sing Slovak hymns," he said.

At Eastertime, food is taken to the church in special Holy Saturday baskets for the priest's blessing, then taken home and covered — not to be eaten until Easter morning, when "the first taste is blessed food."

"That tradition is more prominent now than in the past," said Yurechko.

Yurechko's description of Slovaks as hard-working people determined to succeed without anger and rebellion is expressed in "Out of This Furnace," the story of a Slovak immigrant much like Peter Levanda, who was a teenager in the 1880s when he left Slovakia for Johnston, Pa. He married Susan Ligda and they moved to Gary after Victor, the oldest of six children, was born. Victor, who became a steelworker like his father, and his Slovak wife, Mary Harwys, had three sons and a daughter. One of the sons is Terry Levenda, principal at Fegely Middle School in Portage where another Slovak, Mike Berta, is assistant principal. One son, Larry, teaches in Lake Station, and the other, Jerry, is vice president of a real estate firm in Palos Heights, Ill.

The Levenda family and that of historian Jaroslav Pelikan and astronaut Eugene Cernan reflect the upward movement of the Slovak Americans, who were quiet and unrecognized laborers through the early migration period, 1860 to 1905, fleeing their homes in Saris, Spis, Zemplin and Abov districts to find opportunity at $1.50 a day in the coal mines and steel furnaces of America.

But they dreamed of progress through education for their children.

The children then moved out of the mills, and out of the mill area.

The bishop, whose early years were spent in the mills, has an explanation.

"Heavy industry has a brutalizing effect," he said. "It takes something crude, like iron ore and makes it beautiful and

Slovenes / 85

useful, like stainless steel. But in the process, the people are brutalized."

It was common for steelworkers — Slovaks as well as others — to say to their children, "you better go to school so you don't have to do the kind of work I'm doing," he said.

"Now they've graduated into highly technical skills and can't find work here," he added, making a plea for diversification of jobs in Northwest Indiana.

* * * * * * * * *

Artwork by: Chuck Lazar

Mary Stolzman called to say there are many more prominent Slovaks, such as the Konrady and Malinka families, and John Oleska, the father of Mrs. Robert A. Pastrick.

Carl Yureckho, proud of being "pure Slovak," reported the Slovak story is being printed in the American Slovak newspaper.

18. Norwegians

"We're a small group, but we're together," says Norman Renning, secretary of Trollhaugen Lodge 417 of the Sons of Norway, talking about "a minority among minorities."

They are the Norwegians, who in the 1920s could be contained in the 600 block of Harrison Street in young Gary. They've been dispersed since, to Portage, Whiting, South Haven, elsewhere in Northwest Indiana.

Wisconsin-born Mrs. Renning, a former Hammond teacher, tries to keep the few — about 75 families — Norwegians unified with the 100,000 Norwegians in the Chicago area.

"Think Norse," she said, as Sons of Norway prepared for the annual Ethnic Festival sponsored by the Hammond Public Library and the Lacare Art League at Hammond Morton High School, 169th and Grant, which usually draws 100,000 people for the ethnic arts, crafts, foods and folk music.

Some 25 ethnic groups, including Egyptian, gypsy, American Indian, Asian Indian and Norwegian participate, said coordinator Alice Foster.

The Norwegians displayed their costumes and some of their foods — lefsa bread, raspe kumla dumplings, Norwegian stuffed cabbage, pickled herring, and blodpolse blood sausage, and cream cakes, said Mrs. Renning.

Norwegian Americans who migrated in waves from 1860 to 1920 have become predominantly Midwest people. While Norway has a population of 4,152,780, close to that number of Norwegians, 3,453,839, reside in the United States, with 712,258 of them are in Minnesota and 391,650 in Wisconsin, according to the U.S. 1980 Census.

In Indiana, the census counted only 21,725 Norwegian Americans, compared to 167,995 in Illinois, 153,187 in Iowa.

Few as they are in Northwest Indiana, Mrs. Reidun Paulsen, 83, of Portage, who came from the Oslo area, and her daughter-in-law, Mrs. Ellen Paulsen, who grew up in the ancient coast city of Stavanger, are maintaining Norwegian culture through their shop, the Nordic Cellar, which they call "a little bit of Norway."

Reidun Paulsen and her husband, George, were married in Chicago in 1918, three years after she arrived from her native village near Oslo. They moved to East Gary, then to Gary, where three of their six children were born. They lived near the Norwegian Evangeligal Lutheran Church on Harrison Street, she recalled.

Paulsen worked in the rolling mills, but he was forced to "retire" in 1931 during the depression when the mill was closed down. He took his family back to Norway.

Their son, George, now 59, was eight then. He spent the next two decades in Norway, and met his wife, Ellen, during World War II. They lived through the German occupation and George recalled some precarious times, when he was forced to work in a labor camp.

"But they weren't that bad. They didn't torture us," said Paulsen, who returned to America after the war, settled in Gary and became a steelworker too until his retirement. Now, he's a grandfather.

His brother Ragner, was in Canada in April 1940 when Hitler's troops stormed through Denmark and Norway. Unable to join his family, he joined the Royal Norwegian Air Force and later provided his mother "the greatest joy of my life" when he flew over Oslo as a liberator.

"I can never forget it, April 7, 1945," said Mrs. Paulsen. "It was a joyous day. We celebrated for two days, without sleeping ... My husband looked up to the sky, and said, maybe Ragner is in one of those planes. That night, we got a telephone call. It was Ragner. He was the one buzzing by."

On May 8, 1945, 350,000 Germans surrendered to the Norwegian government, ending the five-year occupation.

Another Norwegian "pioneer" of the area is Leif Sandersen, 73, who retired a dozen years ago from the engineering department at U.S. Steel's Gary Works.

Sandersen was 2 years old in 1912 when his Norwegian parents — his mother came from Oslo and his father from Bergen — moved to Chesterton.

During the early years of his life, he also spoke only Norwegian, although he learned Swedish through an elderly couple in his neighborhood who couldn't speak English.

"I discovered Swedish and Norwegian were close enough. I became their interpreter," he said.

Sandersen, who has never been to Scandinavia, said he would like to go someday, "just to test out my vocabulary," to see if he can speak the way they do across the North Atlantic.

Although Norwegians, Danes and Swedes look and speak alike — many are blonde and blue-eyed — Sandersen and Paulsen drew out the distinction. "We're Norwegians. There's a difference," said Sandersen, aware that there are more Swedes in the area. The Swedes were the early settlers of Miller. Across

Indiana, they number 67,697, and there are 4,345,392 of them in the United States.

The Danish population of the United States is smaller, 1,518,273, with 12,490 in Indiana.

The three groups claim Leif Ericson, the Viking who sighted Newfoundland and called it Vinland in the year 1000, as their very own.

Congress in 1964 declared Oct. 9 as Leif Ericson Day, a special day in Nordic towns such as Stoughton and Blair and Iola in Wisconsin and Decorah in Iowa, and in the Humboldt Park area, North and Kedzie, Chicago, where the National Norwegian Memorial stands.

Ericson, descended from the Germanic people who lived in Norway 11,000 years ago, was the son of Eric the Red, who migrated to Greenland from Norway during the reign of the first Viking king, Harold I. Ericson led the expedition that settled in Vinland, then returned to Greenland. His brother, Thorwald, traveled west to the new lands too, and Norsemen believe he was killed by Indians somewhere in America.

Norwegians were converted to Christianity by King Olaf I in 995-1000; King Olaf II is the Norwegians' patron saint.

The Norwegians — sailors and fishermen — were ruled by their own kings until 1397 when they were united with Sweden and Denmark. They didn't achieve independence for centuries.

The country was devastated in 1349-50, when half if its population was killed by Black Death. The bubonic plague that swept through Norway, Russia, Germany, Italy, France and England from 1347 to 1352 diminished Europe's 100 million population by one-fourth.

Decimated Norway became a province of Denmark in 1536. In 1814, Denmark ceded the land to Sweden, and it wasn't until 1905 that an independent Norwegian kingdom, under a Danish prince, Haakon VII, was re-established.

It was during those years that the first waves of migration started, as America attracted Europeans to settle the vast land. As recruiters sought workers for the railroads, coal mines and steel mills, the numbers multiplied.

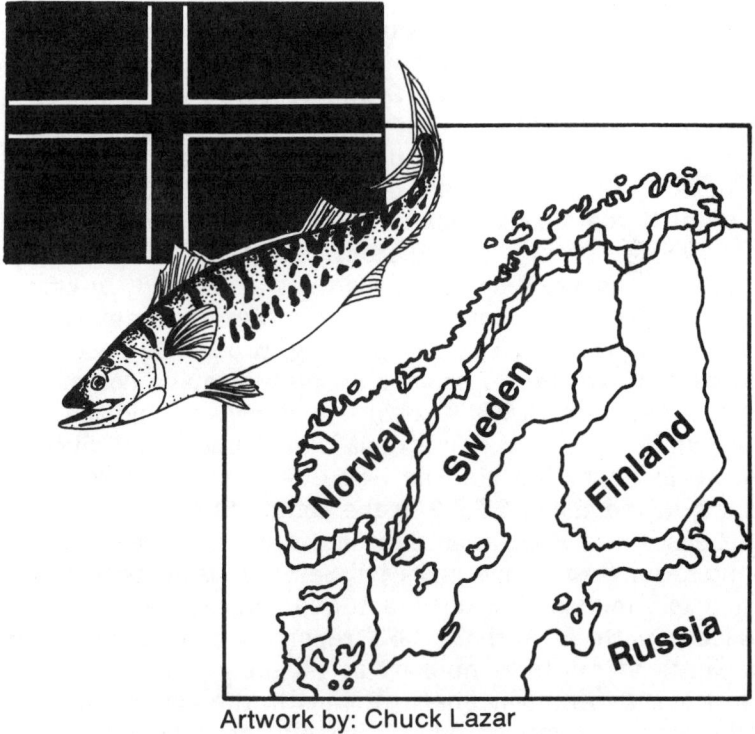

Norwegians / 89

Artwork by: Chuck Lazar

19. Mexicans

"We're proud of our Mexican heritage, and we're proud we are American." — **Jose Arredondo, educator, politican**

"Our time has come," says Tony Avila, speaking about the 14.6 million Hispanic Americans, a majority of them identified as Mexicans.

"The Latinos are getting it together, Mexicans, Puerto Ricans, Cubans, all the Spanish," said Avila, 46, of Lake Station, president of the 50-year-old, 200-member Sociedad Mutualista Mexico, one of a dozen Mexican organizations in the area.

Mexicans, joined by other Hispanics, celebrate Mexican Independence Day each September, commemorating Sept. 15, 1810, when a creole priest, Miguel Hidalgo, launched El Grito, the cry for independence from Spain, achieved in 1921.

The annual Independence day parade is part of the celebration. Traditional fiesta queens are crowned. El Grito and Viva Mexico are shouted amid confetti, mariachi music and south-of-the-border foods such as tacos, tortillas and enchiladas.

Avila, whose father migrated from Vera Cruz, was born in Gary in 1937 and grew up in Gary's Central District, around 13th and Madison. He represents today's Mexican-American — U.S.-born, English- and Spanish-speaking, proud and hopeful.

Francisco Maya, Post-Tribune's Spanish-language columnist, estimates there are 60,000 Mexicans in Northwest Indiana, and Union Benefica Mexicana President Daniel Lopez said about 37,000 are in East Chicago. The 1980 U.S. Census recorded 49,829 Mexicans in Indiana, 7,692,619 in the United States.

The Census and Population Subcommittee of the U.S. House Committee on Post Office and Civil Service, using census data, reported 14.6 million Hispanics, a 10-year increase of 5.6 million. The subcommittee's April 21, 1983, report estimated the number of Hispanics at "15 to 21 million" by including three million in Puerto Rico, two million Puerto Ricans in the continental U.S., 800,000 Cubans, 3.1 million other Hispanics and about six million illegal aliens.

Nearly 90 percent of the Hispanics are in metropolitan areas, two million in Los Angeles-Long Beach, 1.4 million in New York, 580,000 in Chicago, reports the U.S. Population Reference Bureau while projecting the Hispanic population at 47 million by

2020. Harvard Encyclopedia of American Ethnic Groups noted a high percentage of the Mexicans are in Southwest states, Arizona, California, Colorado, New Mexico and Texas.

The data point to President Reagan's vigorous courtship of the Hispanics in his bid for re-election, and the Latinos' drive, with $2.5 million to register one million Hispanics, was launched by 200 leaders, spearheaded by AFL-CIO's Labor Council for Latin American Advancement and New Mexico Gov. Toney Anaya.

Here, that drive is led by LCLAA's Henry Montemayor and Mexican American lawyer Roy Dominguez.

Recognizing the Mexican potential, Benjamin Fernandez, who grew up in Indiana Harbor, declared himself a Republican candidate for president again.

The Mexicans — 84 percent of them are U.S.-born, with 55 percent of them born to parents also born in the U.S. — are bound not only by the new political hope, but also by their lingering language and their proud history.

Uniformly, the family-oriented, Roman Catholic Mexicans favor bilingual education and they glow with pride at the prehistoric triumphs of the Aztecs and the Mayas, their ancestors.

Today, they are united in support of two similar causes — the cases of Ruben Rodriguez, fired from his job as dean of counseling and student activities at Thornton Community College, and Carl Allsup, who has been denied tenure at Indiana University Northwest, where he coordinates the Chicano-Riqueno Program.

Rodriguez is no longer employed by the Illinois college, and legal action is pending. Allsup, a Ph.D. in his ninth year at IUN, has his job until May 1984. The Latin groups are rallying behind him.

Mutualista, UBM and League of United Latin American Citizens are in the forefront of the Latin groups, which also include Latin American Family Education Program, VFW De La Garza Post, and Caballeros.

Jose Arredondo, assistant superintendent of the East Chicago Public Schools, a former Lake County sheriff and auditor, said "we're proud of our Mexican heritage, proud of what our families have been through, and proud to be Americans."

His parents, Miguel and Maria, came from Salamanca, Guanajuato, in 1926 and raised six sons and four daughters in Indiana Harbor. All became professionals, and one of them, Lorenzo, is Lake Circuit Court judge.

The family histories of other Mexicans are similar. Ben Luna, principal at Chase School and former aide to the late U.S. Rep. Adam Benjamin, grew up in the Mexican neighborhood at 19th and Massachusetts as one of eight children of Inez Luna, who came from Mexico in 1920 and worked at U.S. Steel's Sheet and Tin Division.

Lindy Betancourt, acting dean at Indiana Vocational Technical College, was the first Mexican graduate of Portage High School. His father, Ederlindo, came from Michoacan in 1926 and met his mother in East Chicago. Her father, Sebastian Diaz, also came from Michoacan, in 1918, and worked in Kansas City, Mo., before coming to Indiana. Her brother is attorney J. Salvador Diaz of Portage.

Florentino Equihua, 78, one of the founders of Mutualista, along with Antonio Roque, Leovardo Sosa, Reginio Gomez and Santiago Ramirez, was one of the first Mexicans in Indiana, arriving from Arandas in 1927. He worked in the Gary mills for almost 42 years. His son, Salvador, was Gary's first Mexican policeman, now retired. Salvador's son, Miguel, 25, works at Inland Steel. Miguel's son, Mike, will be bilingual, the father insists.

Florentino, treasurer at Mutualista for many years, lived at 14th and Adams, near the first Mexican hall. He recalled the early days as tough ones.

"No union, no pension, no insurance," he said. But he preferred his job, which started at $5.50 a day, because it was better than the $3.28 that New York Central Railroad paid him earlier.

Mutualista's first president was Roque, who came from Cuba in 1923 and formed a group of Mexican baseball players as Club Azteca, which eventually became Mutualista.

Amado Villanueva, who died in 1979 at the age of 114, came from Jalisco in 1922, according to his son, Genaro, who joined him in 1928. They worked in the mills until 1929. In 1934, they started farming the land around 15th and Clay, near the Little Calumet River. Today, Genaro and Celia run a garden store.

Abe Morales, who grew up in Indiana Harbor, said the first Mexicans arrived there in 1909 and lived in boxcars along the New York Central tracks on Block and Pennsylvania streets.

"They were not so bad. They were free. They were well insulated," he said about the wooden cars in use until 1940.

UBM of East Chicago emerged in 1956 from three groups, including Benito Juarez Lodge which had been celebrating Mexican Independence Day in mid-September since 1926.

Gloria Magallon of Gary visits the homeland whenever she can. Many of the Mexicans here are from Michoacan, Durango,

Jalisco, Nuevo Leon and San Luis Potosi states, she noted.

"You should go to Mexico someday, and see the small towns, the silver mines, the Aztec remains," she said.

The Mexicans, descendants of native Indians and Spanish conquistadores who arrived in the New World with the discovery of Mexico in 1517, are proud of their heritage. Ancient Indians lived in that land in 10,000 B.C., grew corn and beans and pepper by 5,000 B.C., developed pottery and villages in 1500 B.C., and built flat-topped pyramids in 500 B.C. when Olmecs developed their own calendar.

The years 300 to 900 A.D. were classic, as Zapotecs developed the Teotihuacan pyramids. The Tolmec empire followed, until it was replaced by the Aztecs, skilled in medicine, music and poetry.

Then came Hernan Cortes and the Spanish Conquest, the defeat of Montezuma II, and 300 years of Hispanization — until El Grito de Dolores in 1810.

The independent young Mexico, with vast lands, didn't last, however. Texas, populated by Americans, seceded in 1836, and the Lone Star Republic joined the U.S.A. in 1845. The U.S.-Mexican War followed and American troops reached Mexico City and Vera Cruz, and the Treaty of Guadalupe Hidalgo gave half of Mexico — California, Nevada, Utah, most of Arizona, parts of Colorado, New Mexico and Wyoming — to the United States for $15 million.

The people in those annexed areas, some 800,000, were the first Mexican-Americans.

In the 1920s during the Cristero Revolution, some 500,000 more Mexicans arrived as the U.S. economy expanded with railroads and steel mills. But immigration declined during the Great Depression, and many Mexicans went back south.

During World War II, as the United States needed manpower for the Bracero Program, the Mexicans were welcomed again, and the flow continued. Operation Wetback (1950-55) expelled 3.8 million illegals.

Mexicans brought their culture to the cities, and the Anglos, as white non-Hispanics are called, are being converted. They're flocking to fast-food outlets like Pepe's Tacos, Taco Bell, Casa Gallardo, Chi Chi and other Mexican chain restaurants.

Tacos have become as American as hot dogs, said Julian Diaz, an East Chicago travel agent, while noting that Anglos like them milder.

* * * * * * * * * *

94 / Mexicans

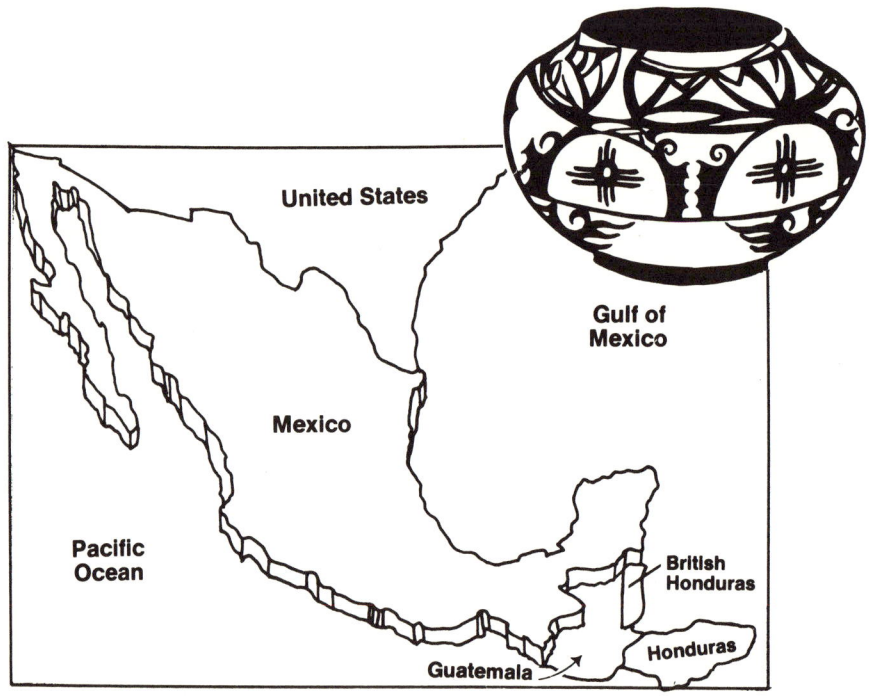

Artwork by: Maryann Bartman

An angry Mexican woman called, asking "where did you get that list?" of Mexicans mentioned in the story, and objecting that a "newcomer," that is, only recently active in the Mexican community, was given recognition. There's no list as such. It was, is, impossible to list all the oldtimer and prominent families of each ethnic group.

20.
Spaniards

> "Every time we get up in the morning, we should kiss the ground. Nothing can come close to the United States. There's no place finer." — **Exequiel Gonzalez, 82**

The golden era of Ferdinand and Isabella, when Spain ruled half the world, has long passed. But four centuries later, their language prevails.

Spanish is spoken by 258 million people, and is the official language of 18 South American nations — all but Brazil, Haiti and Guyana.

In the United States, with 14.6 million to 21 millionHispanics, the number of Spaniards who — like Exequiel Gonzalez of Merrillville and Beatrice Haro of Gary — came directly from Spain is relatively low.

Since 1820, only 250,000 people have migrated from Spain, one-half of them from 1900 to 1924, according to the Harvard Encyclopedia of American Ethnic Groups.

They are the European Hispanics, some of them blond-haired and blue-eyed from Germanic ancestry, who speak Castillian, who delight in the flamenco and bolero dances and eat paellavalenciana, the national dish of 40 million Spaniards.

The U.S. 1980 Census reports that 94,528 Americans described themselves as Spaniards, while 2,686,680 claimed Spanish descent and 7,692,619 identified themselves as Mexicans. All of them, of course, along with Puerto Ricans, Cubans and South Americans, are under the ethnic umbrella called Hispanic.

"We are a small group. Maybe we are getting smaller," said Diego Perez, president of the Spanish Society of Gary, which has 240 members and an active "old-timers" club which meets every Friday at 1500 E. 49th Ave., Gary.

The children of the Spanish immigrants, who formed the first club, Union Espanola, in 1907, with Frank Escudero as president, have long been assimilated into the American mainstream.

Yet William S. Suarez, Porter County Democratic chairman; Dr. Paul Alvarez, a Valparaiso physician; Angeline Prado Komenich, head of the modern languages department at Indiana University Northwest; and others whose parents came directly from Spain maintain their identity through the Spanish Society.

They also maintain it through the kind of Spanish they speak — Castillian, with the silent H and the strong th sound, as in Hernandez pronounced er-nandeth.

Spaniards are a small minority among this country's Hispanics, who are mostly Mexican. But there is no animosity between the groups, even as Mexicans celebrate their motherland's Mexican Independence Day.

"When I was in Mexico, I thought at first I shouldn't speak Castillian," said Basil Fernandez, 67, of Valparaiso. "But someone said speak the way you know and I did, and I got the red-carpet treatment everywhere I went."

He is one of 10 children of Spanish pioneer Lucio Fernandez (1879-1940), who migrated from Zamora Province in north-central Spain in 1912, followed in 1914 by his wife, Erminia, and their four children.

Lucio, who had worked in ore mines near Palentia, went to Panama to work on the canal. Erminia, with Andy, Alex, Anita (Asnar) and Maria (Carmona), joined him in Cuba.

They went to North Carolina, then to Gary in 1923. There were seven children then, including Basil, Frank and Morgan. In Gary, Nena (Jurcic) and Lola (Coster) were born.

Lucio became a foreman at U.S. Steel's Gary Sheet and Tin Works.

They grew up in the house he built at 2nd and Polk, an ethnically mixed neighborhood.

Andy, the firstborn, now in his 70s and living in Chesterton, became a crane operator and an insurance salesman and an interpreter for the FBI and the International Institute.

The Lucio Fernandez family was typically Spanish — strict, loving and bilingual. "We were told to learn English," said Morgan, of Merrillviille.

Basil remembers his father's advice — "Good people always are home by midnight."

Maria Carmona, 71, who helped support the family during the Great Depression, remembers her mother's diligence.

"She never stopped working," Mrs. Carmona said.

The large family lived upstairs; their mother also did the cooking, washing and cleaning for eight Spaniard boarders downstairs.

Other Spanish families in Northwest Indiana for many years were those of Dominic Caballero, Hipolito Fernandez, Frank Rodriguez, Feliciano Rodriguez — in 1907 — and the Urquia, Bobillo, Ramos, Perez, Lavin, Agudo, Conde, Montes, and Garcia families.

Diego Perez, 53, Spanish Society president in 1983, 1979, 1973 and 1972, is of the third generation, although born in Spain. His grandfather came first from Asturias, followed by his father, who returned to Spain, got married, and brought his family over.

Exequiel Gonzalez, 82, of Merrillville, came from Santander in 1919 and was co-founder of Centro Espanol at 1338 Adams St. in 1921. In 1924, on his first of 26 trips to Spain, he brought his parents to America. In 1931, he journeyed again to Santander to marry his high-school sweetheart. He became an electronics man and established Cosmopolitan Radio, which his son, Martin, developed later as MG Electronics.

Gonzalez boosts Americanism. "Every time we get up in the morning, we should kiss the ground. There's no place finer than the U.S.," he said.

Aurora Gonzalez, 69, from Asturias, remembers the Spanish plays and dances she and her sisters, Rosario and Oliva, and their parents, Mr. and Marcelino Montes, attended at the Spanish Castle, 11th and Van Buren. Her nephews are Pepe and Marce Gonzalez, who were athletes at Tolleston. Marce became a teacher and principal.

Also in education are the daughters of Lorenzo Prado, from Asturias. Zulina was the 1940 valedictorian at Froebel High School. Now Mrs. Scales, she's an administrator in Illinois. Olive Prado Bistransky is an administrative assistant at Lake Ridge Schools, and Angeline Prado Komenich, a Ph.D., is language chairman at IUN.

Frank Ramos, 76, was 16 when he arrived in Gary in 1923 from Almaria by way of Havana. A retired steelworker, he lived at 521 Monroe St. from 1938 to 1972 with his wife, Eva, who also was from a pioneering family. Her father, Frank Rodriguez, came from Spain in 1909.

Anita Menor's father, Antonio Garcia, was a Spanish Society co-founder too, active in 1951 in unifying the Spanish groups. He came from Spain in 1921 by way of England and Canada.

Mary Lavin Kujawski, the present treasurer, is one of two female past presidents of the Spanish Society, along with her sister, Elena Harris. Her husband, Louis Kujawski, also is an ex-president, although Polish.

The Spaniards take great pride in their language, developed from Latin by the Romans who occupied Spain from 200 B.C. to 300 A.D. and enriched with 4,000 words from the Moor invaders.

Creature comfort words like almohada (pillow) and alfombra (rug) are derived from Arabic.

The Spanish later passed on words like alfalfa, alligator, lasso, mosquito, potato, ranch, rodeo, tobacco and tornado into the English language in America.

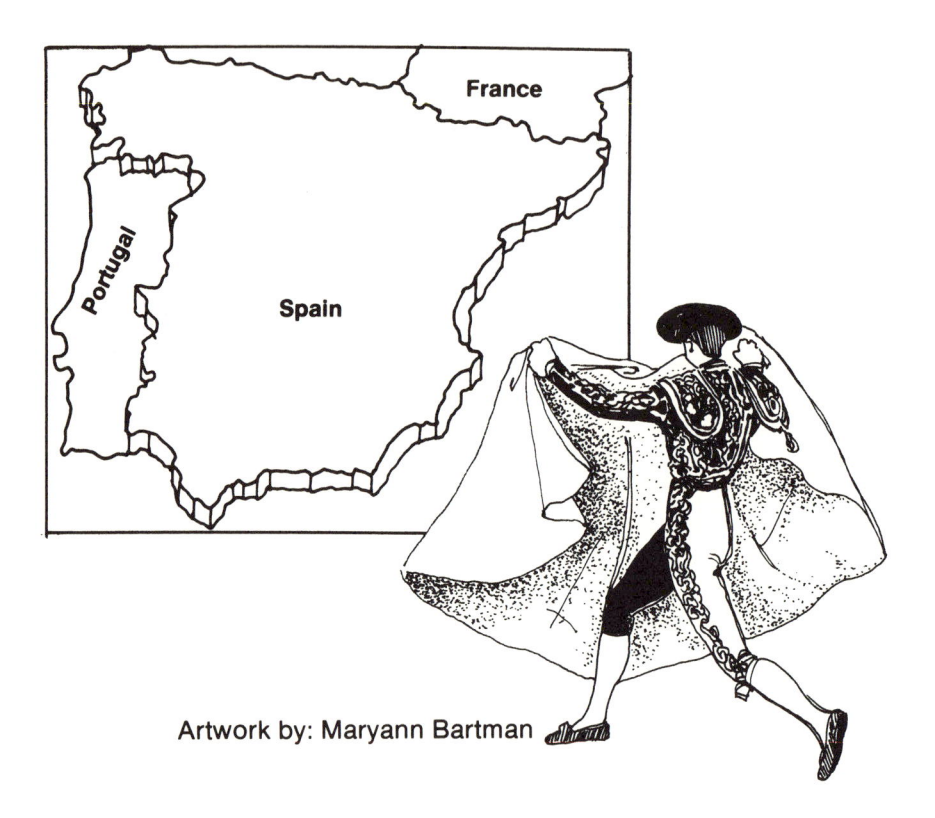

* * * * * * * * * *

Artwork by: Maryann Bartman

Anita Menor and Elisa Harris were two female presidents of the Spanish Society; Mary Kujawski, treasurer in 1983, was never president, according to an angry respondent to the Spanish story. She's right.

Another called about the Spanish Basque people, in the Spain-France mountain border area north of Barcelona. The Basques who speak a language not related to any other have few descendants in the area. But one of prominence is B.G. Snyder, adopted son of the late former publisher and owner of the Post-Tribune, H.B. Snyder.

21.
Chinese

"We put all our hope in the future generation," said David Huang with Confucian simplicity, explaining how such a small group can produce so many whiz kid.

The Chinese in Northwest Indiana are few — no more than 50 families, according to Julie Hsu Lindsey, who runs a travel bureau in Munster.

The United States recorded 894,453 in the 1980 Census, a mere 5,212 in Indiana, while California counted 341,429, New York 144,403 and Hawaii 91,305.

Throughout the world, the Chinese are the most numerous, with 1,063,510,000 in mainland China, the third-largest nation in area, next to the Soviet Union and Canada. In addition, there are an estimated 50 million ethnic Chinese in Singapore, Hong Kong-Kowloon, Macao and elsewhere in the Far East.

Huang, who arrived in America in 1977 from Taiwan and came to Gary with his wife in 1980, is an architect employed by Gary's Department of Urban Planning.

He's one of the "new" Chinese Americans, part of the large migration spurred by the 1965 U.S. Immigration Act, which did away with national quotas. In 1970, there were only 435,062 Chinese in America, more than half of them U.S.-born, notes H.M. Lai in the Harvard Encyclopedia of American Ethnic Groups (1980).

Huang was speaking of the Chinese whiz kids, 1983 version, when told about the flurry of valedictorians.

Lucy Yu, 1982 valedictorian at Munster High School, may have started it.

In 1983, the Munster topnotcher was also Chinese, James W. Yang, while Highland High School's top graduate was Ernest Tseng. At Culver Military Academy, the 1983 valedictorian was Kemin Tsung, son of Dr. and Mrs. Swei H. "Jeffrey" Tsung of Valparaiso. Dr. Tsung is a pathologist at Methodist Hospitals and a former president of the U.S. Chinese Medical Association.

Another Chinese student, Harold Tsai, was 1983 salutatorian at Lake Central High School.

At Culver, the salutatorian was Norman Dy of Portage, whose father, Dr. James Dy, comes from Chinese ancestors in the Philipines, like heart specialist Dr. Felipe S. Chua. (Ernie Hernandez of The Post-Tribune, author of this book, is part-Chinese, from the Ochangco and Tantungco families in Manila.)

Ni Kung-chao, director of Chinese information at the Coordination Council for North American Affairs, the quasi-consular Chicago office of the Republic of China in Taiwan, said that 80 percent of the boat people, refugees from Vietnam such as the Tran Thuy family in East Chicago, are ethnic Chinese.

Huang, whose daughter attends the Gary Banneker School's program for gifted children, said Chinese parents motivate their children toward education. And the children, following the Confucian doctrine of family loyalty, eagerly comply.

That quest for excellence was exemplified by Dr. Wei-Ping Loh and his wife, Dr. Hwei Ya Chang. Dr. Loh, the son of a Chinese landlord, was the chief pathologist at Methodist Hospital for 25 years until he left in 1981. Their children, Terry, Gary and Judy, all born in Gary, never got grades below A.

Loh was among the "pioneer" Chinese in Gary, along with Paul Huang, who started work at U.S. Steel in 1949. Huang is a former president of the International Institute, and only recently was transferred to Minnesota.

"(We) were non-existent then," Huang recalled. He didn't know any Chinese people, although he knew of a laundry on Washington Street.

That was probably Lee's Laundry at 522 Washington St., operated by Dong Ming Lee, whose son, Herbert Lee, was the first known Chinese-American graduate of Gary, at Froebel High School, class of 1931.

"I remember a Chinese boy named Lee," said fellow graduate Helen Meyerick Stolzman of the class with Mildred Uzelac, Sonia Kalember, Dorothy Wade and Orval Lasko.

"He was tiny, brilliant and always immaculately dressed. He wore a suit. I wonder what ever happened to him?"

Abe Lee, the Chicago-born owner of the Pagoda Inn in Griffith, whose Chinese immigrant father came from Boston, is related to another pioneer family which had a Chinese laundry in Indiana Harbor.

The father, descendant of Chinese railroad workers brought to America in the 1870s, had three sons — Percival Lee, who became a lawyer; Raymond, who became a dentist; and Martin, a merchant.

Percival and his wife continued the laundry business, and had Albert, now a businessman in Chicago; Philip, a Ph.D. chemist; William, a physician; Jane, a computer specialist; Susie, a nurse; and Helen. All are college graduates.

"There was a large family of Lees, above the laundry. all the children became high achievers," said Walter Leuca, a

Merrillville lawyer who grew up in East Chicago.

Marcella Otasevich, a former International Institute executive director, recalled Yick Fong, who worked in the mills in the 1930s and 1940s.

Although the Harvard Encyclopedia notes the claim by Sinologists that a Buddhist priest, Huishen, came to America in the 5th Century — well ahead of Leif Ericson and Christopher Columbus — and Chinese were known to be crew members on the Manila-Acapulco galleons from 1565 to 1870, there are no accounts of Chinese in the United States until 1815. Then, a cook, Ah Nam, worked for the governor of Monterey. California was a Spanish colony at that time.

But as the United States expanded after absorbing the western states of Texas, New Mexico, Arizona and California in the Mexican-American War, Chinese immigration proliferated. Conditions in China, the opening of world trade in 1842 after the Opium War, the 1851-1864 Taiping Rebellion, forced widespread emigration. From 1840 to 1900, 2.4 million laborers departed, 322,000 of them to the United States between 1850 and 1882.

They worked on the railroads, then at the gold mines after the 1848 Gold Rush. By 1880, there were 150,000 of them, mostly in California, and they made up 70 percent of the wool workers, 90 percent of the San Francisco cigar makers.

In Hawaii, they become dominant businessmen. One of their descendants, Hiram Fong, became the first Chinese-American U.S. senator, in the 1960s.

Little is known about the descendants of the railroad workers. Lai reported they gravitated to the cities. In 1870, there were so many Chinese in San Francisco that the city passed the first of many Chinese exclusion laws, banning the use of poles (used for carrying heavy loads on a man's shoulder) on sidewalks.

After 19 persons died in an anti-Chinese riot in 1871, California excluded Chinese. The Geary Act of 1882 prohibited the immigration of Chinese for 10 years, and it was extended 10 more years in 1892.

Then, in 1902, the U.S. Exclusion Act, extending the ban throughout the nation, was passed by Congress. It wasn't repealed until Oct. 27, 1943, during the height of World War II, when 10,000-plus Chinese Americans were in uniform.

As early as 1895, the children of those first Chinese immigrants asserted their American loyalty and formed Native Sons of the Golden State, which became the Chinese American Citizens Alliance in 1915. The organization focused on the unique heritage of the Chinese Americans, coming from the oldest civilization in the world to the newest.

Many Chinese believe they're descended from the first humans on Earth. The Peking Man, unearthed near what is now Beijing, is believed to have lived a million years ago.

Chinese history parallels the Western World during the Age of the Pyramids, 3000 BC. The first of Chinese dynasties, Hsia, was 2200-1766 BC, followed by Shang, Chou in 1122-256 BC, Chin in 256-207 BC during the construction of the Great Wall, Han in 207 BC to 220 AD when the Chinese invented gunpowder, Tsin in 220-420, Sui in 589-618, T'ang in 618-906, Sung in 960-1279, Mongols in 1215-1368 in the European ventures of Genghis Kahn and Kublai Khan, Ming in 1368-1644, including the Portugese colonization of Macao in 1557, and finally, Manchu from 1644 to 1912, when Dr. Sun Yat Sen's republic was founded.

Today, Chinese Americans, whose major holidays are the U.S. Fourth of July and the Chinese New Year which starts in February (1984 is Year of the Rat), celebrate the Double Ten — Oct. 10, 1911 — regularly.

Oct. 1, 1949, also is a key date in Chinese modern history as the declaration of the People's Republic of China under the leadership of Mao Tse-tung.

In 1934, Mao led the Communists to Shensi province in what is called "The Long March." The 6,000-mile march lasted more than a year, and welded the survivors into a tightly-knit group under Mao's control.

Chinese Americans identify more with the exile government moved to Taipeh by Chiang Kai Shek in 1949, although there's a growing rapport with the mainland government of Deng Xioping since Mao Tse-tung's death in 1976 and the end of the "Cultural Revolution" he promoted.

The newer immigrants, like David Huang and Hsiu Lien Perez, arrived while Mao was in power in China. Both came from Taiwan.

Mrs. Perez, who met and married her husband, Rayfield, when he was a U.S. soldier in Taiwan, arrived in Gary in 1970 with their son, then four months old. She quickly adapted to American ways, even as she "converted' her mate, who is of Mexican descent, to Chinese gourmet cooking.

He isn't alone. Americans from all ethnic backgrounds are flocking to the 10,000 Chinese restaurants run by Chinese in the United States. There were 4,304 in 1949, 9,400 in 1970, even as the number of Chinese laundries dwindled from 10,232 in 1949 to virtually none now.

Ming Ling, started by the Cohen family in Miller, was one of the first in the area, along with China Inn in Whiting, Charlie Sang's Ho sai Gai in Highland and Don Lee's New Moon in

Munster. New Moon expanded to Merrillville, and other Chinese restaurants emerged throughut the area — Wah Yuen in Merrillville, Jade Palace in Portage, Wing Wah on U.S. 20 in Gary, Lung Wah in Hammond, China House and Golden Dragon in Valparaiso.

Run by Chinese, usually with Chinese immigrants, they make up the bulk of the local Chinese population, which also includes a dozen physicians and about 20 professionals.

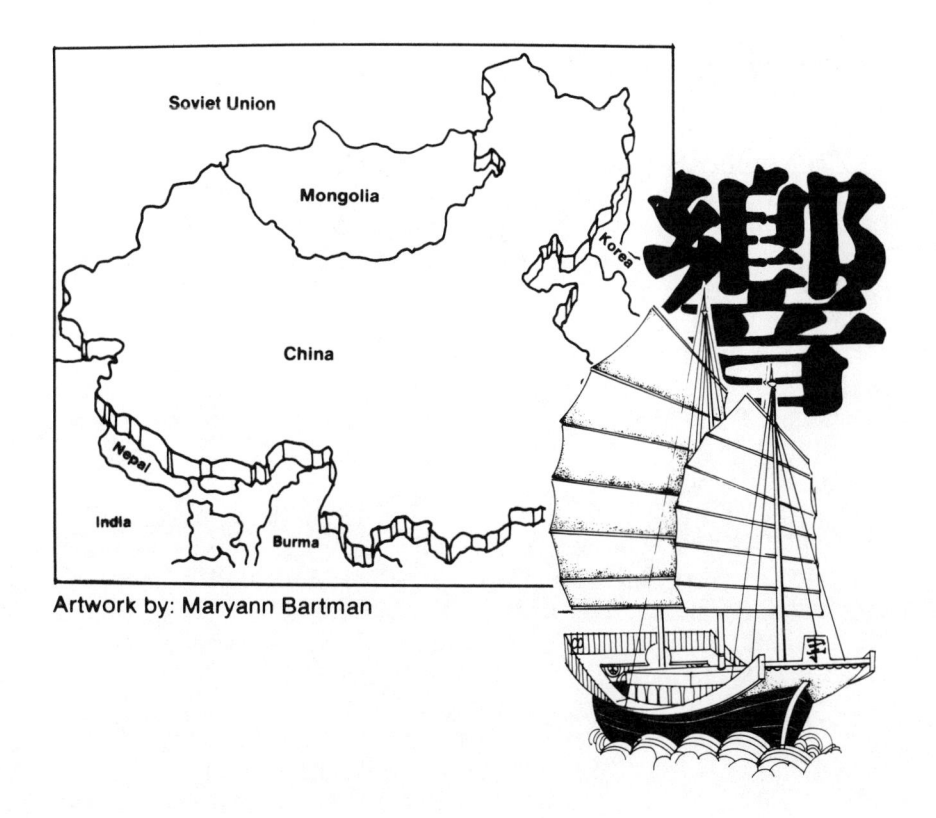

Artwork by: Maryann Bartman

22. Pakistanis

When, in 1947, Great Britain gave up the subcontinent of India and partitioned it, more than 13 million people moved hastily from one part of the land to the other.

In that rapid cross-migration, the largest in human history, six million Sikhs and Hindus fled from Pakistan while seven million Moslems departed long-established family homes in India.

M. Akbar Ali of Gary, an Urdu, was one of those migrants, fleeing with his family from Bihar Province in Southern India, to Calcutta and Delhi, then to Lahore, Pakistan, his new country.

The dramatic scene of the two-way exodus is shown in the popular movie, "Gandhi," but Akbar Ali's case was different. His family migrated by rail and air, rather than oxcarts and foot.

"I remember it well," said Ali of the historic move.

His wife's family, also Urdu from Bihar, chose to stay in India, despite scattered rioting. Later, however, Nasreen also migrated to the Moslem territory, and became Mrs. Ali by their parents' arrangement.

The family migrated to London, then New York in 1977, and Ali — who ha worked earlier in Saudi Arabia — earned his master's degree in urban planning at New York University with the thesis, "The Role of Nuclear Energy in the Development of Pakistan." In 1979, when he became a planner for Gary, he moved his family west.

The Ali family is among 25 in Northwest Indiana, along with Amanullah Khan, who works for U.S. Steel, Asad Sadi, general manager of Gary Sheraton Hotel, and Dr. Mohamed Arshad, psychiatrist. The local Pakistanis have their ethnic organization, the Ittehaad Society, and many attend Masjid Al Amin, the Muslim mosque at 3702 W. 11th Ave., Gary.

The Pakistanis make up a small segment of the Asian minority. In Indiana, there are only 358 of them, according to the 1980 U.S. Census. There are 3,294 in Illinois, 5,231 in New York, 25,963 across the nation — compared to 88.5 million of the Turk-Aryan, Urdu-speaking people of Pakistan, which is the size of Texas and Louisiana combined.

They're understandably few, since their nation is young, established only in 1947 after Britain agreed to the formation of

Hindu and Moslem states within the British Commonwealth of Nations.

The Moslem part became East and West Pakistan, separated by 1,000 miles of India's territory, but 90 million Bengalis in the eastern province rebelled in 1971 and won with the help of the Indians in the third India-Pakistan War, and achieved independence as Bangladesh.

Pakistan's name itself is made up of the first letters of the four comprising states, Punjabi, Afghan, Kashmir and Sind, plus stan which means "land." In Urdu, the official langauge, pahk means "pure," hence, "land of the pure."

The nation was founded by Mohammed Ali Jinnah and the Moslem League, which in the 1940s demanded a separate state. Britain agreed, and the nation was born, although turmoil followed. Pakistan was at war with India in 1948 over Kashmir, and in 1965 and 1971.

Since then, however, as India's Indira Gandhi and Pakistan's Mohammad Zia ul Hap have moved for peace, Pakistan is surging ecnomically.

Pakistanis express pride in their land, which some call the cradle of civilization.

Ancient cities, dating back to 3000 BC, Mohenjodaro and Harrapa, have been unearthed, bringing evidence of an advanced Bronze Age culture that developed at the time of the Sumerians and Babylonians on the Tigris-Euphrates Rivers.

Pakistani customs brought to Indiana are essentially Moslem. They consider Friday their holy day, and note that Thursdays and Fridays are "weekends" in Saudi Arabia. They pray five times a day. They don't eat pork. Their families are closely knit, in constant communication. And they enjoy their time-tested meals, polawo fried sweet-smelling rice with meat, kofta meat balls and kurma beef or mutton. They use their fingers, delicately, in putting food in their mouth, a practice prevalent also in Arabia, India and the South Pacific.

And, Mrs. Ali proudly verified a practice by which Pakistanis are well known. They are so devoted to their children that their parents take them everywhere they go. They never use babysitters.

Ali added something else: The new Pakistani Americans are patriotically American. Although few are U.S. citizens, they will become so, he said.

106 / Pakistanis

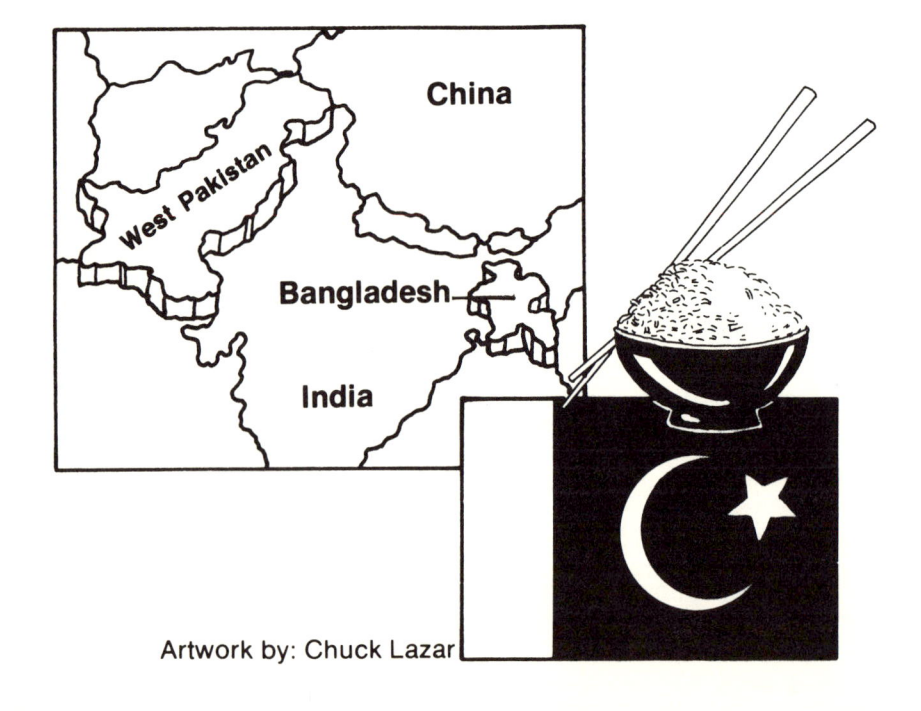

Artwork by: Chuck Lazar

23.
Germans

"I'm part German."

It's a common expression, and description of Americans. Karen Padley said it. So did Christy Walsh, Darla P. Hernandez, Mary Grabczyk, Edna Briggs, Jack Krupa — people we know.

German Americans — on the 300th anniversary of the first 13 Mennonites aboard the vessel Concord who arrived in Philadelphia from Krefeld on Oct. 6, 1683 — indeed are everywhere, and from everywhere.

Counting 42 million in the (East) German Democratic Republic, 62 million in (West) Federal Republic of Germany, with 51 million in the United States and 15 million elsewhere in the world, there are 170 million people who are German or of German descent.

German Americans totaling 49,224,146 make up 26.14 percent of the U.S. population, according to the U.S. Census. That doesn't include the German Americans who came as Austrian, Swiss, Romanian, or Russian immigrants.

The 1980 Census reported 32,270 German Americans in Lake County, 13,123 in Porter County, 15,846 in LaPorte County, 1,776,144 in Indiana, as the most numerous nationality group, as they are in Michigan, 2,487,871; Minnesota, 1,767,770; Missouri, 1,575,432; Ohio, 3,605,411; Pennsylvania, 4,054,472, and Wisconsin, 2,413,992.

Only the English-descent Americans, 49,598,035 — .20 percent more — exceed the Germans in number in this country.

William C. Schmidt, whose grandfatehr, Fred, came from Berlin, is among those Germans who take pride in their heritage as industrious, frugal, disciplined, skilled and nature-loving people. Schmidt's father, William A. Schmidt, who died in 1976 a the age of 81, was one of those Gary pioneers, who settled Clark Station in 1900, even before Gary existed.

Eleanor Schmidt, 84, recalled those bygone days, when Germans lived together at Clark Station and Tolleston, founded by George Tolle. When she arrived as a bride from Oak Park, Ill., in 1918, steeltown Gary was already growing fast, Mrs. Schmidt said. Clark Station had a bathing beach, commercial fishermen, mink and muskrat trappers, she noted.

Prominent then were the families of Dr. Walter M. Behn, and the Scheuers, and Lucks.

108 / Germans

Even then, Germans were already established. Hammond, built in 1850 when the Michigan Central Railroad put up tracks, was a German town, founded by Ernest W. Hohman, from Konigsberg, East Prussia, and his Welsh wife, Carolyn Sibley, whose sister, Louisa, was married to another German, William Sohl.

There were German settlements in 1852 at Lake Station and Chesterton, and George Tolle founded Tolleston in 1856. It was annexed to Gary in 1910.

Regina M. Koch, who was head of the foreign language department at Purdue University Calumet in 1978, taught a class on German Heritage in Northern Indiana, and noted Germans as first settlers in St. John Township, Hammond, Valparaiso, Whiting, Miller, Hessville and Schererville.

In Hammond, Jacob Rimbach hosted the first church service in 1871. In Tolleston, the Rev. Herman Wunderlich was founder and pastor of St. John's Lutheran Church.

Other pioneers were John L. Knoerzer, who organized St. Joseph's Catholic Church, and J.M. Hirsch, who opened a glue and fertilizer factory.

St. John was one of the first German-built towns, in 1838, by Joseph Schmal, Peter Orte, Michael Adler and Mathias Reder, while Henry Sasse Sr. was prominent in Cedar Lake; Henry Von Holler and Lewis Herlitz in Crown Point, and Herman Doescher in Hanover Township.

Although pioneers in Indiana, they were relative newcomers among Germans from the steady stream of migrants that started with the 13 Mennonites seeking religious freedom. As early as 1507, a German, Martin Waldseemueller, writing about the voyages of Amerigo Vespucci, suggested the name America for the New World.

Before the American Revolution of 1776, there were 225,000 Germans in North America, one-tenth the population, many called Palatines because they came from Palatinate in southwest Germany from 1709 on. In 1763, after more than 100,000 had arrived, Benjamin Franklin estimated that Philadelphia's population was one-third German. From 1820 to 1970, when 45 million Europeans arrived in the United States, seven million of them were Germans, according to Kathleen Neils Conzer in the Harvard Encyclopedia of American Ethnic Groups, 1980.

They came not only from the German Empire — Hanover, Rhine, Alsace Lorraine, Bavaria, Westphalia, Silesia, Pomerania, Prussia, Saxony — but also from German lands elsewhere, the Sudetenland Germans from North Bohemia, now

Czechoslovakia, the Siedenburger Saxons from Transylvania, now southeast Romania, the Danube Swabians of Banat from southwest Romania, the Volga German Catholics from Saratov, and the Mennonites from Khortitsa on the Dneiper River.

The Germans-from-Russia, distinguished from Germans from Germany and those Saxons from Transylvania, Romania, are a unique group — invited to Russia in 1763 by the German-born tsarina Catherine II, but forced out by Russian reforms in 1862. A million of them are among America's Germans today, while 1.6 million were banished to Soviet Siberia.

Northwest Indiana's German Americans, of the fourth or later generations from Germany, are assimilated in the community, and no longer speak German, although there's a revival of ethnicity.

Inge Laser, who came from Hamburg with her husband, Erhard, in 1953, with their son, who was then 3, is active in the German-American National Congress, known as DANK for Deutsch-Amerikanischer National Kongress, which was established in 1958. It has 53 chapters in the nation, including Gary-Merrillville, with 150 members, formed in 1960, with Rudi Wein as the first president. Max Bassler was the 1983 president. "Most of our members are immigrants, many refugees from East Germany," said Mrs. Laser, whose husband was with the German Navy in Norway in World War II. They came to America as soon as they could. The war was "horrible," she noted. "There was no future for young people then."

In 1978, she visited communist East Germany and found it "shocking." Her daughter, Christel, 17, won't go there again, she noted.

The Hammond lodge, which had 350 members 10 years ago, has half that many now.

Gerhard Winderlich, president who came from Berlin in 1954, said the traditional Oktoberfest is a time of feasting with traditional German foods, bratwurst and sauerkraut and potato salad, and folk dancing. Liederkranz, the German Singing Society, led by Jerauld Reinhart performs. Anohter singing group is Fidelia of Hammond, established in 1896.

American German-American distinguished persons are John A. Roebling, who designed the Brooklyn Bridge; Albert Einstein, scientist; Charles Schwab, steel magnate; Ottmar Mergenthaler, inventor of linotype; Henry Steinway, piano manufacturer; Adolphus Busch, brewer; Babe Ruth, baseball star.

Artwork by: Chuck Lazar

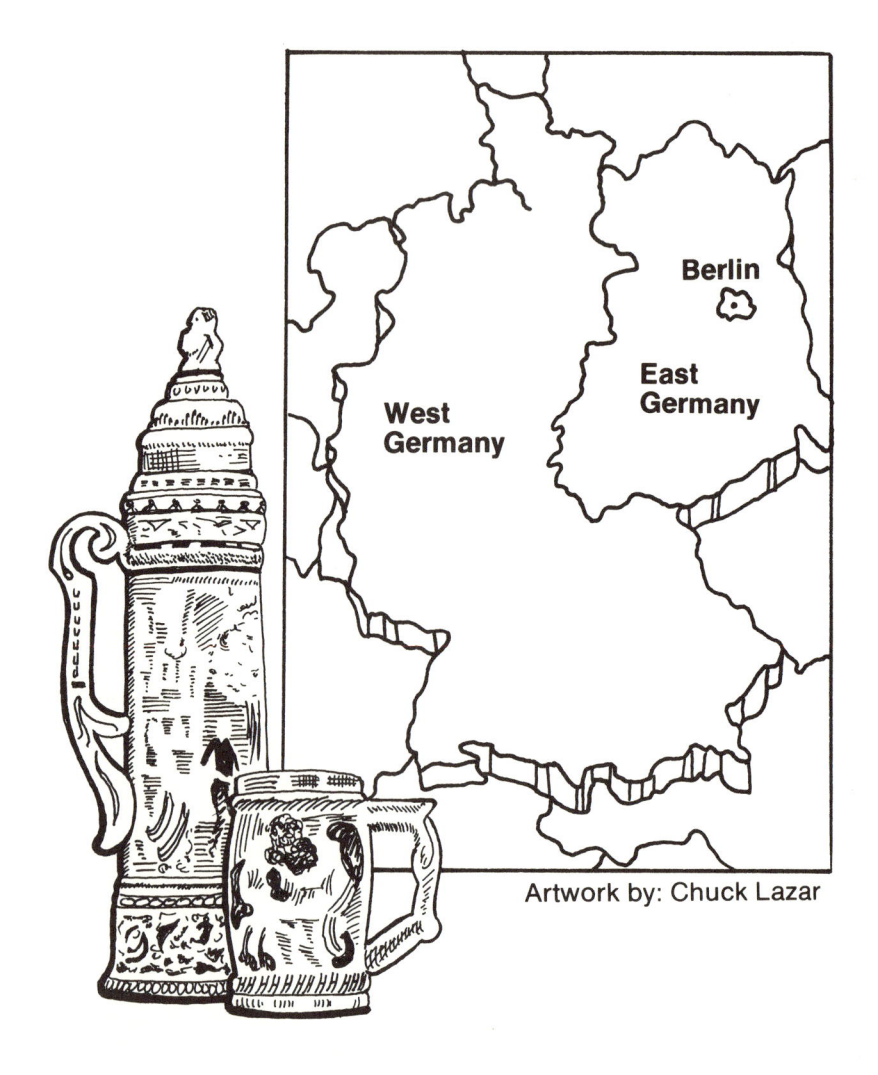

24.
French

"We are not immigrants, we've been here a long, long time," says Gerald B. Hebert about the French.

Indeed, long before the American nation was born, when this land was populated mostly by Indians, Frenchmen set foot on what is now Indiana.

Hebert (pronounced A-bare), a Gary businessman, is one of those with genealogy that defies Alex Haley and the Daughters of the American Revolution's charts.

Going back 12 generations, he is descended from Augustine and Adrianne du Vivier Hebert, from Caen, Normandy, who were among the first 53 colonists who landed in New France in the autumn of 1641 and founded Montreal the following spring.

In July 1982, in Madawaska, Maine, Hebert and his wife, Diane, and 13th-generation Jacques-Rene, 3, and Lora-Marie, 6, were among 850 descendants — quebecois, Cajuns, Falklanders, Americans — at the family reunion. It was relatively small — the Hebert progeny number more than 50,000, he noted.

The French, who lent such names as LaPorte, Vincennes. Terre Haute, Cedar Lake, Portage, Lafayette, LaCrosse and San Pierre to Indiana, rank behind the English, German, Irish and Afro-Americans in size among American ethnic groups. They number 12,892,246, according to the 1980 U.S. Census, which noted then only 3,062,077 of them have a French mother and father.

There are 54.3 million in France and 8 million in Canada, mostly in Quebec.

French Americans number 268,244 in Indiana, 2,330 in Lake County, 949 in Porter County and 586 in LaPorte County, the Census figures show. That does not include the thousands of descendants with one-eighth or less French blood, like this writer's 5-year-old, Peter, whose great-grandfather on his mother's side was a Tyler, from South Dakota.

Then, there are many, like Sue McPherson of Valparaiso, and her French Club students, April Scott and Patty Flynn, Portage High School 9th graders, who admire the French and their speech, which Patty calls "the language of love."

Louisiana has the most French Americans, 934,104; followed by Michigan, 871,912; Massachusetts, 838,475; and New York, 834,540.

The area was claimed for King Francis I in 1954, and

explored by Menard in 1660, Nicolet and Allouvez in 1665 and Jacques Marquette in 1666 and Rene Robert Cavelier, sieur de La Salle in 1680. La Salle built Petite Fort in 1750 in what is now Indiana Dunes State Park.

Joseph Bailly de Messein, for whom Indiana's first nuclear power plant was to have been named, built the first trading post on the Little Calumet River in Porter County in 1822 and the first homestead in 1830.

Few of the French remain in area today. But "we are having an ethnic awakening," said Hebert who mentioned the Arsenault, LeClaire, Berube, Cloutier, Cote, Quesnel and Nault families.

The group that claims to be the oldest in the United States thus has become the latest to organize, as it focuses on the land of the Celtics, which Greek settlers occupied in 600 B.C., followed by Julius Caesar's Romans, the Salian Franks from Germany, and a succession of French leaders, Charlemagne, Capet, Joan of Arc, the Bourbon kings, and Louis XIV in 1643-1715, when France was the greatest power on earth.

Napoleon Bonaparte, Emperor in 1804, controlled Europe for a decade.

Proud of this history, French people in the region in 1983 established Le Cercle de La Fleur de Lis. Now it has 200 family members, and Macel Bolduc, Purdue University Calumet professor of French, a French Canadian from Maine, said Le Cercle's goals are to identify local people of French ancestry and to "raise their level of ethnic consciousness."

The group wants to encourage people to speak French and master the traditions of this sophisticated, fun-loving people with a love for such French foods as crepe suzette, rabbit stew, split-pea soup, steak tartar, pork pie, maple syrup and those delicate pastries whose recipes date back to Charlemagne in the 800s.

The French are most proud, of course, of other French — philosopher Rene Descartes, painters Claude Monet and Pierre Auguste Renoir and Paul Gauguin, authors Jean Racine, Molier and Victor Hugo and Emile Zola and Gustave Flaubert, scientists Marie and Pierre Curie, Jacques-Yves Costeau and J.E. Lenoir, who developed the first internal combustion engine in 1860.

The French invented the neon lamp, the modern airstrip, Braille printing, the parachute, photography on metal, thesewing machine, steamship, steam tractor and stethoscope.

In 1983, French Americans focused on the Statue of Liberty,

dedicated July 4, 1884, a gift from France, although Americans contributed $280,000 for its pedestal.

The year 1984 is the 200th anniversary of the Treaty of Paris, which officially ended the American Revolution, and gave to the United States all the territory between the 13 colonies and the Mississippi River, from the Canadian border south. The French possessed that territory since 1524, and lost it to Britain at the 1763 Treaty of Paris, which ended the French and Indian Wars.

The Hebert family represents the history of the French in America. From Augustine and Adrianne came two sons and two daughters. Hebert is from Ignace, whose forebears remained in Montreal for seven generations, although a member settled in Kaskasia on the Mississippi River and married an Indian. Hebert's grandfather moved to Crown Point, N.Y., in 1850, then to Upper Michigan in the late 1890s. A son, Harry Joseph, Hebert's father, moved to Gary in the 1920s and became a steelworker.

A branch of the family was transported from Acadia, (now New Brunswick, Nova Scotia, Prince Edward Island and northern Maine) to Louisiana in 1755-61, when the British attempted to reduce the number of French citizens. They became the Cajuns of the bayou country.

The British deported some of those Acadians to the Falkland Islands during that same time span. There were Heberts among them.

Among the French of the area is Judge Richard W. Maroc, who traces his family, on his mother's side, six generations and back to Paris.

Gene LeBouef, owner of LeBouef and Bell Diamond Trucking in Gary, also came from French Canadian stock. His grandfather came from Windsor, Canada, and moved to Gary in 1900. His father was born in Gary.

Although migration declined after French dominion ended in 1763, it didn't stop altogether. In fewer numbers, French arrived, even after World War II.

Adolph DeSaintJean, grandfather of Tom De St. Jean, Post-Tribune composing room foreman, and great-grandfather of Gary De St. Jean, a Portage cobbler, arrived from Laventie in 1880. Now, he has 180 U.S. descendants, according to Florence De St. Jean-Cirrincione, who traced the line further, into the 1700s, after she wrote the mayor of Laventie and learned that his secretary's maiden-name was DeSaintJean.

The U.S. De St. Jeans don't speak French anymore. Neither does Robert Farag of Gary, whose Parisian mother met his Egyptian father in Chicago during the Chicago World's Fair in 1922. The children grew up in Gary.

Claudine Wich of Portage arrived from Paris in 1947. Now a grandmother in an English-speaking family, she looks forward to trips to France. She has gone "home" thrice in the last five years.

Liliane Le Sourd Maginot of Hammond, who arrived in 1959, doesn't intend to stay. She's still a French citizen. "Someday I'll go back," she said, as she maintains her French by visiting her mother and brother, Jacques Le Sourd, in New York, where he's a theater critic for Gannett Newspapers. Her daughters, Susan, 13; and Stephanie, 11, and her husband, Jerry Maginot, whom she met when she was in college, speak some French.

Marie-Claude Bley of Chesterton met her husband the same way. She was at the University of Wisconsin when she met a friend who was planning a sailboat trip from La Rochelle, her hometown, to Nova Scotia. One of the sailors was Robert Bley, who visited her family in La Rochelle. Romance developed when he returned to Wisconsin. They went back to La Rochelle, where they were married 12 years ago, and then settled in Porter County. They have two children, who speak French.

Hebert himself doesn't speak the language of his ancestors, but as a founding father of LeCercle, he has taken a vow that "I will be bilingual, and so will my children."

A reborn ethnic, he said "it's not in our best interests as individuals and as a nation to be homogenized. We should maintain our culture and identity to improve the quality of our lives."

* * * * * * * * *

Judge Richard W. Maroc responded, "all my relatives will lynch me," as he noted his French line is Quebecois, 200 years in America, and ultimately from Normandy, and not Paris. Most French Canadians are from French people from Normandy.

Artwork by: Chuck Lazar

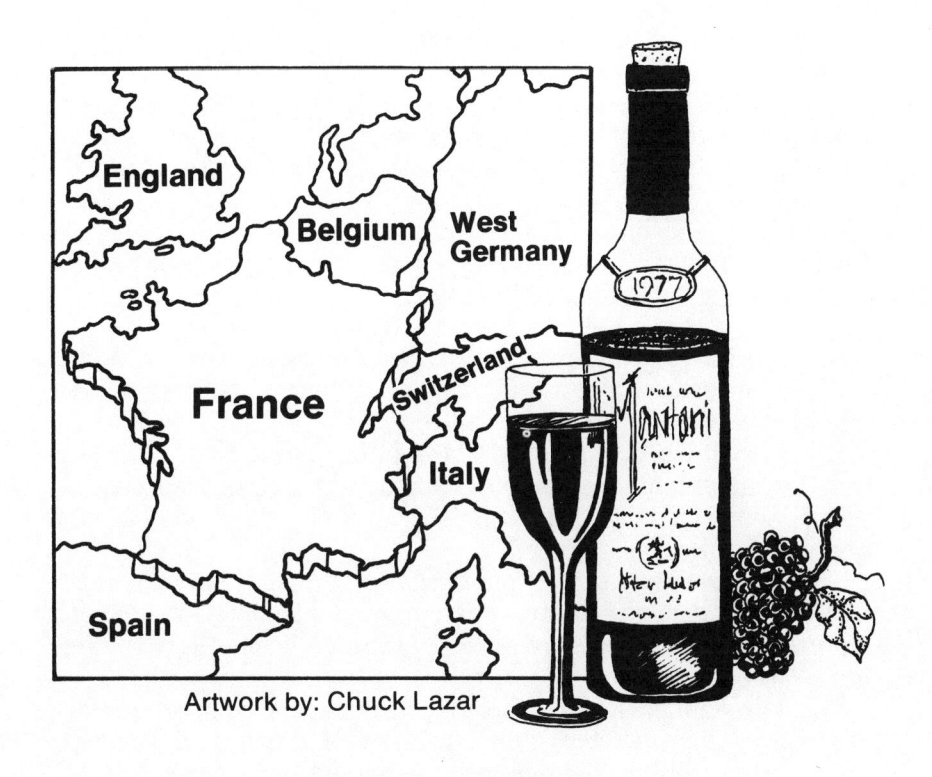

25.
East Indians

"We do not try to propagate," says Ajit Kapila about one of the oldest living religions on Earth.

Kapila, of Portage, an engineer at U.S. Steel's Gary Works, is Indian, from Asian India, a Punjabi who came from Patiala, about 100 miles north of New Delhi, in 1970.

He's a newcomer, relatively, in Northwest Indiana, but among the 100 families who are here from their native land he's virtually a pioneer, and his 22-year-old daughter Adha, a graduate of Fegely Middle School and Portage High School and Ball State University, is as American as baseball and apple pie.

With a little bit of Indian curry, of course. Adha, who works at Allstate Insurance in Chicago, still knows a little Punjabi and quite a bit of Hindi, the Indian national language and the mother tongue of her mother, Tara, a teacher at Gary Wirt High School. Her brother, Ajoy, is the contemplating one.

The Kapilas are Hindus, the religion that ancient Aryans, from across the Khyber Pass between what is now Pakistan and Afghanistan, brought to India, along with Sanskrit, before 1000 B.C.

But it is not a propagating faith, and the India community in Northwest Indiana doesn't have a church or temple, and apparently isn't contemplating one.

"Everyone has a temple at home, where we worship God," said Dr. Vijay Dave, president of the 87-member Indian Medical Association of Northwest Indiana, which had its second annual dinner meeting in 1983.

Hindus believe in a supreme, absolute, infinite being, which they call Brahman, and in the existence of atman (soul) in every being, including animals. This explains why many Hindus are vegetarians.

They believe that the ultimate goal of the soul is union with Brahman in a "bliss beyond change or pain," but that heavenly stature cannot be achieved in one lifetime; hence, karma, the law of re-incarnation.

The fair-skinned Aryans introduced color discrimination, varna (caste), against the dark-skinned Dravidians they had invaded, and in time the doctrines of re-incarnation and caste merged, and levels of Brahman (priest, intellectual); Kshatriyos (warrior, ruler); Vaisyas (artisan, agriculturist); Sundras (unskilled laborer); and Pariah (untouchable, outlawed in 1947) developed.

When Gautama Buddha established his sect in 500 BC, it was in protest of that 500-year-old caste system.

Although Dave and Kapila and other Indians have taught their children about the Hindu diety, recognizing the many "personalities" of God, as Siva for creation/destruction, Kali for goodness/sickness/chaos, and Krishna for love, the new Asian Indian Americans are more tuned to modern co-existence with other Americans. They are rapidly being assimilated in the American ways, without forgetting their heritage of 3,000 years, and the history of India, which was under British control until 1947, when Jawaharlal Nehru became prime minister. His daughter, Indira Gandhi, rules today.

She's not related to Mahatma Gandhi, who is better known to Americans for his principle of civil disobedience.

The 87 physicians in the association include 72 in Indiana. Six are married to doctors, such as P. Sasidharan, the famous neonatologist at Porter Memorial Hospital, and his wife, pathologist Maya Sasidharan.

Although most of the Indians are Hindu, some are Sikhs, like Drs. Surjit Patheja and G.S. Kapoor, from the state of Punjab, the home of 8 million followers of Guru Nanak (1469-1539) who preached a single god and single caste-less people. Guru Arjan (1563-1600) compiled the sacred Sikh writings and the sacred golden temple in Amritsar, which ranks with the white-marble Moslem Taj Mahal in Agra as one of the world's wonders.

Throughout the United States, there are 311,953 Asian Indians, according to the 1980 Census.

The total for Indiana is 3,419. New York has 55,633, California 49,007, and Illinois 30,701 — sufficient for restaurants like Gaylord's and Khyber in Chicago, where appetizers like aloo samosa and sabji pakora and papamus are served along with the tangy katchumber salad, the yogurt-spiced chicken tandoori murgh, baked tandoori, rogan josh cubed lambs for meat-eaters and bengan bhartha baked eggplant for vegetarians.

Food, language, their profession and their tightly knit families unite the local Asian Indians, who still maintain their traditions and follow the news about Indira Gandhi in their subcontinental former home.

In the summer, they picnic often, usually in "Little India," which really isn't a place. It's Shorewood Forest, the Valparaiso subdivision where a dozen Indian physicians live.

India's population is 713,006,000, second only to China, and increasing at 13 million a year in the big cities of New Delhi, Bombay, Calcutta, and Madras and in the country.

Gopal Pati of Gary, Indiana University Northwest professor,

came to America in 1962. He's the son of a physician and lived 75 miles east of Calcutta. Desi Murali, engineer at the Indiana Air Pollution Control headquarters in Indianapolis, is from Madras.

Well-known in the Indian community are Koppolu Sarma, Shodhan Patel, Krishnan Potti, Ramakrishnan Unni, D.M. Shetty, A.N. Damodaran, Arun and Sarla Goel, Arvind Gandhi and A.S. Kochar.

Along with the story about East Indians in the Midwest was this sidebar article about a Hobart Junior High school teacher, who had just returned from a summer of research in India.

HOBART — To Sophie Wojihoski, a world-traveling teacher, India is more than Taj Mahal, mass starvation, sacred cows and learning Gujarati.

Back at Hobart Junior High School, where she's a reading teacher, Mrs. Wojihoski says her Indian summer of 1983 means something else too: A grade of A and three hours of post-graduate university credit.

"I learned a great deal in India. It was an overwhelming experience," said Mrs. Wojihoski, who has traveled to China, the Philippines, the Middle East, Egypt, South Africa, Mexico and Poland.

Her stay in Ahmedabad in the western part of India, north of Bombay, was work, however. She spent the time observing schools and comparing government and private institutions. She submitted daily reports, via air mail, to her professor, Ross Korsgaard.

Then she went home to her husband waiting in Hobart, and together they took a vacation to the land of their fathers, Poland.

Mrs. Wojihokski observed life at Prahash Higher Secondary School, and boarded at the home of its principal, Hemant Shah, and his wife, Bharti, and their 11-year-old daughter, Zaishali.

"I became a vegetarian for a month," she said. She seemed to have liked it.

She was impressed by the closeness of the Indian families, with Shah's brothers and sisters as neighbors, and the strong interest Indians have in education, particularly in languages.

At Ahmedabad, the students were taught English, Hindi (the national language), and Gujarati, the official language of that state.

"They have long school days," she observed, from 10 a.m. to 5 p.m.

Besides languages, they have classes in arithmetic, social science, advanced mathematics, physics, commerce, history, chemistry, bookkeeping, geography, biology, economics, vocational skills, drawing, government and health-physical education.

"Every student has three books for each subject — a notebook, a textbook and a homework book —and they have to have them," she said, comparing the students at Prakash Secondary with her own at Hobart Junior High.

The Indian kids are more serious, more scholarly, she noted.

They're also more studious, at times, and for a very obvious reason. There's a strong emphasis on final examinations for which the students cram. Then, they either pass or fail.

* * * * * * * * *

120 / East Indians

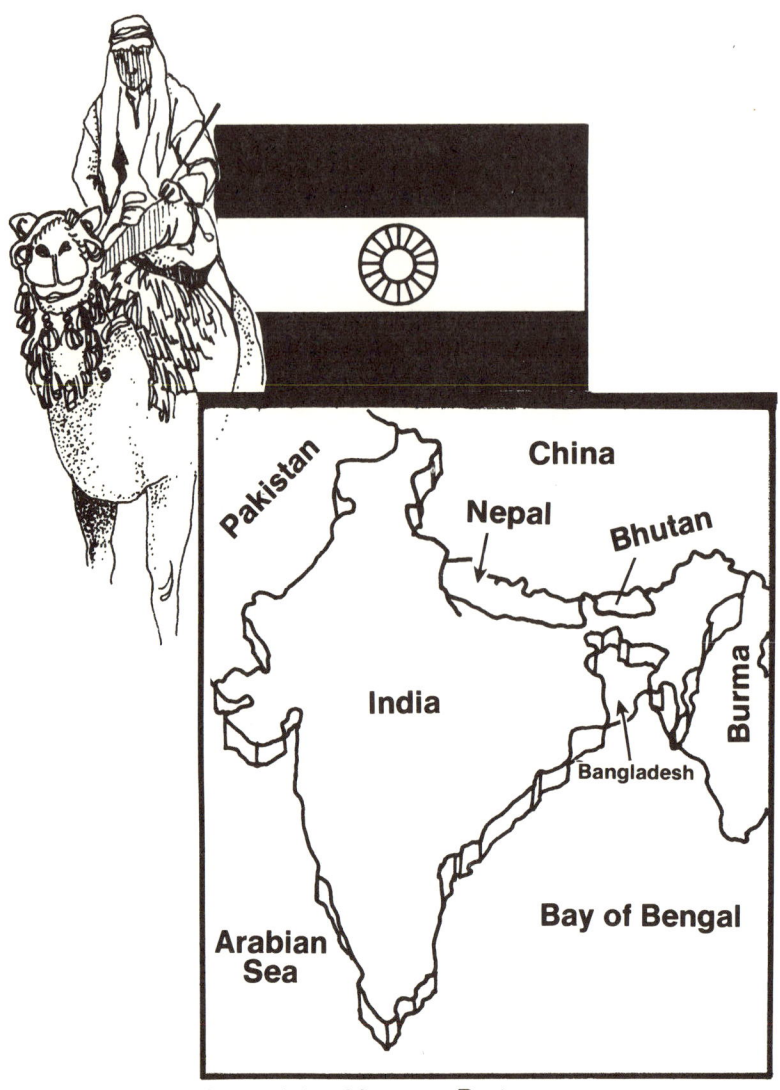

Artwork by: Maryann Bartman

    Professor Gopal Pati of Indiana University Northwest, one of the area's first Asian Indians, said of the series, "I love it, I love it. It's a service to the area." He believes and preaches ethnic pride, with focus on community involvement, an American combination.
    The India story was planned early in May, 1983m when Post-Tribune Editor James G. Driscoll, a guest at the banquet of the Indian Medical Society, found 540 Indians there. "Lake County's newest minority," said Vijay Dave, president.

26.
Czechs

Although Czechs were among the first settlers in Gary, they maintain a low profile in Northwest Indiana today.

"They have died, or moved out. Their children don't speak Czech," said an old-timer.

The frontier city was two years old when Czech brothers started the first meat market, which became an Indiana institution.

That was 1908, when the Tittle brothers — Frank, Joseph, Fred, James and John — established their store at 644 Broadway. Today, their descendants, still prominent in the community, are in other fields. One such relative is Tom Tittle who is in electronics.

The Czechs have never been a dominant group in Northwest Indiana. The first hundred settlers who lived in the Froebel area of Gary didn't establish their own church as many other ethnic groups did.

But their presence was known. They were bsinessmen and professionals, noted Mrs. Marie Sheehy, now retired in Pennsylvania after serving with the U.S. State Department.

Mrs. Sheehy's father, Joseph Pavelka, was a music instructor who maintained a studio at 725 W. 11th Avenue. He taught music in the Gary Public Schools.

"Even then, we didn't pay much attention to nationality," said Mrs. Sheehy, who was born in Kios and joined her father in America after he migrated in 1923.

She was in Froebel High School's class of 1937, which she called "the melting pot," with Irish, Hungarians, Spanish, Filipino, Turks, Slovaks, Polish, and Czechs among the graduates.

Czech Americans are largely assimilated now, and only a few can speak their Slavic language. According to the 1980 U.S. Census, there are 1,892,456 Americans who reported Czech as their ethnic origin, and only 788,724 of them reported having Czech mothers and fathers.

In Indiana, there are 21,954 Czech Americans, while Illinois — which produced a Czech mayor of Chicago, Anton Cermak — has 208,421.

Chicago indeed is the Czech capital of America. The Harvard Encyclopedia of American Ethnic Groups noted that in 1900, Chicago was the world's third largest Czech center, following

Vienna and Prague. Cicero and Berwyn are Czech communities.

The Czechs comprise 65 percent of the 15,624,400 people of Czechoslovakia, which was formed by combining the Czechs in Bohemia and Moravia with the Slovaks of Slovakia. The Czechs come from cities such as Prague, Tabor, Kutna, Hora, Pizer, Brno Olomouc and Ostrava.

The number of pure Czechs has dwindled, however. Many of the immigrants arrived in America early, from 1850 to 1900, prompted by the drought and crop failures in the homeland in 1840, a revolution in 1848, the Austro-Prussian War in 1866, the depression in 1873 and the world grain crisis in the 1880s.

Although the first known Czech immigrant was Augustine Herman (1605-1696), who was given vast lands in Maryland by Lord Baltimore, the migration wave didn't start until 1848.

From 1848 to 1914, 350,000 Czechs arrived in America. The Harvard report showed that in 1940, there were 159,640 Czech-born American residents, while 279,040 were Czechs born to U.S.-born parents, and 81,760 were third-generation (and mixed) Czechs.

"There are no more (Czechs) left in Gary. They have died. The children don't speak Czech," said Mrs. Marie Maly of Merrillville, whose husband, Charles, came from southern Bohemia. He worked for the Tittle brohters and was a close friend of Frank Tittle, who had started the business which had its peak in the 1920s when it had 40 stores in six states.

Mrs. Maly, in her 80s, remembered many Czech gatherings in the late 1920s. The German-influenced Czechs like beer, she noted.

She has three daughters — Marie McLaughlin, Blanche Avery and Donna Odar, who didn't marry Czechs.

The Pavelkas were migrant musicians. Joseph, Jerry and Alois came to Gary as entertainers. Jerry's son, Jerry, was born in Bohemia, and also grew up in the Froebel neighborhood. His wife is Serbian. They live in Hobart.

Another prominent Czech family is Zavada. After arriving in Pennsylvania in 1910, Valentine Zavada had five sons. The five brothers, Vladimir, Oldrich, Joseph, Bush and Stanley, settled in Northwest Indiana.

Vladimir Zavada operated a garage on Chase Street. His son Ervin, now residing in Griffith, fathered Ervin Jr., who is a director and producer in Hollywood. Another son, Emric, is a commerical artist in Hollywood.

Oldrich Zavada's widow, Susan, 81, recalled that her husband also worked for the Tittles. In 1917, he served with the U.S. Army as an ambulance driver in France, but never returned to

Czechoslovakia. Their children are Roland, who is with the Eastman Kodak Co. in New York, and Doreen, a researcher in Chicago.

Mrs. Susan Zavada, who is Slovak, said there's no animosity between Czechs and Slovaks, although there was a time when the Slovaks resented Czech control.

Their language is similar. "The Czechs speak softer vowels, roll their R's more," she said, noting that the early Czech immigrants came from the cities and the steel mills, while the Slovaks, like her grandfather, came from the rural areas.

"We have the same language, the same culture, the same foods," she said.

The first settlers of Moravia and Bohemia were Celts, who were invaded by Germanic tribes in 100 B.C. By 400 A.D. Slovak settlers from the east displaced the Celt-Germans. In the 500s, Slavs settled in the area and absorbed it. Today's Czechs and Slovaks are Slavs.

Christianity was introduced in the 800s.

It was not until 1918, after World War I, that Czechoslovakia became a separate nation. Today it is one of the satellites of the Soviet Union after the Moscow-directed coup in February 1948 and the Soviet invasion of Aug. 21, 1968.

* * * * * * * * * *

Marie Maly of Gary wrote thanks for the research on area's Czechs, but "you caused a little stir by mentioning my age."

Marian Bloksha Morganelli of South Holland, Ill., was thrilled to read about her Czech group, which is becoming "a silent faction," and mentioned Amalie and Vladimir Bloksha, Norma Olsen and Irene Faga as other Czechs in the area. Post-Tribune Metropolitan Editor Paula Ellis also is of Czech descent.

Artwork by:
Rich Kandalic

27. Russians

Fellow Americans, don't be too harsh on the Russians among us.

They're a proud and determined, long-suffering, God-fearing, warm-hearted, loving people. They're survivalists.

And they're a valuable element in the U.S. melting pot — despite some negative opinions about the government in the land of their forefathers.

"We were the first enemies of the Bolshevik Revolution," noted Michael Grisak of Merrillville about the Russians whowere converted to Christianity by Prince Vladimir in 988 A.D.

"I'm proud I'm Russian. But I consider myself more Orthodox than Russian," said William Drozda, former state representative, whose maternal grandfather, Vasily Krochta, was one of the founders of the church.

Their church, St. Mary's Russian Orthodox Church, founded in 1911, was at 17th and Fillmore when it was splattered with red paint at the start of the Bolshevik revolution in 1917.

Today, at 45th and Maryland, with the Rev. Peter Rozdelsky as pastor and 400 members, it's one of three area churches that maintain the Christian Orthodox traditions from old Russia.

The others are St. Nicholas Carpatho-Russian Orthodox Church, 4707 Pierce St., Gary, with 75 famillies ministered bythe Rev. George Havrila, established 48 years ago; and the smaller Holy Ghost Russian Orthodox Church at 4001 Olcott St., East Chicago, with the Rev. Michael Rosco as pastor.

Notwithstanding Americans' contempt for the Soviet Union, Russian Americans don't hide their ethnic identity. They tell of it with pride.

"I'm not ashamed of my roots. I'm American, half Russian, half Italian," said Dave Barancyk, public information officer for Lake County Prosecutor Jack Crawford. Barancyk's grandfather, John Barancyk, came from Russia.

Dave Barancyk never heard his father, George, nor his uncle, William, who's dean of students at Andrean High School, speak Russian. They're U.S.-born too.

The leadership of Soviet communism — Lenin, Trotsky, Stalin, Malenkov, Bulganin, Khrushchev, Brezhnev, Kosygin, Andropov and Chernenko — has a record of tyranny and cruelty as the U.S.S.R. absorbed Latvia, Lithuania, Estonia, the Ukraine, part of Finland and dominated Poland, Czkechoslovakia, Hungary, Romania, Bulgaria, East Germany, Albania and Yugoslavia since the 1940s.

There are 272,535,000 of them in the world's largest nation, with 15 states in 8,649,538 square miles — one-sixth of the world's land.

In the United States, there are 2,781,432 Russian Americans, according to the 1980 Census, which reported 16,973 in Indiana, 384,080 in California, 654,489 in New York, 230,308 in Pennsylvania, 185,887 in Florida, 143,921 in Illinois.

Lake County has 1,358 Russian-Americans, Porter County has 274, and LaPorte County has 204, the census shows.

The national census also counted 7,381 Belorussians, 8,485 Ruthenians, 172,696 "other Slavic" who could be of Russian descent, and 730,056 Ukrainians.

Grisak, who speaks fluent Russian and has written a book based on 276 pages of "genealogical gleanings" handwritten by his father, Joseph Grisak (1878-1950), said most of the Russians in this area are Carpatho-Russians — Russian-speaking people from the Carpathian range in parts of the Ukraine, Poland, Czechoslovakia, Hungary and Yugoslavia.

Although Russians occupy the Soviet Union from Leningrad on the Baltic Sea to Valdivostok on the Pacific Ocean, there are few immigrants here from outside Carpatho-Russia.

Joseph Grisak, son of Andrew, who died in 1902, came from Slovinsky, in Spis, one of three Russian-speaking counties in Slovakia. Joseph was among 750 immigrants aboard the ship, Hanover, which arrived in Baltimore July 12, 1901.

Michael Grisak married Christine Frentzko, one of the daughters of Michael Frentzko, at whose home the first church service was conducted in 1907. On Sept. 28, 1911, at the home of Kondrat Krenitsky at 1632 Jackson St., with $263 in donations, St. Mary's was organized by Peter Romanyak, Vasil Misko, Efrem Shevcik, Vasil Krochta, John Shevtchuk, Timofey Lescisin, Krenitsky and Frentzko.

The first church building was at 17th and Fillmore, dedicated Sept. 12, 1912. Later it was moved to 45th and Maryland.

The only living co-founder, among 83, is 86-year-old Bertha Kowal, of Lake Station, the Polish wife of Russian John Kowal. She and her mother had come to Poland in 1908. When she got married at 14½, she did what her mother did — take boarders.

Frentzko's daughter, Ann, who now lives in Merrillville, said he came from Swatkova, a Russian community in Galicia in what is now southern Poland.

"He came to America in 1894, and he walked from Pittsburgh

to Chicago, and back," Miss Frentzko said.

Frentzko married his wife, Anna, in 1900, and they relocated in Gary. He worked at American Bridge Co. at $12.50 a week, while she was at a cigarette factory at 75 cents a day.

The Frentzkos later opened a grocery store and butcher shop and went into real estate.

Also in real estate was Daniel Krochta, younger brother of Vasily Krokchta, the father of retired Lake County Clerk Nick Krochta. Nick's sister, Mrs. Mary Drozda, mother of William Drozda, is considered the family historian.

"They (Vasily and Daniel) came from the town of Zmigrod (which is now part of Poland) in 1899," she said. "When my father (Vasily) was 16 he joined the Austrian Army. Then, he and his brother went to Budapest, bought two goats and sold milk to raise money to come to America."

Daniel built one of Gary's first cabins at 1704 Madison St. in 1907 and became a real estate dealer and friend of Mayor Tom Knotts. He was one of the six donors of St. Mary's Cemetery on West Ridge Road. Vasily was U.S. Steel's first gatekeeper. He died in a mill accident in 1940.

Nick Krochta, the oldest of seven, married the daughter of Peter Romanyak, who opened Gary's first dairy at 14th and Madison.

The early Russians of Gary included Bartosh, Belko, Guba, Huminik, Markovich, Matuzak, Misko, Ordinsky, Pillar, Saporsky, Savich, Tokash and Sawochka, father of Teamsters Local 142 Secretary-Treasurer Don Sawochka, and Gregory Truchan, the father of the late Sheriff Michael Truchan; and Efrem Shevick, formerly of Gary and now of Valparaiso.

The first priest of the parish was Benjamin Kedrovsky, 1911 to 1957, whose son, Victor Kay, formerly coached at Mann High School. Father Rozdelsky has been pastor since 1961.

Former Gary Mayor Peter Mandich was baptized by Father Kedrovsky.

Russians traced their ancestry to the first Slavs who appeared in the 8th Century from the East, possibly India, and created the first Russian state at Kiev.

****

"Had you been at our St. Mary's church services this morning, you would have had an opportunity to share the favorable comments from our parishoners who read your well-prepared and factual article on the Russian Americans," wrote Michael J. Grisak on Nov. 6. 1983. "The enthusiams expressed can well be summed up in the words of one of our parishioners: 'I would say that such an article is long overdue.' "

Russians / 127

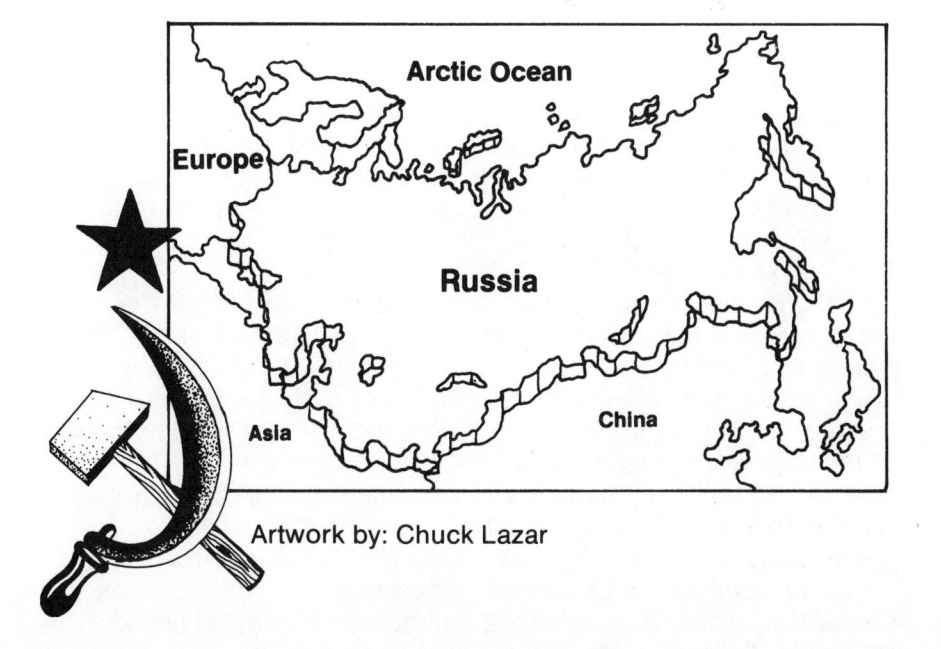

Artwork by: Chuck Lazar

28. North American Indians

"I'm just a wee bit Indian," says Jackie Flotow, who traces her Cherokee blood to her grandmother's grandmother in the Blue Ridge Mountains of Virginia.

Although she's only one-sixteenth Indian, and among 6,715,819 Americans who claim some Indian ancestry, Mrs. Flotow of Michigan City affirms "inside, I'm Indian through and through."

Indian blood indeed is part of what will someday be designated as the American race, a commingling of English, German, French, Slavic, black and other peoples.

Mrs. Flotow, who points to Thanksgiving as the American Indians' prime contribution to the U.S. culture, is one of the local authorities on Indian history and lore, with a private collection of some 2,000 volumes. She's in charge of the American Indian section of the Michigan City Public Library.

Indians consult her to learn about the people — first the Miamis, then the Potawatomis — who lived along the southern shores of Lake Michigan until they were forced out in 1832.

There are no Potawatomis left in the area.

The U.S. Census notes that while 6.7 million Americans — the 10th largest grouping — claim Indian ancestry, only 1,920,824 of them reported having both Indian mothers and fathers.

Another way of counting, based on registration as Indians through enrollment in the 173 recognized tribes, lists the total at 1,421,367, including 7,682 in Indiana, 655 in Lake County, 161 in Porter County and 195 in LaPorte County.

The U.S. Bureau of Indian Affairs accounts for 755,201 "in or near" reservations, while noting that more than half of the people who identify themselves as American Indians live in urban areas, and have little or no contact with the bureau.

Some 25,000 live in Chicago, 8,000 of them in the neighborhood of the American Indian Center, 1630 W. Wilson Ave.

Of the 6.7 million who claim Indian ancestry, 200,932 live in Indiana, one of 24 states with more than 100,000 Indian descendants. California has the most, 750,945. Illinois has 222,134.

Not included in the census are thousands of others, such as Chuck Dillard of Gary, whose grandmother was a fullblooded Cherokee. Dillard's wife, Geraldine, has Indian blood too.

Local American Indians — fullblooded Felix M. Roubideaux (Sioux) of Valparaiso, Winfred and Russell Skenandore (Oneida) of Dyer, Josephine Fox (Omaha) of Griffith, and Francesca Veltri (Apache) of Beverly Shores and those with traces of Native American ancestry — in 1983 took part in two pow-wows.

One was a Veterans Day program at the American Indian Center, for Indians who served in World War II, Korea and Vietnam. Some 25,000 American Indians fought in World War II.

The other was the biggest event, the annual American Indian Center's Pow-wow at Chicago's Navy Pier, when 200 dance groups and two dozen drummers from tribes throughout the nation performed in competition.

In 1982, 200,000 people showed up at the national pow-wow, learned the rudiments of sacred dances, bought stone jewelry and blankets, ate Indian fry bread and tasted some of the Sioux and Algonkian cooking, such as kan stohale, corn and kidney bean bread, and o lah na soup with Indian corn and pork hocks.

Indians point to the pow-wow as an authentic show, with real Indians, doing real dances they learned from their parents. It's with pride that they say this, because of their contempt for "apple Indians" who perpetuate the image of stonefaced, storefront Indians who say nothing but "how" and "ugh."

"Indians are more, much more than that," said Gary-born Francesca Veltri, who has devoted her life to raising Indian children in the tradition of her forefathers.

Just what's an American Indian?

From her, Roubideaux, Mrs. Flotow, Mrs. Fox and Mrs. Skenandore came the answers.

"Indians like to be free, to be outdoors. They don't like fences. They don't understand the concept of buying land, which belongs to all the people," said Mrs. Flotow, who has made a lifelong study of Indians, tracing their history to 6000 BC, when Indians were believed to have crossed over from China by way of the Bering Strait.

"We're resourceful. We make do with what we have," said Mrs. Veltri, whose home is open to anyone anytime for any duration.

"We love our children," said Mrs. Fox, who has two, Cindy, 23, a coordinator of the pow-wow, and Larry, 17, an ardent golfer.

Indians universally resent the myths about them as migrant, warlike peoples and the loss of their tribal lands to the white man. "Everyone feels that way even though they don't say it," said Mrs. Skenandore, expressing sentiments best described in the book, "Bury My Heart at Wounded Knee."

The Harvard Encyclopedia of American Ethnic Groups reports that contrary to popular belief, most of the 850,000 Indians in North America when the white man arrived were not wandering, nomadic hunters, but farmers with stable villages, like the Pueblos along the Rio Grande, who had multilevel masonry homes and irrigated fields.

"The Potawatomis — they also had their Trail of Tears," said Mrs. Flotow, refering to 1830 when the Five Civilized Tribes (Creek, Cherokee, Choctaw, Chickasaw and Seminole) were removed from the Southeast states to Oklahoma. Of 70,000 in the march, 20,000 died.

The Potawatomis, an Algonkian-speaking group with the Chippewas and Ottawas, were a farming-fishing-hunting tribe on the eastern shore of Lake Michigan in 1500 until they were forced to move south and west by the warring Iroquois around 1635.

They dominated the southern part of Lake Michigan, replacing the Miamis, who moved south.

Joseph H. Cash, in "The Potawatomi People," an Indian Tribal Series published in 1976, recounted the removal of the Potawatomis after they ceded five million acres of Northwest Indiana in the Treaty of Tippecanoe Oct. 26-27, 1832.

The 6,000 Potawatomis were moved first to Wisconsin, then to Iowa, then to a 576,000-acre reservation near Topeka, Kan., in 1837. Four years later, the land was parceled out to the individual Potawatomis. Many of them moved to Oklahoma, which now has the largest concentration of Potawatomis, 11,000.

Now, there are no Potawatomis in the area, although Cindy Fox said she met one recently among the 100 tribes represented at the American Indian Center.

Indians here today are from other places, descendants of people who lived on reservations. Among the local Indians are Jean DuFault (Chippewa), Goldie Tucker (Shawnee) and Corine Knight (Chippewa) of Highland, Ben Doxtator (Oneida) of Lake Station, and Chief Lone Eagle of Hammond.

They gravitate to the American Indian Center, social and cultural headquarters for Indians within 100 miles of Chicago. There also are tribal clubs, where old languages, such as Huron and Chippewa, are taught.

Native Americans / 131

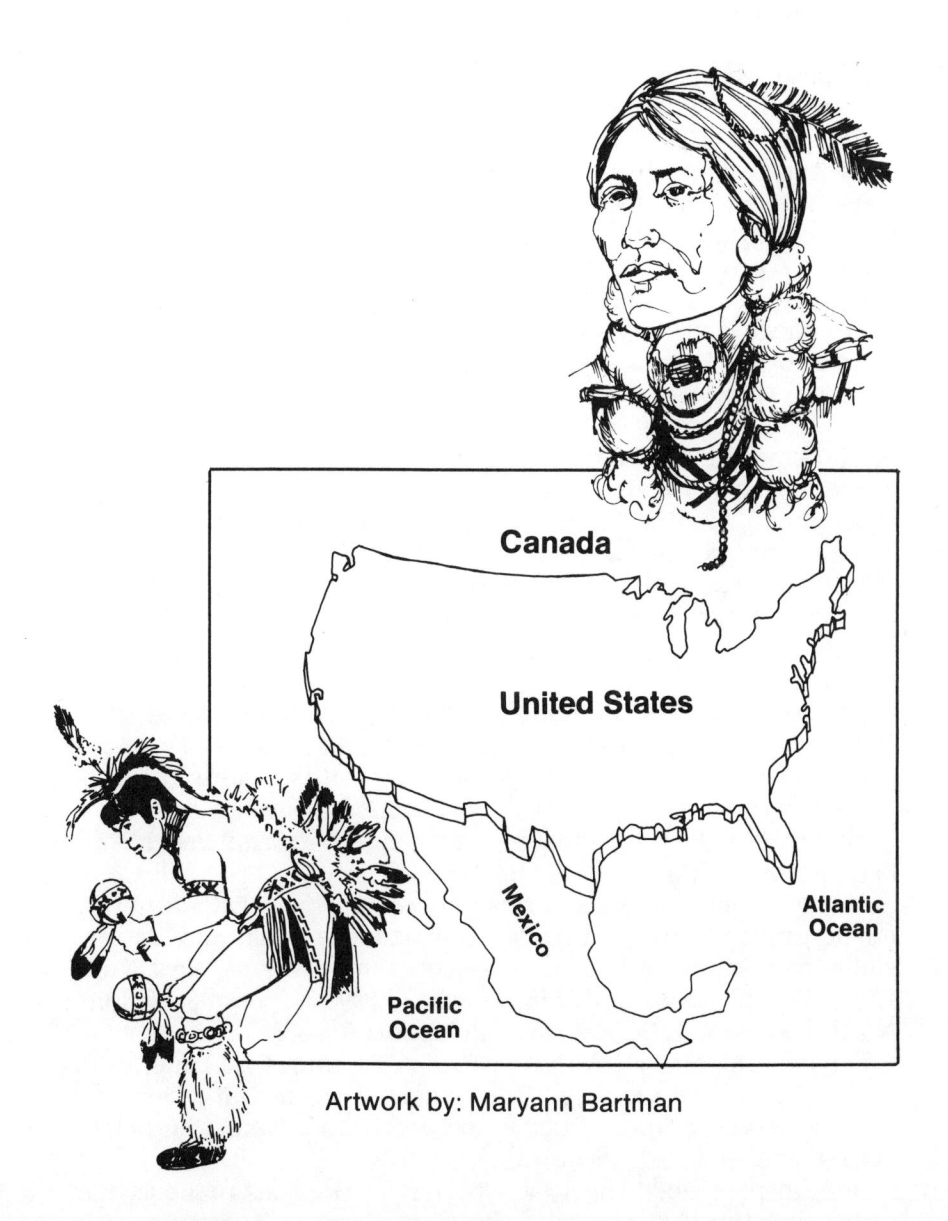

Artwork by: Maryann Bartman

29.
Afro Americans

One of Gary's pioneers — Kathryn Lorraine Duncan Washington — is also one of its most hopeful.

"Thank God I'm still here," said Mrs. Washington, at 74, in the house where she was born, 2649 Washington St.

Gary's first black baby, the daughter of Samuel J. Duncan, a co-founder of the First Baptist Church in 1908, has seen her city grow and decline. It will blossom again, she believes.

Her father came to Gary in 1906 when U.S. Steel's plant was under construction.

There were few blacks then, and Mrs. Washington called her neighborhood "a mixed group." She graduated in 1927, four years ahead of Henry Coleman, former Gary city controller, from Froebel High School.

Today, Gary, led by Mayor Richard Gordon Hatcher, who came from Michigan City, is predominantly black — and proud of black people's accomplishments in sports, music, science and education, and proud of greats such as Martin Luther King, Muhammad Ali, Joe Louis, George Washington Carver, Crispus Attucks and Jackie Robinson.

Lake County, with 522,955 people, is still mostly white, but its black population is 126,051. There are 8,662 blacks in LaPorte County, and 299 in Porter County, according to the U.S. 1980 Census.

The census tallies the nation's black population at more than 21 million, with 20,944,729 Afro-Americans as many as 13 generations away from their African ancestors. There are also 258,000 immigrants from Africa and 253,268 from Jamaica.

Indiana has 355,670 Afro-Americans, 2,393 Africans and 1,992 blacks from Central and South America.

The 20.9 million Afro-Americans make up the fourth-largest ethnic group, following English, German and Irish, and six states have more than a million black Americans — New York, 1,546,486; California, 1,517,815; Illinois, 1,399,204; Texas, 1,351,011; North Carolina, 1,034,398; and Michigan 1,025,538.

Indiana University Northwest Professor James B. Lane, in his book "City of the Century," said blacks were in Gary from its inception. With Samuel Duncan arrived 200 workers who helped lay out the mill and the town.

Duncan persuaded the Rev. Charles E. Hawkins of Louisville to become the first pastor of the First Baptist Church. In 1907, the city's blacks included John Preston, an ice vendor; Shepherd King, a cook; William Elston, in real estate; William Seaton, an electrician; and Charles Beard, a street paver.

By 1910, there were 400 blacks in Gary and by 1918, one-tenth of the millworkers were black, Lane reported.

Among the old-time families are Means, Williams, Holliday, Whitlock, Allen, LeBrois, Banks, Battle, Beckwith, Epps, McHenry, Griggs, Streeter, Simpson, Rankin, Washington, Patton, Bolden, Montgomery, McFarland, Tatum, Anderson, Leek and Wesson, noted Hoyt C. Brown, 63, whose father, William Brown, came from Andersonville, Ga. in 1920.

Hoyt C. Brown, who was Calumet Township justice of the peace from 1962 to 1977, grew up in an integrated neighborhood, 16th and Jefferson, and was one of seven black graduates of the 171-member Froebel class of 1940.

Gary in his youth was a segregated town, divided at the Wabash Railroad traks, observed Brown. "We couldn't be caught north of it," he said, "unless we were coming from the Plaza Theater."

Blacks then were allowed one place for fishing, Pine Beach off Clark Road; and one facility for golf, at North Gleason Park. Until 1953, black people weren't allowed to swim at the Lake Michigan beach.

Curtis Parrish, owner of the City Castle, 11th and Broadway, since his retirement from the Police Department in 1978, said there were 20 black policemen when he joined in 1958.

A native of Memphis, Parrish served in the South Pacific in World War II, and was lured to the Gary mill in 1946.

Among the post-war immigrants from the south were Roosevelt V. Haywood, the first of the families that transferred wholesale from Mound Bayou, Miss. His son became a city councilman.

Another ex-Mound Bayouer became a teacher and legislator, U.S. Rep. Katie Hall.

Among those old-time residents was Sherman George Banks, who arrived in 1920, recalls his grandson, 43-year-old William Banks.

The first of the prominent Leek family was John Leek, who moved from Mississippi to Arkansas in 1890. Later, in 1921, he came to Gary with his son, James, to work at Cudahy Packing.

James married Ardenia Patton, from another pioneer family, and they had 12 children — Donald, Barbara, Geraldine, Dorothy, Ardenia, Joan, Martha, Johnetta, Clay, Judi, Robert and Bruce.

Donald Leek is the Gary school system's athletic director,

and Barbara Leek Wesson is city clerk.

George C. Smith, 64, who retired recently after 35 years as a millworker, was born in Gary in 1924. His father, George, had worked railroads in Topeka, Kan., until he moved to 22nd and Jefferson in 1921.

Another Smith, Daniel, came from Shelby, Miss., in 1923, and then called for his family. His son Buse T. Smith, grew up in what he called "the melting pot at 21st and Jefferson," and graduated from Roosevelt High School, where H. Theo Tatum reigned as principal and Warren "The Hawk" Anderson was assistant.

Buse T. Smith lived in Chicago for 15 years after World War II, then returned to teach art and social studies. He also became a city councilman, and retired in 1981.

His third wife, Theodosia, 43 years ago opened a liquor store bearing her name, one that is perhaps the oldest existing liquor store in the city. She also operates the Elbow Room, one of the city's popular restaurants, a haven for black favorites — souse, chitterlings (called chit'lin'), greens, blackeyed peas, baked sweet potatoes and the best of "soul" food.

Black culture, American-style, is soul indeed, as explained by Frieda Dawkins of East Chicago when the Indiana Committee for the Humanities and Tri-City Community Mental Health Center undertook an indepth project, "Pass the Culture, Please," to show how ethnic groups transmit their traditions.

Religion and family pride, soul food and American holidays — these are the things that black families maintain, she told the researchers.

And black history does, too — a long tale of intercultural suppression and suffering and a steady struggle for freedom, recognition and a better way of life.

Emmma Lou Thornbrough in "The Negro in Indiana Before 1900," published by the Indiana Historical Bureau in 1957, noted that black slaves were in Vincennes as early as 1746, and they were outnumbered then by Indian slaves.

There were 630 Negroes in the state in 1810, and 237 of them were slaves. The Indiana Constitution, adopted in 1816, provided "there shall be neither slavery nor involuntary servitude in this state."

But even while blacks escaped from slavery in the South, aided by Indiana's "underground railroad" and the Quakers, they weren't encouraged by law.

In 1851, they were banned from settling in the state, from serving in the militia, from voting, from testifying in court against people accusing them, from attending public schools.

In 1850, Daniel Crumpacker, the Lake-Porter delegate to the Constitutional Convention, made an impassioned speech against racial discrimination, but the immigration ban passed anyway, 93-40, wrote Thornbrough.

Intermarriage with whites, miscegenation, was banned by law, with fines up to $1,000 until those 1816 statutes were repealed in 1965.

University of Michigan Professor Thomas C. Holt, in the Harvard Encyclopedia of American Ethnic Groups, wrote that a vast majority of United States blacks are descended from 427,000 slaves sold to colonial America during a short span of time, 1741-1810.

Half of them, 200,000, were from Angola and southern Nigeria, while 50,000 each came from Ghana, Senegal, Gambia and Sierra Leone, and small numbers came from Mozambique and Biafra, the professor noted.

"One of every five inhabitants who witnessed the inauguration of the new American nation in 1789 was black, and only about one in five of these had been born in Africa," wrote Holt. He noted that while the first 20 slaves were sold by a Dutch frigate to Englishmen at Jamestown in 1619, it wasn't until 1740 that British North America and French Louisiana bought slaves in a large scale.

Slaves sales, at 5,000 a year from 1741 to 1760 legally ended in 1807. By 1860, however, there were 3,954,000 slaves in the United States.

The first slaves were born free in farm villages in Central West Africa, as Alex Haley in his book, "Roots," discovered. They were enslaved by opposing African tribes, or snatched away by slave traders, a business that evolved after Portugese explorer Vasco de Gama discovered the Cape of Good Hope in 1497.

Slave trade became important after America was discovered. From 1450 to 1865, 10 million slaves were imported, most of them for the sugar plantations in Brazil and the Caribbean.

Half a million of today's black Americans are descended from those West Indians, including Roy Inns, James Farmer, Malcolm X, Shirley Chisholm and Stokley Carmichael, and Gary educator Montague M. Oliver.

Slavery, an ancient tradition, had almost disappeared by 1300 when exploitation of black Africa began. It was in 1516 that King Charles I of Spain gave colonists in the New World permission to take slaves.

The African slaves weren't savages from the jungles. Many

136 / Afro Americans

came from civilized villages, and, as Haley found, they claimed histories dating back hundreds of years.

Africa had great empires — Kanem in 1000, Ghana in 1000-1200, Mali in 1200, Songhai in 1400, and Kongo, Luba, Mwanamutapa and Karanga.

* * * * * * * * *

Rubel Shelton of Gary, born in 1927, offered her grandmother, 96, as one of the notable Afro Americans.

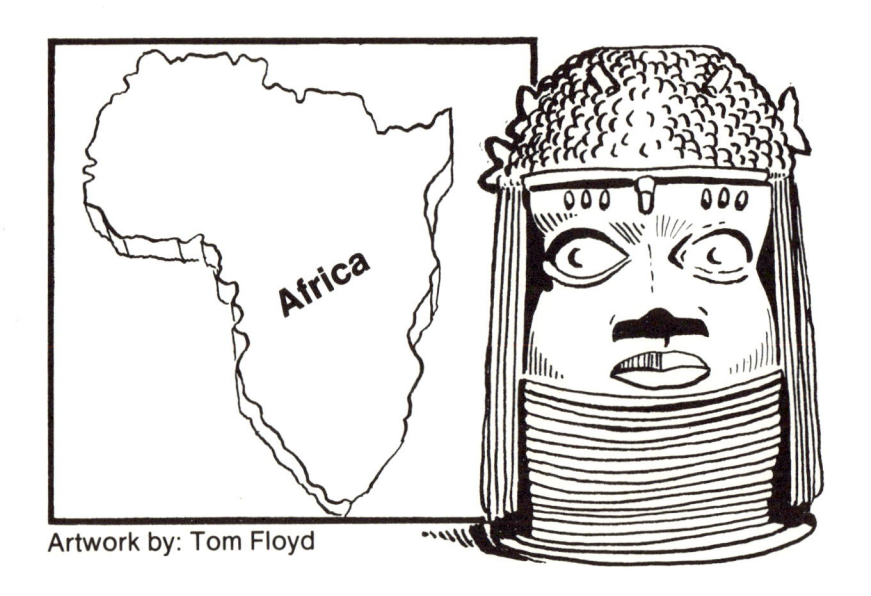

Artwork by: Tom Floyd

30.
Puerto Ricans

Puerto Ricans — they're making themselves known in Lake County.

The year 1983 was a landmark year for these Spanish-speaking Americans from the tropical Caribbean island of Puerto Rico.

Three were elected councilmen in their communities — Jose de la Cruz and Secondino Cruz in East Chicago, where Ramon Colon is a school board member, and Pete Mendez in Lake Station.

Although their number is small, reported at 9,255 in Lake County by the 1980 U.S. Census, they include some people of prominence.

They include the four Latino lawyers, Carmen A. Fernandez, Itsia D. Rivera and Lettice Otero, second-generation Puerto Ricans who graduated from Indiana University Law School and passed the Indiana bar in 1977, and Blanca Bianchi de la Torre, who fled from Cuba as a child and grew up and studied law in Puerto Rico.

And there's Colon's daughter, Judy Surdzial, and Dino Cruz's daughter, Margie Benzinger, who teach English at Block Junior High School in East Chicago.

And Hector Lopez, one of a dozen Puerto Rican policemen in Gary, who's coordinating a coalition of Puerto Rican groups.

And Ray Sanchez, a 33-year veteran at Inland Steel, who was Indiana's first elected Puerto Rican Democratic precinct committeeman in 1960. He is Gary City Judge Charles Graddick's chief civil court bailiff.

The first Puerto Rican lawyer in the area, who represented the Latin community in the 1960s and 1970s, was the colorful Marrero de Ibern, now deceased.

"We're getting it together," said Lopez about the Puerto Ricans, who number 5,572 in East Chicago, 3,415 in Gary, and 1,041 in Hammond, according to the updated census figures. There are 555 in Porter County. The Indiana total is 12,854.

Not only are Puerto Ricans consolidating their groups; they are working in unison with other Hispanics, the Mexican-Americans, as never before.

At the Puerto Rican Parade Committee's installation banquet in 1983, there were about as many Mexicans as there were

Puerto Ricans. And Daniel Lopez, president of Union Benefica Mexicana, noted that Puerto Ricans helped celebrate UBM's Mexican Independence Day.

Hector Lopez, whose father, Pedro Lopez, arrived in Gary in 1950 to work at Inland Steel, was 10 years old when he left the town of Camuy. But he's not the first Puerto Rican policeman in Gary. That was Sam Muniz, now retired.

Lopez said a plan to consolidate the Puerto Rican groups in Gary is in "the talking stage" with Marie Marquez of Puerto Rican Benefit Society, Tom Orocho of Caballeros de San Juan, Justiniano Bonilla of Central Latino, and Juan de Jesus of Organizacion Civil Actionales Borinquena.

"We have the same ideas, the same goals," he said of the lively Puerto Ricans, who love to play dominoes, dance the salsa and merengue, feast on lechon (suckling roast pig, as it's also known in the Philippines), **leche flan** (caramel custard), and speak their brand of Spanish which is faster than the Mexican version.

And Puerto Ricans are learning Mexican delicacies such as tacos and tamales, dancing to Mexican mariachi, and distinguishing word meanings. Banana for instance is **platano** to the Mexicans, **guineo** to the Puerto Ricans.

In East Chicago, the Puerto Rican clubs are Hijos de Borinquen, Puerto Rican Parade Committee and Brotherhood Commercial Club.

Across the nation, Puerto Rican migration from the tiny, crowded, 3,459-square-mile island has steadily increased, even as its population grew 17.9 percent from 2,712,033 in 1970, to 3,196,250 in 1980.

New York has the largest Puerto Rican population, 703,072; followed by New Jersey, 171,600, and Illinois, 98,782.

The inhabitants of Puerto Rico, claimed for Spain in 1493 by Christopher Columbus and acquired by the United States in the Spanish-American War in 1898, are U.S. citizens, since the island was declared U.S. Territory in 1917. The island became a constitutional commonwealth in 1952.

That's the form of government apparently favored by Puerto Ricans, who by a 60 percent vote on July 23, 1967, chose to retain it, while 1 percent voted for indepedence, and 39 percent to become the 51st state of the United States.

Another referendum is anticipated in 1984, following the 1979 U.S. Congress resolution favoring a popular vote. On Jan. 12, 1982, President Reagan pledged support for statehood if the islanders want it.

"Most of the people don't want it," predicted Sanchez. "They like it the way it is; the taxes are lower."

But he noted an increasingly strong sentiment for statehood, which would mean that the Puerto Ricans can elect their representatives in Congress and vote for president.

As a commonwealth, the Puerto Ricans aren't exempt from most federal laws; including the draft. They served in the Armed Services in World War II, Korea and Vietnam. Sanchez noted six of the Marines who were killed in the Beirut terrorist bombing were Puerto Ricans.

Puerto Ricans, descended from Spanish settlers who arrived in 1508, or from black slaves taken to the island between 1513 and 1873, didn't migrate to the United States in large numbers until the end of World War II.

The first immigrants were political exiles, Ramon Emeterio Betances, in 1898, in the fight for freedom against Spain.

Sanchez noted that his uncles, Angelo Martinez and Pedro Menendez, were among the first Puerto Ricans in Northwest Indiana, in 1948. He followed them in 1951.

Judy Colon Surdzial may have been the first Puerto Rican baby born in East Chicago, in 1950.

Carmen Fernandez, one of the four children of Pedro Fernandez, said he came from Villalba during the big post-war wave of immigrants in the late 1940s. He first worked at Standard Forge, then at LaSalle Steel.

Itsia Rivera, the second of 10 children of Carmen and Candelario Rivera, is the family's first high school graduate, first college graduate, and first lawyer.

"He instilled in us the idea that education is important, and that we should be bilingual," she said.

Miss Rivera is president of Latin American Family Education Program and the Hispanic Bar Association.

Her father came from Yabucoa, while her mother's from Arecibo. They met in Gary. He worked for U.S. Steel, and retired in 1981.

Lettice Otero, the third of 10 children of Victor Otero, who came from Morovis in 1953 and became a Gary steelworker, also is a graduate of Emerson High School and is the family's first lawyer.

She ran for city judge in Lake Station in 1979, and again in 1983, when Miss Fernandez ran for city judge in East Chicago. Their efforts failed this time.

Although Blanco Bianchi de la Torre isn't Puerto Rican, she's well aware of the island's traditions. She and her husband, also Cuban, grew up in Puerto Rico.

She was 12 years old in 1962 in Communist Cuba when Fidel

Castro allowed her to leave. With the help of Catholic Welfare Services, she migrated to Nogales, Ariz., until her parents were able to flee. They were reunited in Miami, then in 1963, they moved to Puerto Rico, where her father resumed his profession, as a transportation consultant.

She remembers the revolution well, the Bay of Pigs fiasco, and the Castro treatment of Cubans.

"They apprehended everyone except my grandmother, grandfather and me. They confined all the people in airport hangars. They were afraid the people would join the Bay of Pigs invaders," she said.

Blanca Bianchi finished high school and college in Puerto Rico. She passed the bar in 1975, shortly before her husband, who had studied engineering, obtained a job at Bethlehem Steel's Burns Harbor Works.

They moved to Chesterton. In 1978, she took the Indiana bar examination and passed it. She and Miss Rivera are now law partners in East Chicago.

* * * * * * * * * *

Councilman Joe de la Cruz staked his claim as one of the first Puerto Ricans born in Northwest Indiana, in 1948. Inland Steel brought Puerto Ricans to East Chicago in 1946, he said, and his father was one of them.

Mirna de Jesus of East Chicago called too and called it "bad research" because Fred de Jesus, Isabelina Candelario and Jose Cruz and Mirna de Jesus were not among those recognized, she said.

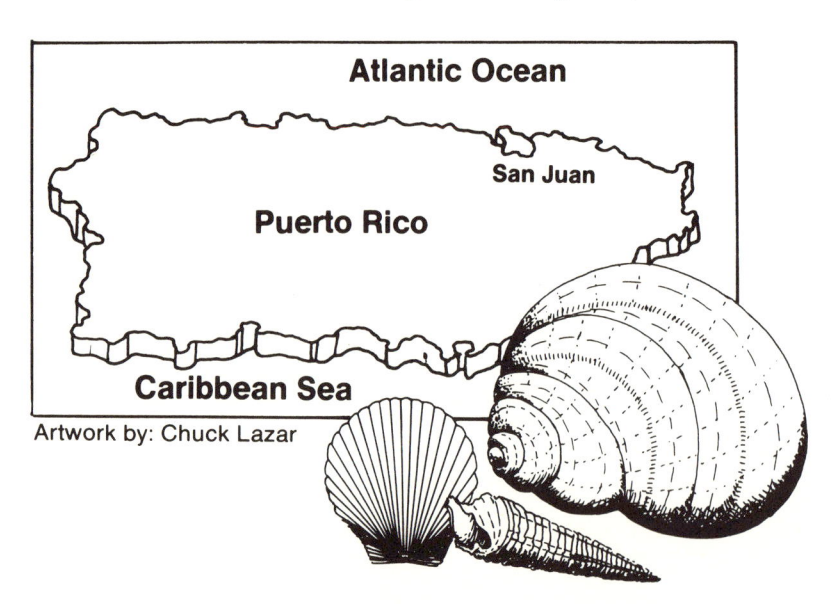

Artwork by: Chuck Lazar

31.
Japanese

A couple of generations after Pearl Harbor, Japan has become a part of the American way of life.

Common as household words today are Toyota, Datsun, Honda, Kawasaki and Sony, as well as karate, kamikaze, geisha, kimono, hibachi, teriyaki, sukiyaki, harikiri, shogun, samurai and sayonara.

Nipponese bombers devastated Pearl Harbor Dec. 7, 1941, embroiling the United States in war, which put 16 million Americans in uniform, killed 405,399 and cost $263 billion.

President Franklin Delano Roosevelt called it "a day that will live in infamy." It led to the defeat and occupation of Imperial Japan, destruction of its cities and military deaths totaling 2,144,507.

That ugly war had another day of infamy, Feb. 19, 1942, when FDR signed Executive Order 9006 which took 110,000 Japanese Americans, 71,484 of them U.S. citizens, from western Washington, Oregon and California and placed them in barbed-wire concentration camps.

Among two dozen Japanese-American families in Northwest Indiana today are two Nisei (second-generation) who experienced that internment — Purdue University Calumet mathematics professor Theodore S. Chihara of Highland, and Catherine Yamamoto of Crown Point, children's librarian at the Lake County Public Library in Merrillville.

Neither became embittered by their confinement, but they recall the anguish of their parents.

"Under the circumstances, we accept," said Miss Yamamoto, who was 11 when her family was taken from their farm home near Auburn, Wash., and confined. If they had never been interned, she and her sisters would have stayed on the farm for life, she rationalized.

On the other side of the globe, in World War II, were Dr. Takamitsu Nakamura of Munster, ear-nose-throat specialist in Hammond; Theresa Tatko Takahashi Ozug of Merrillville; and Yukiko Dawson of Valparaiso. They endured B-29 bombings which flattened their home cities, Osaka, Tokyo and Yokohama, and shuddered at the atom bomb explosions, which killed 92,000 in Hiroshima, 40,000 in Nagasaki.

Nakamura was 7 when his family fled to the mountains from their home in industrial Osaka. There were air raids almost every day, he said. When the war ended, "I was so glad. We had been so hungry," he recalled.

Mrs. Ozug, mother of six, is from Yokohama. She was 14 when nightly raids began in June 1944. "I can't talk about it," she said when asked about the atomic bombs.

Sam Schultz, who owns the House of Kobe restaurant in Schererville, had a different experience. The son of a Japanese mother from Kamakura and born in Seattle, he was in Japan when war broke out. As Americans, his family was imprisoned by the military. His mother and sister died when the camp was hit by U.S. bombs.

Among the other Japanese in the area are Toshio Fushimi of Valparaiso, who was a Japanese pingpong champion in the 1930s; Mrs. Yoshio Fujioka Pacific, a Japanese war bride; Dr. Tsuyoshi Toyama of Munster, anesthetist at St. Margaret Hospital; Matthew Ikeda of Valparaiso, psychologist of the Porter-Starke Services, whose wife uses the Suzuki method of teaching at Children's World School; Dr. George Y. Kino of Merrillville, and Sue Yoshuko Yoshizaki Kendall of Valparaiso, whose daughters, Margaret, 23, and Janet, 19, are studying in Indianapolis, while their brother, Fred, a Wabash College engineering graduate, is employed in Japan.

The Kendalls are hosts to 17-year-old Irie Nakano, who is learning English while she is an exchange student from the same Osaka High School that Mrs. Kendall attended.

Janet, a future flight attendant, spent six weeks in Japan when she was in high school. "They're very friendly, very disciplined, very hardworking," she observed.

She pointed to the quest for excellence. In May 1982, Nature magazine reported the Japanese mean IQ at 111, world's highest, and that 10 percent of the population has an IQ of 130 or higher.

Japanese-speaking restaurateur Schultz, whose maternal family line is Inouye, and his wife, a native of Saga, 20 miles north of Nagasaki, serve as liaison for the Japanese community. Many of today's third- and fourth-generation Japanese are descendants of immigrants from the Hiroshima area, he said.

Until Commodore Matthew G. Perry opened trade with Japan in 1853, there were no Japanese in America. Today, according to the 1980 U.S. Census, there are 791,275, the 27th largest ethnic group. There are 3,806 in Indiana, 283,392 in California, 246,000 in Hawaii, 20,808 in Illinois, 30,753 in Washington.

They came from a crowded land — with 120 million people today in 145,809 square miles, smaller than Montana. Only 20 percent of their land is arable.

The first 12,000 Japanese immigrants worked in Hawaiian sugar plantations in 1890. By 1920, there were 300,000. By 1970, they made up 28 percent of Hawaii's population. After Pearl Harbor, 900 Japanese-born people suspected of war activity were detained at Sand Island.

It was a stark contrast to the mass arrest of men, women and children, who were trucked to camps at Tule and Manzanar, Calif.; Minidoka, Idaho; Heart Mountain, Wyo.; Granada, Colo.; Topaz, Utah; and Rowher and Jerome, Ark.

What did they do there?

"We went to school. The older people farmed. We weren't allowed to leave," said Miss Yamamoto, who was interned in California, then Colorado.

Chihara and Miss Yamamoto, who don't know each other, were released after two years, while others were confined until 1946 when the U.S. Supreme Court, in **Endo vs. United States,** ordered them freed.

President Gerald Ford revoked FDR's Executive Order 9006 in 1975, saying "we now know what we should have known then — not only was the evacuation wrong but Japanese Americans were and are loyal Americans."

According to Japanese myth, discarded by Emperor Hirohito, he is descended from the sun goddess, whose son founded the empire in 660 B.C. Anthropologists say Chinese colonized Japan in 200 B.C., after forcing the original inhabitants, the Caucasian Ainus, north to Hokkaido. The Japanese were converted to Buddhism in 500 A.D.

Like other Orientals, they were subject to discrimination. California anti-Japanese laws in 1913 prohibited them from owning farm land or employing white women. It wasn't until the McCarran-Walter Act of 1952 that the Japanese-born were allowed to become naturalized citizens, hence the right to vote.

Schultz noted that the first-generation Japanese (**issei**) got around that. They sent for wives in Japan. Ultimately, they were able to buy land — in the names of their U.S.-born children.

The Japanese didn't move to the Midwest in large numbers until 1946 when about 30,000 of the internees moved to the Chicago area.

Masako M. Osako, University of Illinois professor, writing in "Ethnic Chicago," said there were only 390 Japanese in Chicago in 1940, but there were 10,829 in 1970, and 15,732 in 1980. The Japanese centers are Hyde Park and Near North.

144 / Japanese

Lack of space that particular day of newspaper publication forced some information on Japanese Americans to be edited out. Deleted was mention of Fred Korematsu, who defied the military order for concentration camp in 1942 and was convicted as a spy. In 1983, he was cleared in federal court when documents of FBI Director J. Edgar Hoover were disclosed, showing no proof that West Coast Japanese had signaled Japanese worships. In 1984, Ellison Onizuka will be the first Asian-American astronaut to be aloft in space.

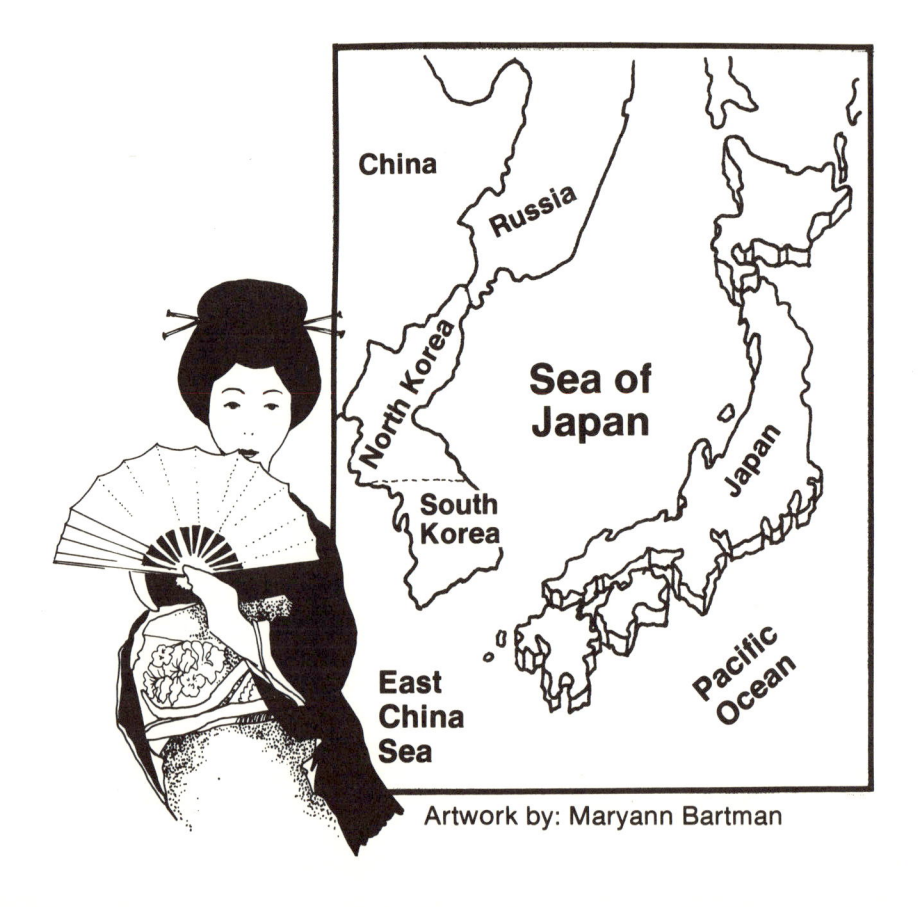

Artwork by: Maryann Bartman

32.
Koreans

"How can you not love a child," declared Karen Scheeringa, hugging Julie Yoon, 2, her daughter from Korea.

Mrs. Scheeringa, 27, and her husband, Melvin, an auto-body mechanic in Griffith, have three adopted daughters and one "home-grown," as they call their own 4-year-old Dutch-American Dayna.

Julie Yoon Scheeringa is actually the third child in their family, following Dayna and 5-year-old Melanie, born of Filipino-German parents. The latest is Daniela, 1, from Guatemala.

Julie is among more than 40,000 Korean children adopted by U.S. parents since the 1950-53 Korean War, which killed more than a million South Koreans and cost the United States $67 billion and 54,246 lives.

The children, such as Kimi Ambelang, 14, of Valparaiso, and Matt Wetklow, 16, of Portage, are almost totally assimilated in the American way.

Kimi was 16 months old when she arrived at the home of Joel and Lois Ambelang. For the adopting parents, it was a 3½-year wait. Kimi joined their son, Mark, and three months later, Beth, now 12, was born.

"She's just like any American girl," said Ambelang, noting that Kimi, a delight to her family, has shown no real interest in the land where she was born.

Matt was 7½ and couldn't speak English when he brought joy to the H.R. Wetklow home, which was ready for him with Korean story books and records. Now, he's more occupied with the business of being 16 — track, cross-country, soccer — although he inquired about the 1988 World's Fair in Seoul and liked M*A*S*H, the television series based on the Korean War.

The Korean War, M*A*S*H, the North Koreans' 1968 capture of the USS Pueblo, the Soviet downing of a Korean Air Liner with 269 aboard in 1983, and the presence of 38,000 U.S. troops in Korea today are focal items when considering the 376,676 Americans of Korean descent, as determined by the 1980 Census.

They're a rapidly growing, cohesive group. Time magazine recently reported there are now 150,000 in Los Angeles, up from 8,900 in 1970, with Korean blocks in Hollywood, Beverly Hills, Palos Verdes, Hawthorne, Monterey Park, like Chicago's North Clark Street.

There, one can hear strains of Korean string music, buy Seoul-made toys, and eat foods like the hot **kimchee,** essential in every Korean home.

The 1980 census counted 96,421 Koreans in California, 22,884 in Illinois, 31,742 in New York, and 4,059 in Indiana, mostly in Northwest Indiana and Marion County.

There are about 50 Korean families in the area, including new immigrants, brides of armed forces veterans who served in Korea and the adopted children.

Encouraged by adoption agencies, the parents haven't kept the children's heritage secret from them. "We try to teach families as much about Korean culture, to bring it to the home," said Phyllis Lowenstein, director of the International Adoption Agency in Newton, Mass., which processes Korean adoptions in six Northeast states. "The Korean government insists that they maintain pride in being Korean."

The U.S. Immigration and Naturalization Service reported over 40,000 U.S. adoptions since 1950. Among the earliest were eight infants adopted in 1955 by Harry and Bertha Holt of Eugene, Ore., who founded the leading agency for foreign adoptions.

In Indiana, the only agency for adopting Korean babies — a two-year wait — is Bethany International, Indianapolis.

Julie Yoon came to Griffith with encouragement from Kenneth and Gail DeVries of DeMotte, who had adopted three Korean children. "They're an inspiration to us," Mrs. Scheeringa said of them.

Julie's arrival, through an agency in Tulsa, Okla., led to Mrs. Scheeringa's involvement in children with special needs. Now, as a volunteer for Families Adopting Children Today, she meets arriving children at the airport, and she is Midwest coordinator for "Heal the Children," an international group which provides medical assistance, usually corrective surgery, for poor children in foreign lands, like the two Korean children brought to America by President and Mrs. Reagan.

Mrs. Scheeringa, who lost four babies by miscarriage after the birth of Dayna, said she had wanted a large family. The experience with Julie made it possible, although financially taxing.

"Whenever we get a new child, we get a home improvement loan. And that's what adoption is, a home improvement," she said.

The latest child from Guatemala, Daniela, stresses the family commitment to Heal the Children. Daniela was born with no roof in her mouth. The first of six surgical operations was completed in 1983.

For the sake of their Korean child, the Scheeringas are learning Korean ways. Mrs. Scheeringa can cook Korean dishes. The family attended a Korean Christmas party.

Korean families in the area include those of a dozen physicians, such as David Min, Young Rock Kim, Young S. Kim, Young S. Koo, S.W. Kim, Kang I. Koh, Young Kyoo Kah and K.J. Ahn.

"Old-timer" Koreans, who have been in the area more than 10 years, are Chun Chong, who has a Korean grocery and specialty store in Highland; his sister, Ann, at New Moon Restaurant in Munster, and another sister, Sue, who works at Lever Bros.

Jung Shin and his ex-wife, Young Shin, run Peacock Cleaners in Gary, a business they acquired and expanded in 1982. They came to America from Seoul in 1975.

Among the Korean brides, a dozen of them, is Kim Kum Ye Middleton, from Yongsanpo in southwest Korea, who met her husband, James, when he was in the Signal Corps in 1967. Now, she works for Joyce Manufacturing in Gary. Their daughter, Marie, 15, is a sophomore at Portage High School, and son, James A., 13, is at Willowcreek School.

"We teach them about Korea," said Middleton, a U.S. Steel employee. "Four years ago, they spent seven weeks and went all over Korea. They loved it."

But they don't speak Korean, except phrases like **Anya ha sumiko** (How are You) and **Kum up sum nida** (Thank you), said Middleton.

While language is disappearing, the taste for Korean food has not. Rice and **kimchee** are still favored in the homes of the Middleton, Hancock, Kang, Kim, Huang, Soong, Pak and Park families.

Perhaps the first Korean in the area was Junko Linedecker, who was born in Japan, where she met her husband, Cliff, while he was in the Navy in the 1950s. He became a reporter in LaPorte in 1959, then they moved to Fort Wayne, Philadelphia and Chicago.

Divided Korea, with 20 million people in North Korea and 38 million in South Korea, has a language distinct from Japanese and Chinese.

148 / Koreans

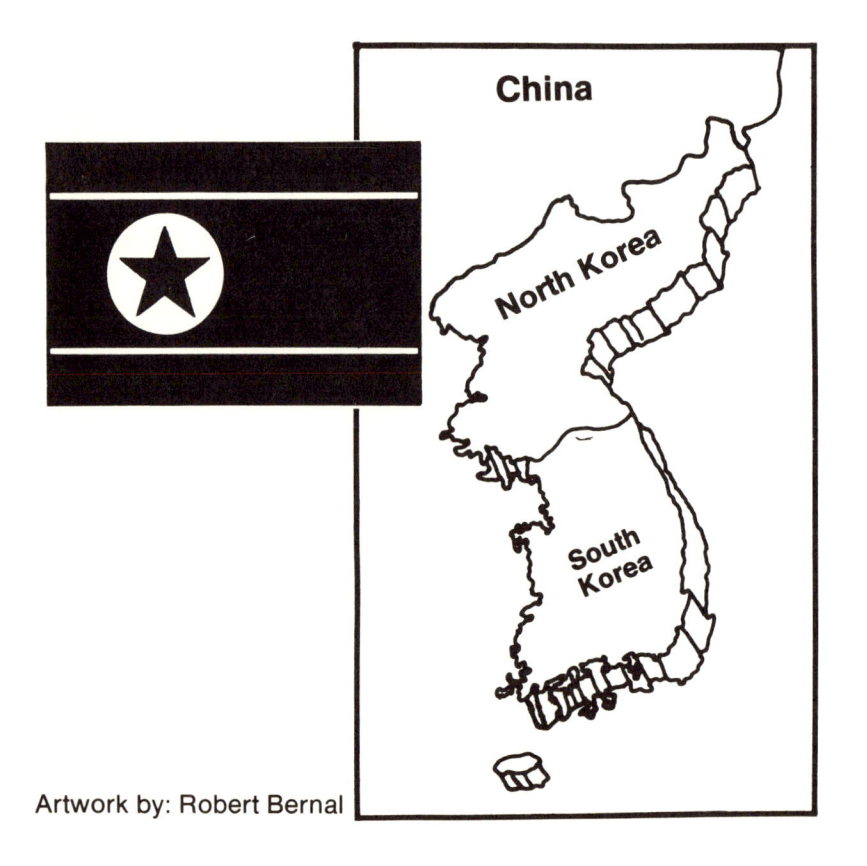

Artwork by: Robert Bernal

33.
Swedish

Santa Lucia and the elves Juul Toote and Juul Nisse reign supreme during the Christmas season in the Peterson, Swanson, Anderson and Johnson homes — where Swedish is no longer spoken.

Christmas time is a special season for all, particularly the ardently religious Swedish Americans — 4,345,392 of them according to the 1980 U.S. Census.

"When the first Swedes came to Baillytown in the 1840s and 1850s, they had nothing but their Bible and their knapsacks," said William Ahrendt, 80, historian of the 125-year-old Augsburg Lutheran Church of Porter and grandson of Nils Johnson, one of those first 31 pioneers.

The Swedes, with mass immigration movements from 1840 to 1925, brought with them their religion and tradition, such as Santa Lucia Day, Dec. 13, which for them marks the beginning of the Christmas season.

On Santa Lucia Day, the oldest daughter dresses in white and wears a green wreath with seven candles on her head. She offers coffee and buns to the rest of the family.

According to Swedish legend, St. Lucia carried food to hungry folk in Varmland during famine. She was a girl in Syracuse, Sicily, who gave her dowry to the poor instead of becoming a bride. A Christian accused of witchcraft, she was burned at the stake on Dec. 13, 304. She was later canonized a saint.

Today, in Swedish centers such as Galesburg, Ill. (where Carl Sandburg was born); Lindsborg, Kan.; Chisago and Isanti counties, Minn.; and Chicago's Near North Swede Town, Luciafest is still grandly celebrated.

But everywhere else, with third- and fourth-generation Swedes totally Americanized, it's a fading tradition, just as Jolly Old St. Nick has replaced the once-ubiquitous juuls. At Northwest Indiana's Vasa Club, with membership down to 55, president Edna Anderson of Hobart said Santa Lucia is no longer familiar.

"The Swedes were noted for their adaptability to American conditions and for their willingness to work and save their money. They came to this country to stay, and a study showed that no other immigrant group was so quickly Americanized," she quoted from Powell Moore in the book, "The Calumet World."

The Swedes, after all, have been here for a long, long time — some came as early as 1638 when New Sweden was formed north of the Delaware River in what is now Wilmington, Del. In 1776, John Morton, a Swede, cast a vote for independence during the Continental Congress.

The 4.3 million American Swedes are in all 50 states, with concentrations in California, 551,651; Minnesota, 528,081; Illinois, 379,993; Washington, 225,780; New York, 171,907, and Wisconsin, 158,716.

The Census reported 67,697 in Indiana, including 2,580 in Lake, 1,312 in Porter, and 986 in LaPorte counties.

Mrs. Anderson's granddaughter, Michelle, 16, who knows no Swedish words, said all she knows about the Swedes are that they have "blond hair, blue eyes and high cheek bones."

Mrs. Anderson, like her, is American-born, as is Edna Swanson, in Portage. Her father, Herman Swanson, was born in Ogden Dunes, and her grandfather, Carl Johan Swanson, came from Smaland in 1867.

A third-generation Swedish American who didn't see Sweden until 1948, she married "a real Swede," who was among the last immigrants, arriving in 1923 from Gastrikland.

She learned Swedish anyway. She prepared limpa bread, pepparkokor spiced cookies, tapotatis korv potato-pork sausage, and of course glogg the noted Christmas drink, for Santa Lucia Day.

There are many other "oldtimers" in the area, including Martha Anderson Clavey of Hobart, Carl Martinson of Griffith, Edith Nicholson Fleming of Portage, and Mildred Eskilson of Miller, along with members of the Izakson, Johnson, Holmes, Olson, Lundberg, Nordstrom, Ericson, Carlson, Lindberg, Lofgren, North and Frederickson families.

Mrs. Fleming's mother, Ruth Nicholson Linstrom, was born in Miller, on Old Hobart Road, in 1888, before it was a part of Gary. Her great-grandfather was one of the founders of Bethel Lutheran Church in 1874, along with Svanti A. Nordstrom and Hokan Hasselgren, who worked for Aetna Powder Co.

Until 1905, services at that church were in Swedish, noted Indiana University Northwest professor James Lane in his book, "City of the Century."

Bethel wasn't the first Swedish church in Indiana. Bethany Lutheran Church was founded by the Palumblad family, first settlers of LaPorte, in 1857, and Swedish Lutheran Church of Baillytown, later named Augsburg, was organized by Erland Carlson in 1858. Swedish Evangelical Lutheran Church, later renamed Augustana, was started by Carl J. Johnson and 18 others in Hobart in 1862. In 1879, 65 members of the Augsburg church started Bethlehem Lutheran in Chesterton.

Trinity Swedish Methodist Episcopal Church was established by Lars Ericson in Hobart in 1886. In 1887, at the John Nelson home in Michigan City, Zion Swedish Evangelical Lutheran Church held its first service. St. Paul Lutheran Church of East Chicago started in 1890.

Swedish Evangeligal Bethlehem Lutheran Church, founded in 1906 in Gary, was chartered by 44 members at the home of Alfred Carlson in 1910. In 1932, it absorbed Central Lutheran Church of the Norwegian Synod, and it dropped the Swedish designation in 1950. In 1968, it merged with Grace Lutheran Church, which had been founded at 8th and Connecticut in 1912.

Fifth-generation descendants of the Carlsons, charter members of Augsburg, still attend the church. They include children of Jeanette Lee Condeni, church secretary, whose mother, Betty Carlson Lee, was the daughter of Arvid Carlson, son of Carl Oscar Carlson, one of the 31 co-founders with Erland Carlson and Nils Johnson.

Johnson's grandson, Ahrendt, born in Baillytown in 1903, recalls his youth, when pioneer Joseph Bailly was well known. Bailly's son-in-law, Jonas Asp, sought Swedes in Chicago to run his lumber mill. Johnson was among those recruited. They later bought government land acquired from the Potawatomi Indians by treaty.

Ahrendt, who speaks Swedish, said he and his German father learned it from his mother and grandfather, who once scolded him for walking through a wheat field.

"A liar is worse than a thief; you can watch a thief, but not a liar," was the lesson he has taken past his 80th birthday.

Descendants of Nordstrom, founder of Bethel Lutheran in Miller, couldn't be found. There's another Nordstrom family, descended from John R. Nordstrom, from Lassebo, who came to American in 1901 and was known as a carpenter and vocalist. He died in 1983 at the age of 105.

Noted among the local Swedes were William Olander, engineer for the Gary Land Co.; Gus Strom, who built the drainage ditch from Lake Michigan to the Little Calumet River; and Albin G. Witting, who held positions as chief engineer and assistant to the general superintendent at U.S. Steel Gary Works, and who retired in 1943. He came to Gary in 1911.

* * * * * * * * *

152 / Swedish

We couldn't find descendants of Svanti Nordstrom before publication, but when the paper came out, Gabriella Anderson Koppka, 67, emerged. She's related to the founder of Bethel Lutheran Church of Miller.

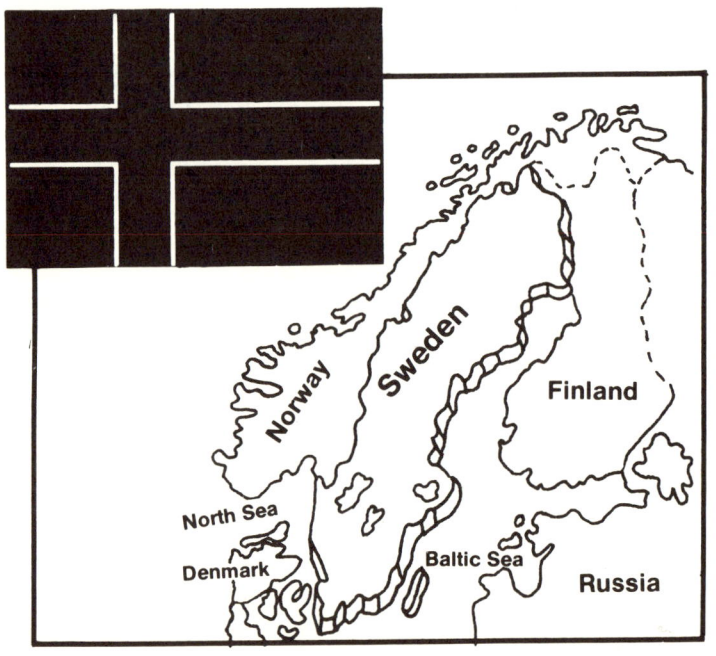

Artwork by: Rich Kandalic

34.
Irish

"I came to be an American," said Patrick John Hall, an Irish Catholic from Ulster, a relatively "new" immigrant who arrived in Chicago just 35 years ago.

Hall, of Highland, is among 40,165,702 Irish Americans (1980 Census). Many are U.S.-born, Irish by name and blood line, who turn on their greens once a year, on St. Patrick's Day — when every American is Irish.

The Irish stress their long history as Christians, dating back to 432 A.D., when the Emerald Isle was converted by St. Patrick. To them also goes the credit for bringing to America, from Druid ancestors, the custom of kissing under the mistletoe at Christmastime.

Hall and his wife, Noreen, from County Cork, haven't forgotten the land of their birth, where they were married after World War II — Irish folk dances, Gaelic football, hurling, and the Christmas eve tradition of visiting relatives and feasting on plum pudding, goose and fruit cake.

"Our Christmases were beautiful, and holy," said Mrs. Hall. Mary Jones of Highland, who left Ireland in 1955, agrees. "There, it's a very religious holiday," she said.

Mrs. Jones, from County Mayo, taught Irish folk-dancing for 16 years. Her daughter, Veronica, now does the same, in Atlanta, Ga.

A bride when she arrived in 1948, Mrs. Hall's three children were born in Indiana. One of them, Patrick, is public information officer for the Lake County Parks. He has yet to visit the old country, but he pays more than a casual interest to the continuing crisis in Northern Ireland, where more than 20,000 people have died in terrorist rebellion since 1969.

Irish, who make up the third largest nationality group in the United States, following English and German, have been coming to America for 400 years, reports Unitersity of Tulsa professor Patrick J. Blessing in the Harvard Encyclopedia of American Ethnic Groups (1980).

In 1586, Edward Nugent served with the English in the Indian Wars. An Irishman, Thomas Dongan, was governor of New York in 1683-86, and Charles Carroll III of Maryland signed the Declaration of Independence. Thomas Fitzsimmons was the only Catholic signer of the U.S. Constitution.

But, while the migration was steady — 4,720,247 from 1820 to

1975 — the greatest masses came after the Great Potato Famine of 1845-51, when one-eighth of the eight million Irish died, and an eighth went to America. Today, the population of Free Ireland, three-fourths the size of Indiana, is 3.5 million.

Twelve states have more than a million Irish, led by California with 3,725,925, New York with 2,977,518, and Pennsylvania with 2,449,110. Illinois has 2,027,692, and Indiana 1,017,944, with 16,284 in Lake County, 4,200 in Porter County and 3,227 in LaPorte County.

In Lake County, the number of people with mixed Irish ancestry is 61,456, largest of any group.

And everyone, even Asian Americans, is Irish on March 17, the day in 432 when St. Patrick, who converted all of Ireland, died.

The Friendly Sons of Erin, whose main function is the annual feast day, observed its 25th anniversary in 1984, at the Hellenic Center in Merrillville, when it presented Shamrock and John F. Kennedy awards for public service.

James Buckley, assistant superintendent of Highland Public Schools, who won the Shamrock in 1977, identified the planning committee.

It includes Joe Radigan, John Foley, James McNamara, Bob Doyle, Tom Clifford, Tom Lynch, Terry Burns, Duane O'Donnell, Jack Mehan, James Knight, Ted Fitzgerald, Joseph Granger, John Quinn and Dennis McGuire.

Of course, when it comes to kissing the blarney stone, drinking Irish whisky, praising Notre Dame, and generally talking of the luck of the Irish, the family names of Walsh, King, Carrabine, Flaherty, Fahey, Mulley, Kane, O'Brien, O'Connor, Nealon, Brown, Ambrose, Mullins, Egan, Kelly, McGrain, Galloway, O'Rourke, O'Neill, Sullivan, Judge and O'Boyle can't be ignored.

Gabriella Koppko of Merrillville, great-granddaughter of Svanti Norstrom, the founder of the first Swedish church in Miller, is part Irish, from her mother, Josephine Ryan Anderson. Mrs. Koppko recalls Gary's East Side, the St. Luke's church neighborhood, which was Irish from the 1920s to 1940s.

McGuire, Gary air pollution control chief, son of Martin and Margaret Gibbons McGuire from County Mayo, grew up there. He recalled the Irish plays at Emerson School, and the parish priests, the Rev. Timothy Doody for many years, then the Rev. William Martin.

Now, St. Luke's, merged with St. Monica's, is predominantly Hispanic.

Football great Tom Harmon was a Gary West Sider, but John

Walsh, who became a dentist, and Tom Clifford, who became a lawyer, and Ed Burns, who became a funeral director, all had their beginnings on the East Side.

John D. Radigan, who founded Radigan Bros. Furniture in 1912 with his brother Michael, also was a Gary East Sider from County Roscommon.

John, who lived at 700 Lincoln St. for 55 years, had seven sons, including William, now 67, still active in the business; Joe, retired; and Edward, who has a travel bureau.

The Irish were politically active from the time of their arrival, writes Blessing.

In 1928, Alfred E. Smith was the first Irish Catholic to be nominated for president, although it would take another 32 years for another, John F. Kennedy, to be elected in 1960.

Great labor leaders Philip Murray of the United Steelworkers and William George Meany of the AFL-CIO were Irish-Americans, as were literary figures F. Scott Fitzgerald, John O'Hara, Eugene O'Neill and James T. Farrell, and entertainers Bing Crosby and Maureen O'Hara, and U.S. Sens. Joseph McCarthy, Eugene J. McCarthy, Robert and Edward Kennedy and Daniel P. Moynihan.

Known for their strong Catholic religion, their pride in being Irish, their conviviality, their adaptability to changing circumstances, the Irish are noted for their love of discourse.

"We are the greatest talkers since the Greeks," wrote Oscar Wilde. The tavern is an Irish — and American — institution.

Their hatred of the English stems from being dominated for 800 years, from Henry II in 1171 to colonization of Ulster by Scottish Presbyterians in the 17th Century and bloody rebellions that ended with the Irish Free State in 1922.

Ireland was occupied by prehistoric people in 6000 B.C., who were econquered by Celtic tribes in 400 B.C. St. Patrick brought Christianity in 432.

156 / Irish

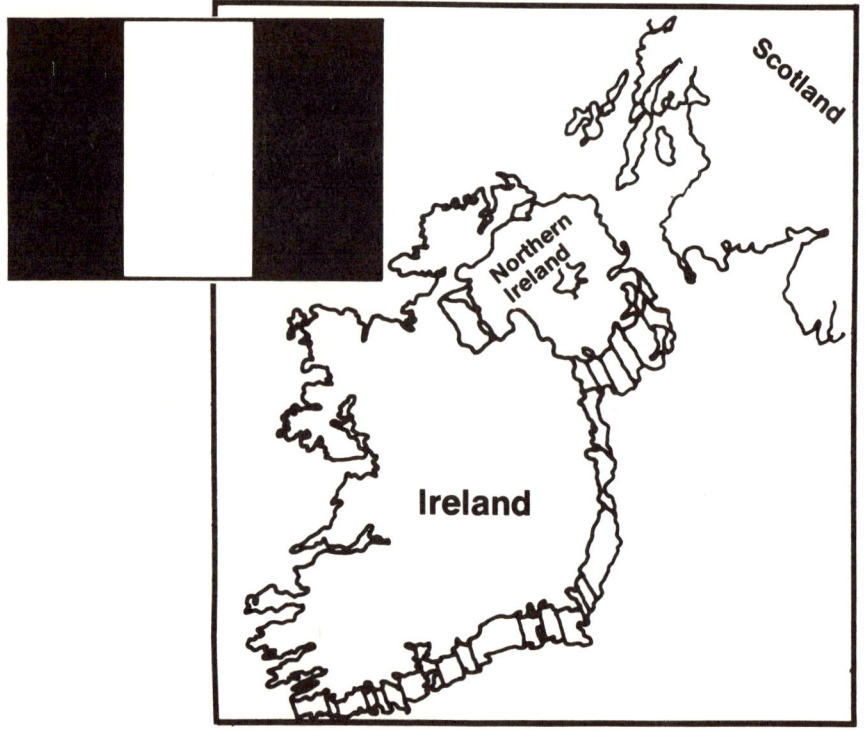

35. Scots

Bliandha Mhath Ur.

Happy Ne'erday.

These are ways to say Happy New Year in Scotland. The first is in Gaelic, as expressed by Allen McIsaac, a Scottish American from Nova Scotia. The second is in Lowland Scotch, said by Isobel Smillie, a native of Glasgow.

What's so Scottish about New Year's Day, celebrated around the world since ancient times?

For those who kissed and were kissed at midnight, New Year's, thank or blame the Scots. They brought the custom to America, as they celebrated Hogmanay on New Year's Eve.

That immortal song, Auld Lang Syne, was written by Robert Burns, Scotland's poet laureate.

Scots in the United States, estimated at 10,048,816 by the 1980 census (which noted that 38.2 million Americans didn't denote their ancestry), are a varied ethnic group whose ancestors came to America as early as 1600.

First came early colonists in 1600, with names like Campbell and Crawford, who set up towns such as Aberdeen, Edinburgh and Glasgow.

Then came the Scots from Hebrides and Shetland and Ulster, 50,000 by 1650, 250,000 from 1717 to 1775, whose descendants we call Scotch-Irish or Ulster Scots. Many of them became the Appalachians, the American frontiersmen, and the group, merged with English and German, who now call themselves "hillbillies."

Then more came from Scotland and Ulster, half a million before the 1840s famine, a million from 1851 to 1899, another half-million from 1911 to 1970.

To the Scots, descended from Gaelic Celts famous for their wit, love of liberty and bravery in battle, belong the credit for inventing golf in 1100. They're known for kilts and bagpipes, for rolling their R's as they speak, for words like wee and bonnie, and for being frugal.

The Scots, herring and oatmeal eaters in their land smaller than Indiana with 5 million inhabitants, celebrate the new year with dumplings and shortbread. Their national holidays are St. Andrew's Day on Nov. 30 and Bobbie Burns Day on Jan. 25, in honor of the Ayrshire-dialect poet's birthday, when the traditional haggis made from sheep's heart, liver, cereal, potatoes and herring cooked inside a sheep's stomach is served.

But Scot tradition no longer is widespread in America. Many Scottish Americans, up to 14 generations from their migrant ancestors, don't know about haggis and hogmanay.

Scottish Americans are spread through the United States. The 1980 census reported 214,514 in Indiana, 1,362 in Lake County, 477 in Porter, 202 in LaPorte.

California has the most, 1,155,239, followed by Texas, Pennsylvania, Florida and New York. Illinois has 379,239.

Isobel Smillie of Schererville and her husband, William, are "just about the last" to arrive, in 1967, they said.

Coming to Gary from Scotland in the last 40 years were familes such as Archibald, Bache, Burcke, Collins, DeVaney, Duncan, Falconer, Ferguson, Guthrie, McGuffney, McGrath and Templeton, assisted by the International Institute.

They found what Smillie called "a little Scotland" on Gary's west side at 7th and Monroe, near the First Presbyterian Church, established in 1908 by Fred E. Walton and others.

While most Scots are members of the Presbyterian Church founded by John Knox, the church in Gary started as all-American. Its first members were the white, upper-class, management people of the new city, noted the present pastor, the Rev Roderic Froman.

Presbyterian churches with Scottish members already existed in Indiana. First Presbyterian of Crown Point started in 1844, with the Rev. J.C. Brown, who came from Valparaiso.

The First Presbyterian Church of Valparaiso was founded in 1840. The present pastor, E. Allen Campbell, is of Scotch-Irish descent, but his congregation is mixed, he said.

Allen McIsaac, who came from Nova Scotia's Scottish community in 1925, said Gary was a booming city then, advertised in Canada as "The Magic City of Steel."

The Nova Scotians, three or four generations descended from Scotland, mingled easily with their "cousins" with similar names, whose ancestors had come to America much earlier from Scotland or from Northern Ireland.

Among the Canadian Scots were John J. Campbell, now 83; Annie Mae MacDonald, who retired from Gary National Bank 10 years ago; and James and Elizabeth MacDonald McKenzie, who met in Gary in the 1920s.

McKenzie had come from Alberta and his wife, whose parents were Scotland-born, came from Nova Scotia. Their daughter, Mrs. Ann Campbell of Merrillville, is about as pure Scot as one can find nowadays.

Scot names can be Irish, too, such as McAdams, McCormick,

MacArthur, McPherson, McGill, McKinley, Macleod.

But Mrs. McKenzie says there's a general rule — Mac is Scot, Mc is Irish.

So the name she acquired from her Scot husband should be Mackenzie. "I get mad every time I write it," she said.

In Gary in 1956, there were 3,000 Scots, including John Bewick, Don McLennen, Dr. Ira Miltimore, Assistant City Engineer William Farquharson, John Beattle, Fred Bowie and William McNeil, who had founded Clan McNeil — one of several Scot ethnic groups which, like the Burns Club and Caledonia Society, have ceased to exist.

McNeil was among 400 Scots, many of them brickmasons, who arrived in 1908-09. One of them, William J. Fulton, became Gary's first fire chief and fifth mayor.

Margaret McGregor of Portage said her husband, Daniel, who died 20 years ago after working at the U.S. Steel tube mills, was a Scotsman whose great-grandfather had come directly from Scotland. But he was very Americanized, and their children know nothing about Scotland except their name, she said.

Scott Duncan, 24, of Merrillville and Mrs. Pat McNeil of Schererville are Scotch-Irish, descended many generations ago from Lowland Scots encouraged by King James I of England to colonize Ulster. Some 200,000 Presbyterian Scots settled in Northern Ireland from 1603 to 1690; 2 million of their descendants subsequently migrated to America from 1650 to 1775.

"How interesting," said Duncan, whose Baptist Scotch-Irish father, Larry, came to Northwest Indiana from Southern Illinois. He's anxious to learn more.

Great indeed was the role of the Scotch-Irish in American history. Patrick Henry was Scotch-Irish, as were Presidents Andrew Jackson, James Buchanan, Chester A. Arthur, James K. Polk, William McKinley and Woodrow Wilson.

John C. Calhoun and Thomas J. "Stonewall" Jackson, Cyrus H. McCormick, John T. Pirie, Samuel Carson, Andrew McNally and Thomas W. Mellon were of Scotch-Irish descent.

Among the Americans descended from Scots who came directly from Scotland were two signers of the Declaration of Independence, James Wilson and John Witherspoon. Also coming directly to America were Hugh Orr (1715-1798), who cast guns for the American Army, and John Paul Jones (1747-1792), who founded the U.S. Navy. Andrew Carnegie (1835-1919), who made his fortune in iron and steel, was the son of a Dunfermilne weaver.

The Harvard Encyclopedia of American Ethnic Groups reports that "Scotch-Irish" is an American compound name that "accurately reflects a historical reality; the people to whom it refers were culturally distinct from both Irish and the Scots."

American Scots and Scotch-Irish today aren't involved in the crisis in Northern Ireland, one-seventh the size of Indiana with 1 million people. Since 1969, 20,000 people have died. Northern Ireland is part of the British United Kingdom.

Scotch-Irish made up the bulk of the frontiersmen who moved westward from the Allegheny Mountains in the 1700s to the Shenandoah Valley in Virginia, the Carolina hills, west Pennsylvania, West Virginia and Kentucky.

Migration being a second nature to them, the Scotch-Irish ignored King George III's refusal in 1763 to let colonists take land west of the Alleghenies. They built log cabins, wore deerskins, fought with the Indians, developed circuit riders, settled the Ohio River Valley and followed Daniel Boone's Wilderness Trail into Kentucky in 1775.

In the 1880s, the Appalachians, made up of descendants of English, Scotch-Irish and Germans, moved on to the Ozarks, to Southern Illinois, Texas and Oklahoma. The McCoys, of the story of the Hatfield and McCoy hillbilly feud, were Scotch-Irish.

* * * * * * * * *

"I want to tell you how very much I enjoyed your 'Blame the Scots for your New Year kiss' " wrote May MacNeill Hake of Valparaiso. "It brought back all kinds of happy thoughts."

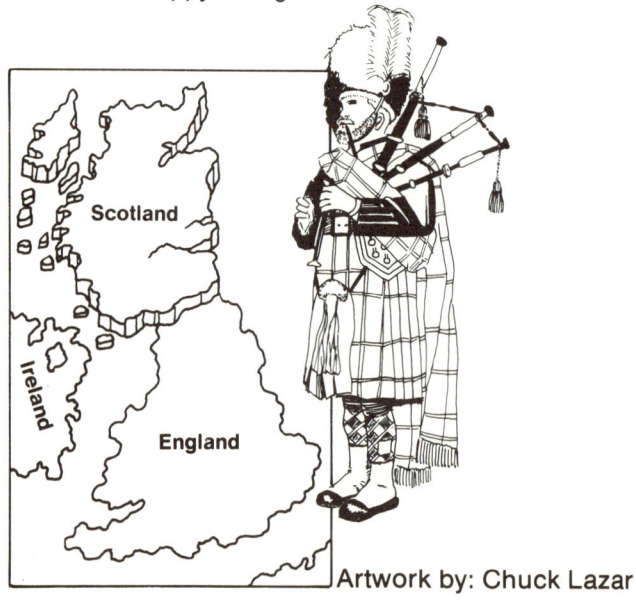

Artwork by: Chuck Lazar

36. Lebanese

"The only way to settle it is to give the lower third to Israel, the top third to Syria, and the middle to the Lebanese Christians," says George Mussallem, 75, whose father came from Lebanon's Bekaa Valley.

"I don't know if there's a solution. The Christians are no longer the majority," said Philippe Joseph, 32, whose natural parents were killed in Beirut in the 1950s.

"We don't have business there. Send the boys home," said Mrs. Julie Sawaya, who was 16 when she left her native town near Beirut in 1930. Now her grandson, 19, is a Marine Reservist.

The three are Lebanese Americans, a relatively small number in the United States whose parents grew up in the land which became Lebanon in 1943.

There are, according to the 1980 U.S. Census, about a million Arab-Americans — from Egypt, Jordan, Saudi Arabia, Kuwait and 15 other Middle East nations. Most of them are of Lebanese descent.

The census counted 294,895 Lebanese, 3,709 in Indiana, and 106,638 Syrians, 2,208 in Indiana.

But Alixa Naff of the National Center for Urban Ethnic Affairs, who wrote the Arab-American chapter in the Harvard Encyclopedia of American Ethnic Groups, said 90 percent are Maronite Catholics, whose families came from the Mount Lebanon coastal area between Beirut and Tripoli, in the Syrian province of the Ottoman Empire.

Lebanon today, one-ninth the size of Indiana and with 4 million people, was the center of world attention, with 1,400 U.S. Marines on a "peacekeeping" mission. A total of 250 Americans died there since that force was established, including 241 in a terrorist bombing in 1983.

Mussallem, of Gary, whose father, Abdoneur Mussallem, grew up in south Lebanon, is American-born and has never been to Lebanon. But through the years, he has followed its history, and "I know more about it than the average newspaperman," he said.

His idea, adopted from Henry Kissinger, is to split Lebanon in three, thereby satisfying all factions — Israeli and protection for its northern territory, Lebanon's Shi'ite and Sunni Muslims — who with the Druse now make up the majority on the land

— and the Lebanese Maronite Christians.

Mussallem, now retired, was married to Helen Fadell, who was supervisor of personnel at Metropolitan Life Insurance in Gary for many years. She died 10 years ago.

The Mussallems are among the few Lebanese families in the Gary area, including Fadell, Haddad, Nabhan, Neimay.

In Michigan City, with a larger Syrian and Lebanese community, the well-known family names are Sam, Kalil, Muckway, Shaia, Joseph, Tadros, Sawaya, Abraham, Farah and Borane.

Among the early Lebanese in Gary were the Nabhans. Abe, owner of Abe's Fruit Market at 9th and Adam in Gary for 50 years, died in 1973 at age 75. Shibley died in 1967 at 72, and was also a grocery-store owner.

Ferhat Naban, who peddled fruits and vegetables in Miller, came from Zahle, east of Beirut, in 1908. He died seven years ago at 67.

One of his sons is Walter Nabhan, who was football coach and assistant principal at Wirt High School. Ferhat also raised his brother's son, Theodore Nabhan, who was a Gary city councilman from 1962-67.

One of Ferhat Nabhan's five daughters, Emily, married Herbert Nabhan, who had come from Massachusetts. The third generation is Kenneth Nabhan, who owns Nab's Lounge in Portage, and his two sisters, Joanne Stephan and Dolores Arvidson, both of Portage.

In Michigan City, where Abe Gibron, the former Chicago Bears football coach, grew up, the Syrian-Lebanese community is a large one.

Other well-known Lebanese are Danny and Marlo Thomas, entertainers, and Helen Thomas, White House correspondent for United Press International.

Glady Bull Nicewarmer, in her 1980 book on Michigan City, noted that the first Syrians came from Chicago in 1900 to work for Haskell-Barker Car Co., which became Pullman-Standard.

Philippe Joseph is the first of four adopted children of the late Michael "Adjo" Joseph, (1916-1975) whose parents, Shamon and Lillian, migrated from the Beirut area in 1905-07.

Mickey Joseph became a famous chef, labor leader and founder of the Labor Beacon newspaper. In 1958, he won the grand prize on the $64,000 Question television program and used the proceeds to buy the 75-acre Cedar Brooks Farms in Rolling Prairie. He then assisted in the immigration of 52 orphans from St. Vincent's Orphanage in Beirut.

Adopted as Americans, the children, such as John Johns and

Mary Roldan and Rolanda Wieze, are grown now. They hold reunions at Cedar Brooks every summer.

Philippe Joseph was a 1958 "Christmas gift," the first of four to arrive at the Joseph home, followed by Andre in 1959 and Louise and Marcelle in 1960. Andre is now a longshoreman union leader, and Marcelle works for Sullair Corp.

Louise is a professional singer in Tulsa. Philippe has become a caterer, like his father.

Philippe, who was 5 when he arrived, has studied Lebanese culture with the help of people in the Lebanese community.

The Arabic foods, laban yogurt, burghul crushed whole wheat, camas bread, lubya lamb stew and warna areesh stuffed grape leaves, are well-known to him.

Shish ke bob is now an American delicacy.

Philippe follows the political developments in Lebanon with intense curiosity, knowing there is little Americans can do.

Christians — Maronite Catholics, Greek Orthodox and Protestant — now make up less than half the population, while they were the majority in 1943 when their nationalist movement started.

The Muslims — the orthodox Sunni and the Shi'ite sect allied with the Ayatollah Khomeini of Iran — are more now, along with 200,000 followers of the Druse secret sect founded as a mixture of Christian and Islam beliefs by Caliph Hakim in 1000, and 350,000 Palestinian Arabs who fled Israel in the 1960s and 1970s.

What is now Lebanon, known for its cedars, has long been a commercial center.

Seafaring Phoenicians settled before 2000 B.C., followed by the Romans in 64 B.C. The people were among the first Christians.

In the 800s, Arabs from the desert brought Islam. In the 1000s, Lebanese Christians welcomed the Crusaders from Europe and started a traditional friendship.

Turks conquered the land in 1516 and made it part of the Ottoman Empire until after World War I, when the League of Nations put Lebanon under French rule. The French granted independence in 1943, and the Christians, wealthier and more numerous, took leadership.

Civil strife erupted in 1958, and President Eisenhower sent 10,000 Marines and order was maintained. But the tensions remain.

Syrian troops, as peacekeepers, came in 1981, and Israeli invaders took the Bekaa Valley and south Lebanon in 1982.

164 / Lebanese

37. Dutch

"God created the world, but the Dutch created Holland." — **Old Dutch saying.**

When Julie Leep, 18, and John Bartel Zandstra, 22, weremarried at the Second Christian Reformed Church in Highland in 1984, it was strictly in the Dutch tradition.

The marriage of Julie and Johnnie, great-grandchildren of Dutch immigrants who pioneered in Lake County before the turn of the century, was a festive event indeed for the close-knit, deeply religious Dutch community.

"We're happy," said their parents, Mr. and Mrs. Allen Leep and Mr. and Mrs. John Paul Zandstra, not so much because it's a merger of two prominent clans but because "they're right for each other."

"I really wasn't looking for a Dutch girl. I wanted a fine one, and she's Dutch," said Johnnie, who works for his father's Zandstra's Store for Men in Merrillville.

Julie and Johnnie have known each other virtually all their lives. They go to the same church, went to Highland Christian School and Illiana Christian High School in Lansing, Ill. — where most of the Dutch children go.

Julie's father is the son of Nick Leep, whose father, David Leep, was one of the first Dutch settlers in Highland.

Johnnie's father, John Paul, is the son of John B. Zandstra, the 8th of 16 children of Batele Hans "Red Bart" Zandstra (1867-1939), who migrated from Ostermeer in The Netherlands' Friesland province in 1890 and settled in Highland.

Highland, Munster, and old Saxony (now Hessville) along 173rd in Hammond, and much of the low, fertile lands along the Little Calumet River were founded and developed by Dutch gardeners, with skills they brought over from The Netherlands.

Zandstra, Leep, Van Til, Scheeringa, Jabaay, Klootwyk, Kooy, Schuringa, Schoon, Roorda, Van Prooyen, Vander Hayden, Terpstra, Kuiper, Kuipers, Van Dellen, Van Dyke, VanHorne, VanDrunen, and Van Gorp today are among prominent Dutch families in Northwest Indiana.

There are, according to the 1980 U.S. Census, 4,644 people of Dutch descent in Lake County, 780 in Porter County, and 536 in LaPorte County.

The Indiana total is 209,722, ranking behind Illinois; 293,056;

Ohio, 356,808; New York, 396,477; Pennsylvania, 420,749; Michigan, 546,678; and California, 612,370. The total in the U.S. is 6,304,499 Dutch Americans, the 11th-largest ethnic group in the nation.

The Dutch, originating in a country half the size of Indiana, came to America as early as 1609 with Henry Hudson, who discovered the Hudson River. Kilinen Van Rensselaer (1595-1643), a diamond merchant from Amsterdam, was one of the first patroon landowners who colonized New Amsterdam, now New York, in 1629.

Martin Van Buren (1837-1841), the eighth U.S. president, was the son of a Dutch truck farmer in Kinderbrook, N.Y., and Theodore Roosevelt (1858-1919), the 26th president, and Franklin Delano Roosevelt (1882-1945), the 32nd president, were descendants of Klaes Martensen van Roosevelt, one of the patroons in the 1640s.

Robert P. Swierenga, writing in the Harvard Encyclopedia of American Ethnic Groups, 1980, said there were 100,000 Dutch Americans in the first federal census of 1790, and 80,000 of them were within 50 miles of New York.

As they increased in number through steady migration, the Dutch — who typically had large families — began their westward move in 1845 and settled along Lake Michigan, from Muskegon to Green Bay, particularly Grand Rapids and Holland, Mich., Roseland in Chicago, and South Holland, Ill.

The first Dutch settlers of Northwest Indiana came from the west, however, says Purdue Calumet Professor Lane Trusty. They came from Roseland.

Such was the story of Bartele Hans Zandstra, a 19-year-old orphan from Oostermeer, who joined his first cousin, B.O. Zandstra, known as "Black Bart," at work at George Pullman's 115th Street shop, which eventually became the Pullman-Standard car company.

According to family historians David and Arnold (Butch) Zandstra, B.H. and "Black Bart" Zandstra moved to Highland in 1890, and B.H. married Tryntje K. DeRuiter in 1893.

B.H. had 16 children. The ninth, Bartel (1906-1983), became Highland's first clerk-treasurer, Lake County clerk and auditor, county and 1st District Democratic chairman, a candidate for lieutenant governor in 1956, and a candidate for U.S. senator in 1958.

The second child, Gertrude Huizenga, had eight children, including Hilda Leep, mother of Bruce Leep, president of the Bank of Highland, and Ken and Bart Leep, owners of Pleasant View Dairy.

The seventh child, Charles "Chuck" along with No. 11 Arnold "Dick" and No. 13 William, established Zandstra Bros. Farms. Two of Chuck's sons, Bartel and Charles, became lawyers; one, Dennis, works at the farm, and the fourth, Duane, took another Dutch migratory leap — he is now a teacher in Buenos Aires, Argentina.

Arnold Zandstra, now 74, at the farm with sons Dave, Butch and Nick, had seven children, and one of them, Bernard H., is a professor at Michigan State University. Dave is the president of the Highland Historical Society.

Butch went to Holland in 1983 and traced the family line in Oostermeer to 1800, when Napoleon ordered the use of surnames.

B.H. Zandstra's No. 8 child, John B., had five children, including Burdette, a real-estate agent, and John Paul, the haberdasher.

Even earlier than the Zandstras were Jacob Schoon and Simon Koedyker, who settled in Roseland in 1866. Schoon acquired 160 acres along the Little Calumet River, west of Broadway in Gary, and Koedyker bought adjoining property between Burr and Mississippi, wrote a descendant, Peter W. Schoon.

Kenneth J. and Margaret S. Schoon wrote "Portraits of a Ridge Family: The Jacob Schoons," in 1981, and related that Jacob and Henrietta Schoon had 11 children, including Kate Schoon Koedyker, who bore 12; Alice Schoon Kaluf, who had 10; Mary Schoon Kooy, who had 14; Eva Schoon Swets, who had 6; and Simon, who had 9. By 1956, the Jacob Schoon progeny exceeded 600.

Cousins abound. Jerry Schoon, 23, employed at Van Til Grocery in Hammond, said he doesn't know all his relatives. He's the son of the late Nicholas C. Schoon, whose parents were Jacob and Kate Schoon.

What is Dutch?

Like the Greeks, they're closely knit and family oriented. Unlike the Hellenes, however, the Dutch generally dislike politics.

"I believe we're expected to marry our own kind," said Jerry Schoon. "We go to the same schools, same churches. We're kidded about being frugal."

They're proud of Dutch accomplishments anywhere — classic painters Vincent Van Gogh and Anton Van Dyke, poet Mark Van Doren, tycoon Cornelius Vanderbilt, their Boer "cousins" who developed South Africa, the famous dikes and canals of Holland.

George Van Til, administrative officer for Lake County Sheriff Rudy Bartolomei, said the Dutch, serious and hospitable, are known for their adherence to the strict Calvinist code of the Reformed or Christian Reformed Church.

They don't gamble, drink, dance, go to movies. They believe in public confession of major sins. They abide by the Sabbath. Their stores are closed on Sundays, when they go to church twice, morning and evening.

"The Dutch are strong on the work ethic, on family togetherness at dinner, on discipline, on Christian education, on tithes," said Van Til, a third-generation Dutch American.

Are Dutch expected to marry Dutch? "Absolutely. It's promoted subtly and overtly," he said.

The hard-working, no-frills Dutch, known for tulips, windmills, wooden shoes, the Dutch treat — indicative of frugality — their forthrightness and their passion for order and cleanliness, rate Christian education a top priority, he noted.

* * * * * * * * *

The search for Dutch people of Northwest Indiana started early in May 1983 after Tom Bakker of Bakker Produce in Griffith said his grandfather came from Holland. George Van Til provided much of the help, when we got around to interviewing the local Dutchfolks.

Artwork by: Maryann Bartman

38.
English

"The Redcoats are coming ... "
— **Paul Revere, 1775**

"The trouble with Americans is that they're overfed, oversexed, and over here."
— **London resident, 1945**

It's no big thing for Laura Barr that she comes from a long line of Americans, the first settlers in America.

"I knew it when I was a child. But nobody believed me in school," said Miss Barr, 24, a scretary at Townsend Pontiac in Merrillville.

She and her brother, Daniel, 25, are of the 11th generation descended from Miles Standish, one of the first Pilgrims on the Mayflower in 1620. Their father, Standish Barr, 52, and grandfather, Harold W. Barr, 76, of Crown Point, have taught them their heritage — to handle it with pride and humility.

The English provided this multi-ethnic nation, a nation with more than 100 diverse and merging cultures, the foundation for unity — a common language — and the basis for its unique, now widely imitated, form of democratic government.

There are some 13,000 Americans today with documented proof of the General Society of Mayflower Descendants, Plymouth, Mass., that they are descendants of the 102 men, women and children aboard the Mayflower who established the second permanent English settlement in America, following Jamestown, Va., in 1607.

The Pilgrims of Plymouth started the first Thanksgiving with Indians in 1621. Forty-one Pilgrims, seeking religious asylum, signed the Mayflower Compact, the first agreement for self-government in America, even before the boat landed, and only 21 of them survived the first winter.

About 4 million people migrated to America from Great Britain, not quite thrice as large as Indiana, since the Susan Constant, Godspeed and Discovery landed in Jamestown. According to the U.S. Census, their descendants number 49,598,035, or 26.34 percent of the 1980 population.

California now has the largest number of English descent Americans, with 4,946,554, followed by Texas, 3,083,323; Ohio, 2,371,236; and New York, 2,320,503. Indiana, 13th, has 1,356,135, with 25,526 in Lake, 7,810 in Porter and 7,969 in LaPorte counties.

Of 38 million Americans who identified their ancestry as "American," many are of English descent, the 1980 Census noted.

There were four distinct waves of English migration, from 1628 to 1642, from 1709 to the Revolutionary War, the three decades after the War of 1812, and the 40 years after the 1845-47 potato famine in Europe.

Charlotte J. Erickson, of the London School of Economics and Political Science, wrote in the 1980 Harvard Encyclopedia of American Ethnic Groups that by the end of the Colonial Period, the English were no longer the majority — outnumbered by French, German, Scotch-Irish and Scot immigrants.

The United States is still a nation of immigrants. In 1970, 7 percent of families were headed by immigrants, compared to 25 percent in 1900, the Census noted.

From 1607 to 1776, the colony's culture was unmistakably English, with English law, language, literature and half the population.

But the country integrated, and English-descent Americans are less likely to proclaim their heritage as British, she noted.

English dominated, even in states predominantly Spanish, and the English descendants who merged with Germans and Scotch-Irish to form the rugged Appalachians, surged westward, defying the Proclamation of 1763, which reserved lands west of the Appalachians for the Indians. That was one of the factors of the Revolution.

In the spread to the Midwest, English communities were formed in New Harmony and New Albany in Indiana in the 1830s. English were among the first settlers when the Fort Dearborn to Detroit Trail was opened and a LaPorte land office was opened in 1833, when Porter County was carved out of LaPorte County in 1836, and when Lake County was created out of Porter Couinty the next year.

George Earle of Falmouth, England, settled in Liverpool, now part of Lake Station, in 1837.

Mrs. Pearl Papka Baboo of Gary, who traces her ancestry back to the Magna Carta era, is descended from the Saxtons who came to America before 1650. One of them, Ebenezer Saxton, her great-great grandfather, settled in Turkey Creek and married Mary Ann Mummery and died in the Civil War.

Their grandson, Henry C. Saxton, was married to Bertha Reissig, from another Lake County pioneer family, and moved to Gary in 1907.

Mummery is an old Hobart name. Well known for years was Allen Mummery, born in a log cabin in Hobart in 1878, whose father, Stephen, had migrated from Kent County, England. Allen Mummery fought in the Philippine Insurrection in 1899. He died in 1973.

Mrs. Baboo, a regional director of Daughters of the American Revolution, and Josephine McKay Bourne, an 11th generation descendant of William Bradford (Mayflower leader who became governor of the colony and founder of Thanksgiving Day), helped compile a list of two dozen descendants of the Mayflower.

She noted that the "old-stock" English descendants have intermarried with other nationalities and races. Somewhere in her line are Indians and Chinese, and she has a cousin married to a woman from Bombay, India.

Descended from Elder William Brewster, who led Separatists to Leiden in the Netherlands in 1608, and then led them back to Plymouth aboard the leaky Speedwell in 1620 and then to the New World on the Mayflower, is Mrs. Olive Hartsough, 77, of Merrillville, and her sister, Mrs. Betty Livengood of South Bend.

"I knew as a child (in South Bend) that I was descended from the Mayflower, but I didn't have proof," she said. It took her a dozen years to trace the line, then she lost the evidence in a 1969 gas explosion that demolished her home in Glen Park. Just before she retired as a teacher at Gary's Melton School in 1970, she retrieved the data and became Mayflower-certified.

She learned her roots went deeper, to the Norman invasion of England in 1066, but it would cost much more for more genealogical research, she said.

Other Mayflower descendants in the area are Barbara and Esther Ann Courtwright of Crown Point (from Richard Warren), Mrs. Helen Dancy of Chesterton and Nancy and Walden McBride of Crown Point (from Edward Fuller), Charles E. and Kathryn Daugherty of Gary and Crown Point (from Richard Warren), Constance Ann Fileff of Gary and Ruth Marie Mader of Crown Point (from John Alden), Joel Janowski of Gary (from Thomas Rogers), Mary Etta Lunstrom of Valparaiso (from Francis Cooke), Elizabeth Munger of Michigan City (from Edward Doty and Richard Warren), Ruth Shawley of Michigan City (from George Soule), and Juanita Bell Thoeson of Chesterton (from John Billington).

Common English names are Allen, Davis, Smith, Hatfield, Jones, Ross and Merrill, from whom Merrillville drew its name. Not so common is Knotts, the first mayor of Gary, (Thomas), whose daughter, Mrs. Susan Mulcahey, 75, still lives in Gary.

English

As early as 1776, the new Americans considered the New World a melting pot. "Europe, and not England, is the parent country of America," wrote Thomas Paine in "Common Sense" that year.

But it was not until 1908 that the first reference to "The Melting Pot" was made, by Israel Zangwill, in his play by that name.

The pot is still melting. This book focused on 38 of 100 ethnic groups recognized by the U.S. Census and Harvard Encyclopedia.

Among some of the groups not featured in this book are Americans of Danish descent (1,518,273), Portuguese (1,024,351), Swiss (981,543), Austrian (948,588), Finnish (615,872), and Belgian (360,277) descent.

They are represented in small numbers in the Calumet Region, such as James Driscoll and Dave Hawk, of Finnish descent; Don Blume, Belgian; Robert Farag and Joan Hac, Egyptian; Eric Madsen, Dane; Graham Wickramakesera, Sri Lanka; Niang Petretta, Thailand; Maggie Verboon, Indonesia; Carrol Moscoso Sharp, Bolivia; Peter Kamanaroff and James Balanoff, Bulgarian; Mrs. Earl Mann, Panamanian; John Boog, Liberian; Margaret Peute, South Africa; Phil Cyprian, Greek Cypriot; Mrs. George Vroheritis, Turk; Jack Parry and E. W. Griffith, Welsh; and Pauline Anastas, Albanian.

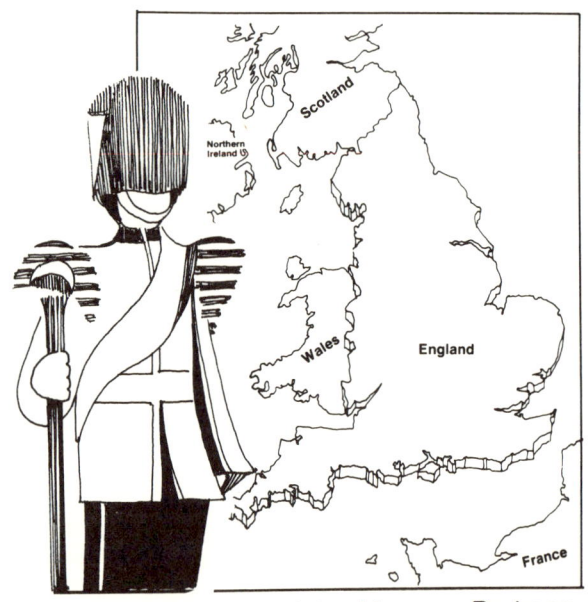

Artwork by: Maryann Bartman